MW01617767

Martin Puryear

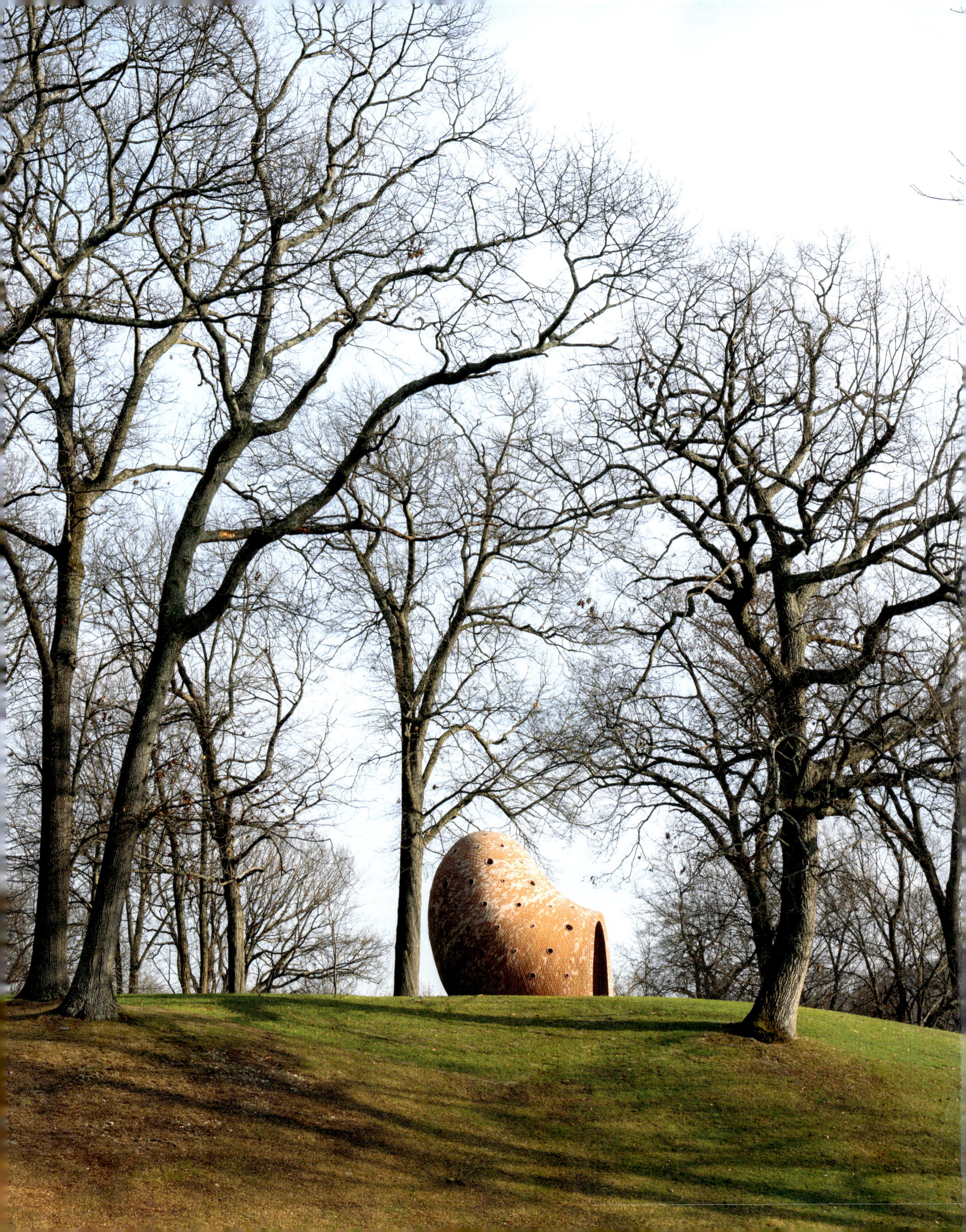

Martin Puryear LOOKOUT

Nora Lawrence
Amy S. Weisser
Martin Puryear
Glenn Adamson
Adela Goldsmith
John P. Stern

Storm King Art Center
Gregory R. Miller & Co.

Contents

Foreword and Acknowledgments 6
John P. Stern

MARTIN PURYEAR: WORK ETHIC 9
Nora Lawrence

LOOKOUT: SEEING, CONSIDERING, FEELING 21
Amy S. Weisser

MARTIN PURYEAR IN CONVERSATION 37
with Glenn Adamson

MAKING *LOOKOUT* 42
Photographs by Carlton Davis

LOOKOUT 54
Photographs by Jeffrey Jenkins

PROCESS AND SCALE 75
Adela Goldsmith, Nora Lawrence, and Martin Puryear

Checklist of the Exhibition 167
Biography 171
Contributors 172
Artist's Acknowledgments 175

Foreword and Acknowledgments

The process of realizing a site-specific commission for Storm King Art Center requires so much more than just an artist and an idea. Although the relationship between Martin Puryear and Storm King goes back more than four decades, our conversations with the artist about a permanent work began in earnest almost fourteen years ago. Several years into our conversations, Storm King's Director Emeritus David R. Collens and I took a cart tour with Puryear all around the Art Center during which we visited a site atop one of Storm King's highest hills, with a sweeping view of the landscape and Schunnemunk Mountain to the west. Once he found that location in the North Woods, Puryear knew that he would have to forgo the drawings and models for his previous ideas and start again, to make a work that responded directly and specifically to the particularities of that site.

Now, after more than a decade of planning and collaboration, *Lookout*, Puryear's permanent work at Storm King, and his first-ever work in brick, has been completed. Puryear has described *Lookout* in many ways: an observatory of diurnal nature, a pouch, a tapestry of brick. It is a work that heightens visitors' awareness of the landscape around them—a simultaneous experience of art and landscape that is uniquely possible at the Art Center.

Realizing a permanent site-specific commission also requires the right constellation of people who believe the work is possible, along with those who possess the technical skills to realize the artwork and see the project through until the end, no matter how long it takes. *Lookout* would not exist without the talent of the masonry team led by Lara Davis, Principal, Limaçon Design, and Rob Horton, Studio Manager, Martin Puryear Studio; with Scott Cafarella, Owner and Mason, Hudson Valley Mason Works; Mario Magana, Mason, Hudson Valley Mason Works; and Aaron Getman-Pickering, Studio Assistant, Martin Puryear Studio.

Instrumental in the realization of *Lookout* were Silman (Structural Engineering), John Ochsendorf (Structural Engineering Advisor), Reed Hilderbrand Landscape Architecture (Landscape Architecture), KC Fabrications (Formwork), and Taylor Clay Products (Bricks). Additional thanks are owed to David R. Collens, Steve Blankenbeker, Mary Ann Carter, Ross Dalland, Edison Coatings, Inc., Jeanne Englert, Chris Hoppe, David Kucera, Inc., Patty Lipshutz, Mark Mendel, Donovan Palmquist, Josh Safdie, and Marin Sullivan for their involvement in bringing this incredible project to fruition. My sincerest thanks to Glenn Adamson, Carlton Davis, and Jeffrey Jenkins for their contributions to this publication. I am also deeply grateful to Storm King's Board of Trustees for their steadfast support of this project as it has grown and changed over time.

Storm King's commission and exhibition by Martin Puryear have been made possible by generous major support from Janet Benton and David Schunter, Bloomberg Philanthropies, Roberta and Steven Denning, Bridgitt and Bruce Evans, Glenstone Foundation, Ellsworth Kelly Foundation, Ohnell Family Foundation, the Hazen Polsky Foundation, Thomas A. and Georgina T. Russo, and Margaret VB Wurtele. Lead support has been provided by Agnes Gund, Barbara Bluhm-Kaul and Don Kaul, The Ronald and Jo Carole Lauder Foundation, and Matthew Marks Gallery. Support is also provided by Robert Lehman Foundation and Sidney E. Frank Foundation and supported in part by Allison Berg, Jennifer Brorsen and Richard DeMartini, Andrew L. and Gayle Shaw Camden, Tommy and Dathel Coleman, Martha Gabbert, Debby and Rocco Landesman, and the Ralph E. Ogden Foundation. This project was supported in part by an award from the National Endowment for the Arts.

At Storm King, a fantastic curatorial team supported the presentation of Puryear's new commission and organized the accompanying exhibition: Nora Lawrence, Artistic Director and Chief Curator; Amy S. Weisser, Deputy Director, Strategic Planning and Projects; Adela Goldsmith, Curatorial Assistant; Gina Guddemi, Registrar and Collections Manager;

and Hanna Washburn, Administrative Assistant, Curatorial. *Lookout* was co-organized by Lawrence and Weisser, and the accompanying exhibition, *Process and Scale*, was organized by Lawrence with Goldsmith. Mike Seaman, Storm King's Director of Facilities and Conservation, led a talented and dedicated crew, including Mike Cook, Jeff Damiano, Shannon Ferrell, Joel Longinott, Armando Ocampo, Florencio Ocampo, Mike Rivera, and Randy Sutton, in expertly assisting with the construction of *Lookout*, starting with laying the foundation on which it sits.

Many other staff members at Storm King contributed to this exhibition. The curatorial team partnered extensively with our Department of Learning and Engagement, led by Hannah des Cognets. Catherine Taylor-Williams and the Development staff worked diligently to fund the commission and organize related events. Jessica Burke, with outside counsel from FITZ & CO, strategized on communications and marketing. Dwayne J. Jarvis and Irene Buccieri lent critical support. I also want to also recognize the invaluable work of our Operations and Visitor Services team, led by Chief Operating Officer Kellie Honeycutt, with Tia Padget, Lakin Corbett, and Colleen Zlock. Storm King's entire staff has assisted with presenting these works in every possible way, and I am so thankful for my wonderful colleagues.

This catalogue has been designed by Miko McGinty Inc. with Rita Jules and Eleanor Morgan, edited by Libby Hruska, and copublished with Gregory R. Miller & Co. Many thanks to Gregory for being such an enthusiastic early believer in this book project.

In 2021 we had the honor of presenting Puryear with the Storm King Award, which is given in recognition of meaningful contributions in the fields of visual arts, landscape, and nature conservation. Looking back on his decades-long history with Storm King on that occasion, Puryear remarked, "Here we are, at least forty years later, and it confirms my belief—and everybody who knows me will tell you this is true—I will hold out until the right time. I've done it." Martin, it is a privilege and pleasure to have your work in Storm King's collection; this is the right time.

John P. Stern
President, Storm King Art Center

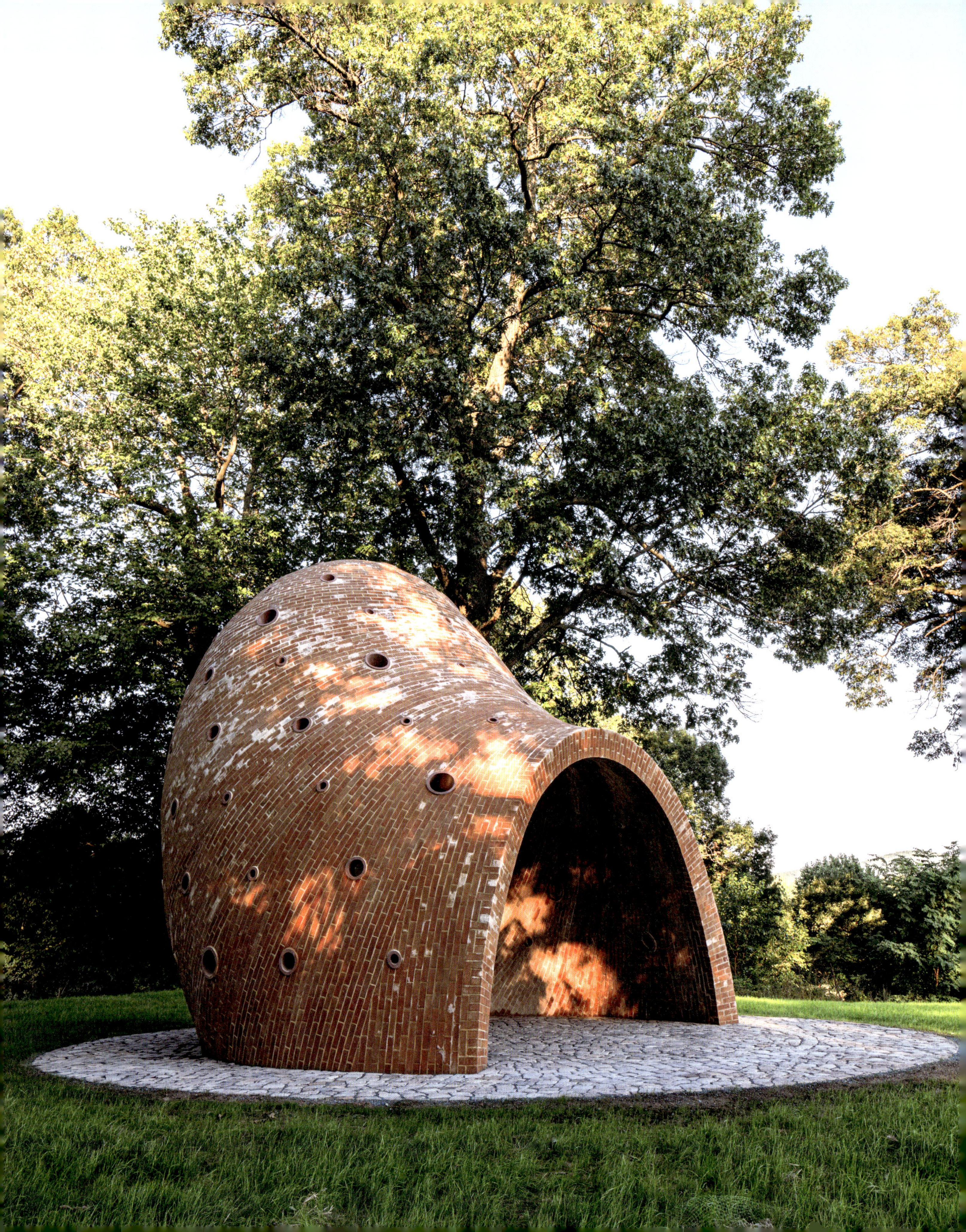

MARTIN PURYEAR WORK ETHIC

Nora Lawrence

Martin Puryear's commission for Storm King Art Center, *Lookout* (2023), sits on a small, protruding plateau that looks southwest across much of Storm King's landscape to Schunnemunk Mountain. A view from within the work encompasses much of Storm King's property; it places the viewer in the significant role of completing Puryear's sculpture with their own perceptual experience of what surrounds it (fig. 1). For Puryear, a public commission is not only an invitation to respond to a site and to work on a larger scale, but also a chance to delve into the study of materials and artisanal practices with which he has long been fascinated. Most of Puryear's sculptures have been made in his studio, by hand and in wood, but few of his large-scale, outdoor projects have been created primarily in wood, or in his studio. Instead, many of these works have been occasions to collaborate with expert makers, artisans, and craftspeople with knowledge divergent from Puryear's own. As he has said, "The one thing that is clearly of interest to me is trades, and ways that things are done. . . . How ordinary things are made. And a kind of dignity in what we call ordinary labor, that's being done very deliberately and with great care and responsibility."[1]

Lookout provided an opportunity for Puryear to work in brick, a material new to him. The planning and building of the work was a chance to demonstrate unusual and beautiful possibilities within brick masonry, elevating and highlighting the trade. The work is the result of Puryear's fascination with histories of formless brick masonry worldwide, and is also locally specific: the Hudson Valley, where Storm King Art Center is located, and where Puryear has lived since 1992, was historically a center for the manufacture of both bricks and the mortar used to hold them together (figs. 2, 3). *Lookout* also bears much in common with many of Puryear's earlier site-specific and outdoor commissions created throughout the artist's career: in philosophy; in the process and method of research and construction; and in aesthetic sensibility.

Puryear was inspired by the hill on which *Lookout* is situated, and the view that opens south from it, leading him to incorporate an embodied, present experience of the work and its surroundings. Storm King's North Woods area, which *Lookout* crowns, is the wildest part of the site—home to large maple trees and evergreens, as well as intimate hiking paths through thick forest. It is a surprise to many who know this landscape better for its expansive fields. Puryear has described his affinity for this specific setting:

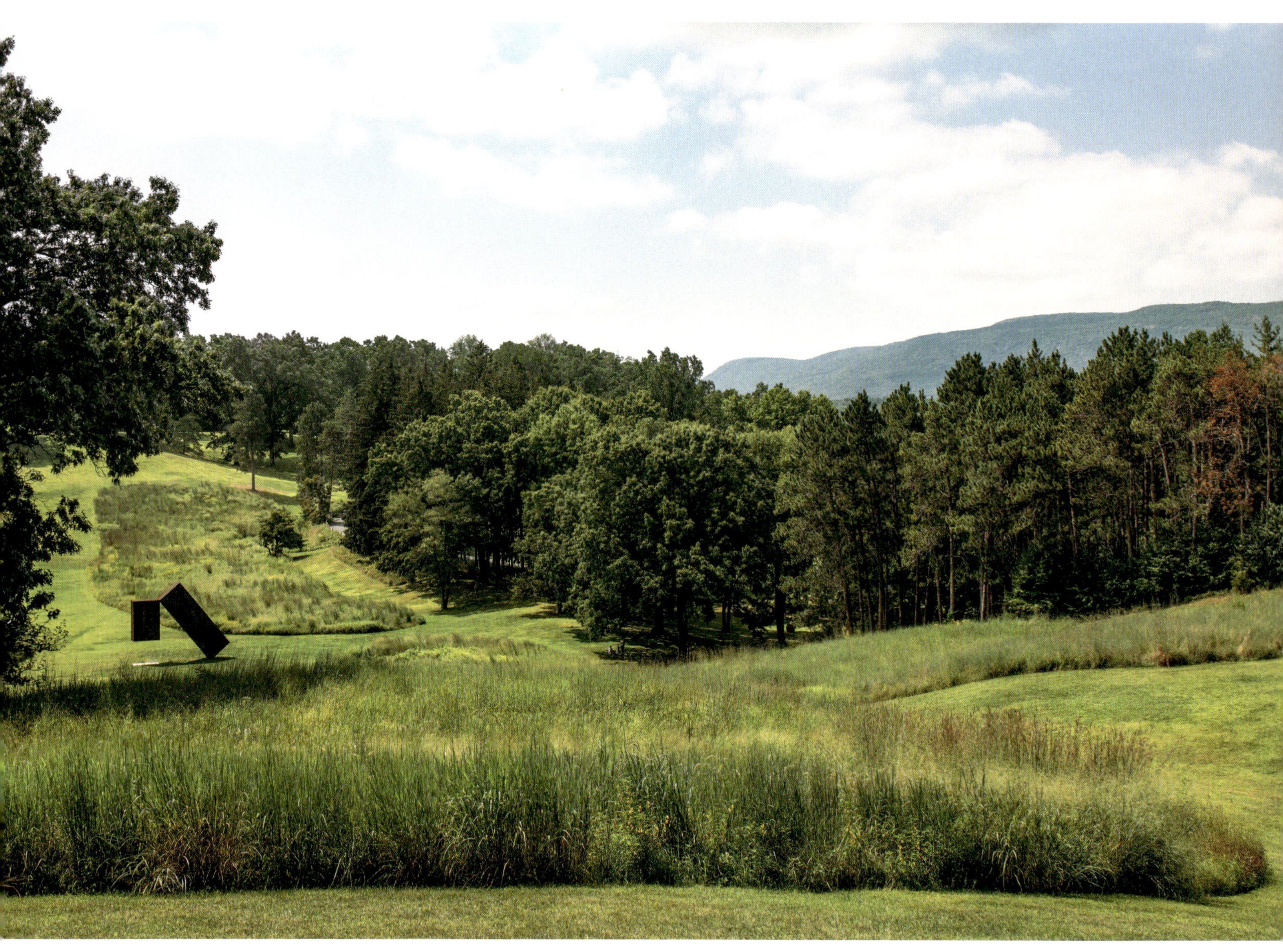

Fig. 1. View of Schnunnemunk Mountain from the future site of Martin Puryear's *Lookout*, May 2021

> It's sort of between two environments. It's on the edge of the woods, and it's looking out. . . . It gives you a sense of what Storm King is about, because you see a lot of sculptures from here studded in the landscape, but you're also, facing the other way, looking back into what almost feels like wilderness, because it's a thickly wooded area with trails through the woods, so it was like that verge between open and closed.[2]

The view Puryear describes includes first a dip down a large hill to an iconic work titled *Suspended*, by Menashe Kadishman (1977), then back up toward Museum Hill, the center of Storm King and where a 1978 site-specific work sits: Isamu Noguchi's *Momo Taro*. Farther toward the west the view opens to the expanse of Schunnemunk, distant enough to be obscured by clouds on occasion.[3] Puryear's sculpture, including the round platform of cobblestones into which it nestles, was designed for, and is right-sized for, the space it occupies.

The title of the work is indicative of the sculpture's incorporation of the landscape around it; it is not just something to be observed, but a tool for viewing beyond. The work begins in an arch at its entrance, with bricks laid vertically. It transitions gradually into a dome, with bricks laid horizontally. The contour of its form traces this transition from vertical to horizontal, as periodic diagonal slices through the laid brick reorient the direction. At an approximate halfway mark of this transition, subsequent bricks tip up far enough from the original arch to meet, and start to form, in layered ovals, a connection between the sculpture's back end and its curved roof. The resultant shape is familiar but elusive: a hat, a shoe, an animal. At regular intervals, open cylinders are embedded into the brickwork, creating ninety portals—radiating up, sideways, and slightly down toward the ground—through which a visitor standing in the work's center can gaze outward in every direction. The work also includes an auditory experience in the amplification and echo of sounds from a central spot in the dome that heightens the experience of being with the work.

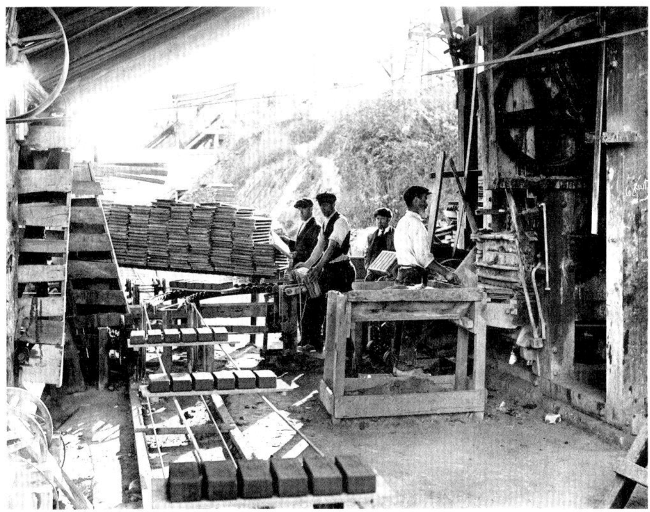

Fig. 2. Workers at the Ver Valen automatic brickmaking machine, Excelsior Brickyard, Dan DeNoyelles Collection, c. 1900. Haverstraw Brick Museum

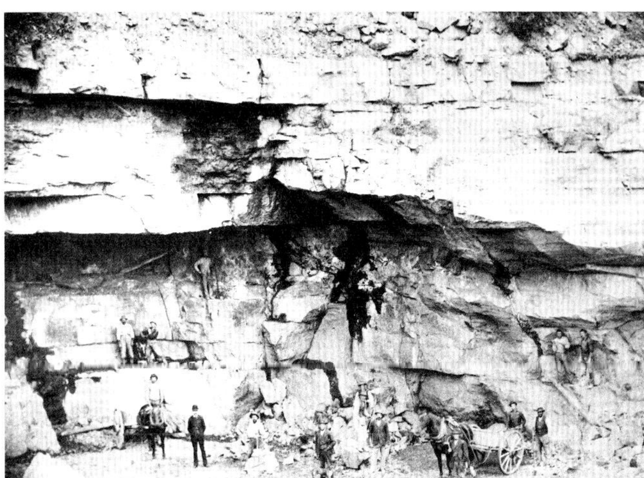

Fig. 3. Beach Mine, natural cement quarry in Rosendale, New York, c. 1800s

While *Lookout*'s shape is biomorphic, it is also bilaterally symmetrical. With the arch framing its front, it suggests the shape of an animal sitting back on its haunches: "I gravitate toward forms that feel like they exude life, like living things have forces that push outward, like our bodies. So there's something rounded about them, but there's no . . . it's not a religion."[4] This form is reminiscent of other of Puryear's

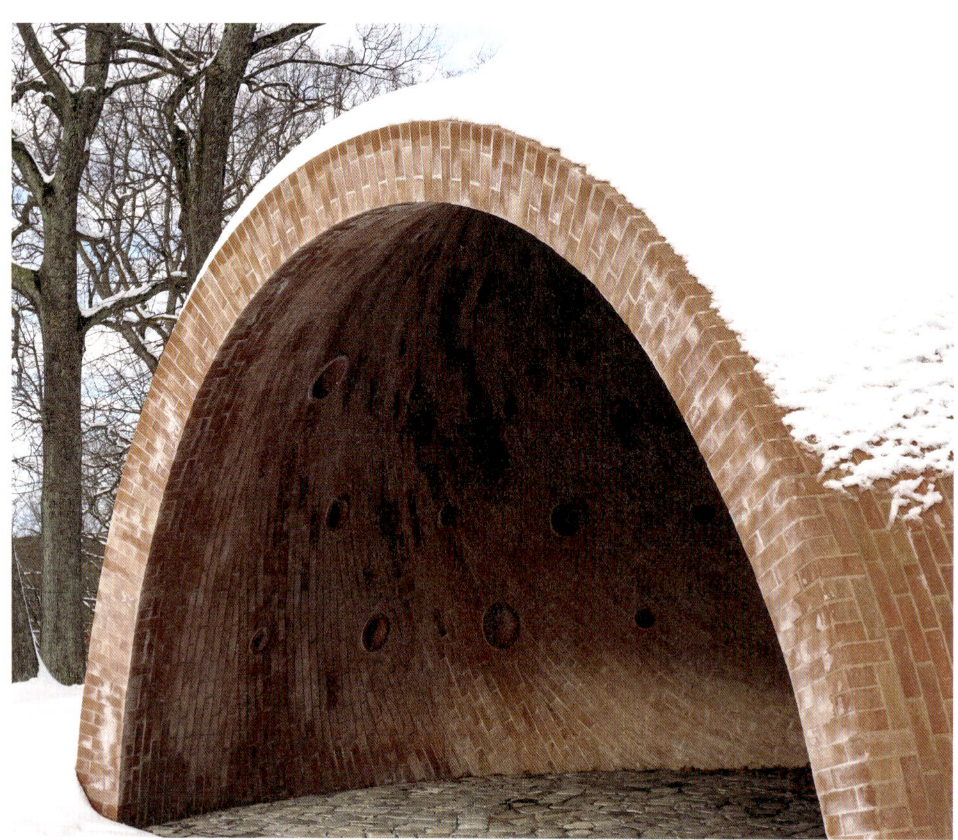

Fig. 4. *Lookout* in the snow, January 2024

outdoor works that recall a highly abstracted animal, specifically *Creature from Iddefjord* (2020; pls. 57, 58), in Oslo, and *Big Bling* (2016; pl. 41), a temporary sculpture created for New York's Madison Square Park: both curled onto tucked-back haunches, their front legs straight and facing forward. Inasmuch as *Lookout* might resemble a frontally oriented face (we are, after all, being encouraged to look out the front of the work), other public sculptures such as *That Profile* (1999; pl. 33), *Guardian Stone* (2001–03; pl. 38), and *Bearing Witness* (1994–98; pl. 26) share the suggestion of the rounded back of a head, curving out from the nape of a neck. The meandering *Connecting* (2018; pls. 47, 48), which Puryear made for the U.S. Embassy in Beijing, also shares this curve.

Lookout is Puryear's first permanent work that viewers may enter. However, since some of his earliest outdoor works, the artist has considered distinctions between his sculpture and architecture, and between object and place. Puryear's 1993–94 *Pavilion in the Trees* (fig. 5, pl. 6), created for Philadelphia's Fairmount Park, which he began constructing models for in 1981, is a raised treehouse-like platform with a latticed wooden roof. Describing the work, which is permeable to the woods around it, Puryear noted that it was not a sculpture but a "public amenity designed by a sculptor," that gave the setting "a bit more poetry than it otherwise might have."[5]

Puryear also considers how his works will interact with the natural surroundings. *That Profile,* sited against the dramatic backdrop surrounding the Getty Center, is constructed from thin steel poles that form a delicate lattice against the Los Angeles sky. The work's height requires viewers to look up and through it, allowing it to frame the landscape beyond its physical materials. The artist has also made use of public projects as catalysts to immerse viewers in natural experiences. *Bodark Arc* (1982; pl. 11), at the Nathan Manilow Sculpture Park outside of Chicago, takes landscape almost entirely as its medium. The edge of the work of art—the line framing and creating it—is a mown, arched path through tall grass (it was originally asphalt), and a hedgerow of trees with a path underneath. This work employs relatively little to announce itself as a sculpture: a bronze chair (designed and created by Puryear, based on a type used in West Africa),[6] and a timber arch made from heavy beams. The semicircular path continues over the edge of a lake as well as over a marsh, following the same curved line of the circumference of a circle with the chair at its central point.

Of all Puryear's outdoor works, his 1994–95 untitled sculpture created for a private collection at Oliver Ranch in Geyserville, California (pls. 23, 24), provides the closest visual as well as technical precedent for *Lookout*. This work marks Puryear's second constructed from fieldstone, more than a decade after his first engagement with the material for *Sentinel* (fig. 6, pl. 10), in Gettysburg, Pennsylvania. Like *Lookout*, the work at Oliver Ranch is symmetrical. One must circumnavigate the sculpture to understand its form, because its flat front does not reveal its bulbous, cantilevered back end. The front comprises a flat stone wall with an arch at the center. It is a hollow form of a scale that a human might enter, but its front opening is barricaded by a gate of diagonally gridded cedar beams. This obstructed entry leads into the rounded fieldstone pouch, rising into the air several feet higher than the front wall. Comparing *Lookout* and the work at Oliver Ranch, Puryear has explained:

> I have done a similar form in its most basic outline or silhouette or whatever you want call it in the project in Geyserville, California. And it came to mind here as a way to open it up and make it accessible. So that viewers could see this form not only as something to be experienced from outside, but something to experience from the inside.[7]

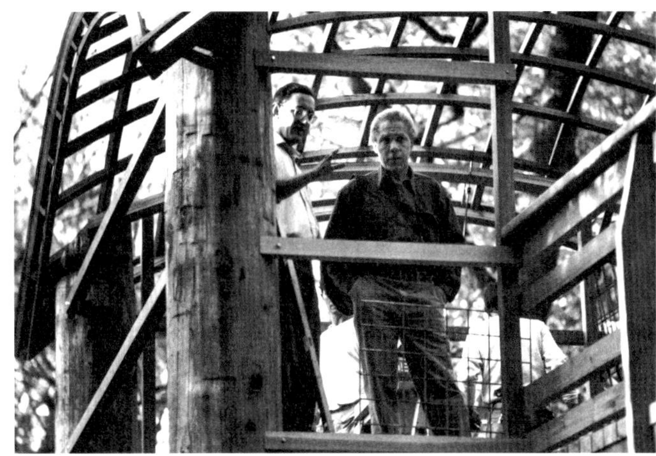

Fig. 5. Martin Puryear at the installation of *Pavilion in the Trees* (1993–94), Fairmount Park, Philadelphia

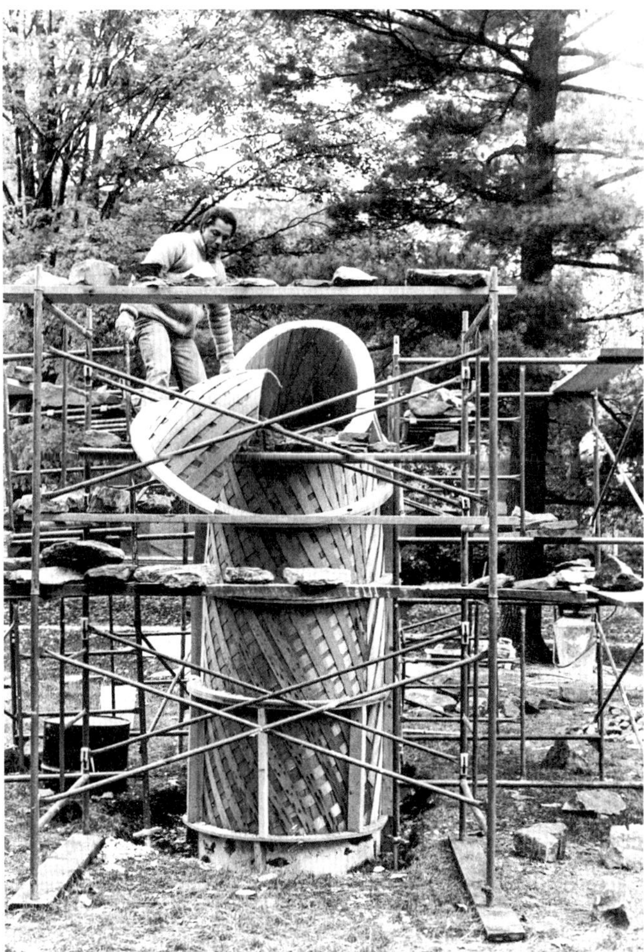

Fig. 6. Wooden formwork used for the fabrication of *Sentinel* (1982), Gettysburg College, Pennsylvania

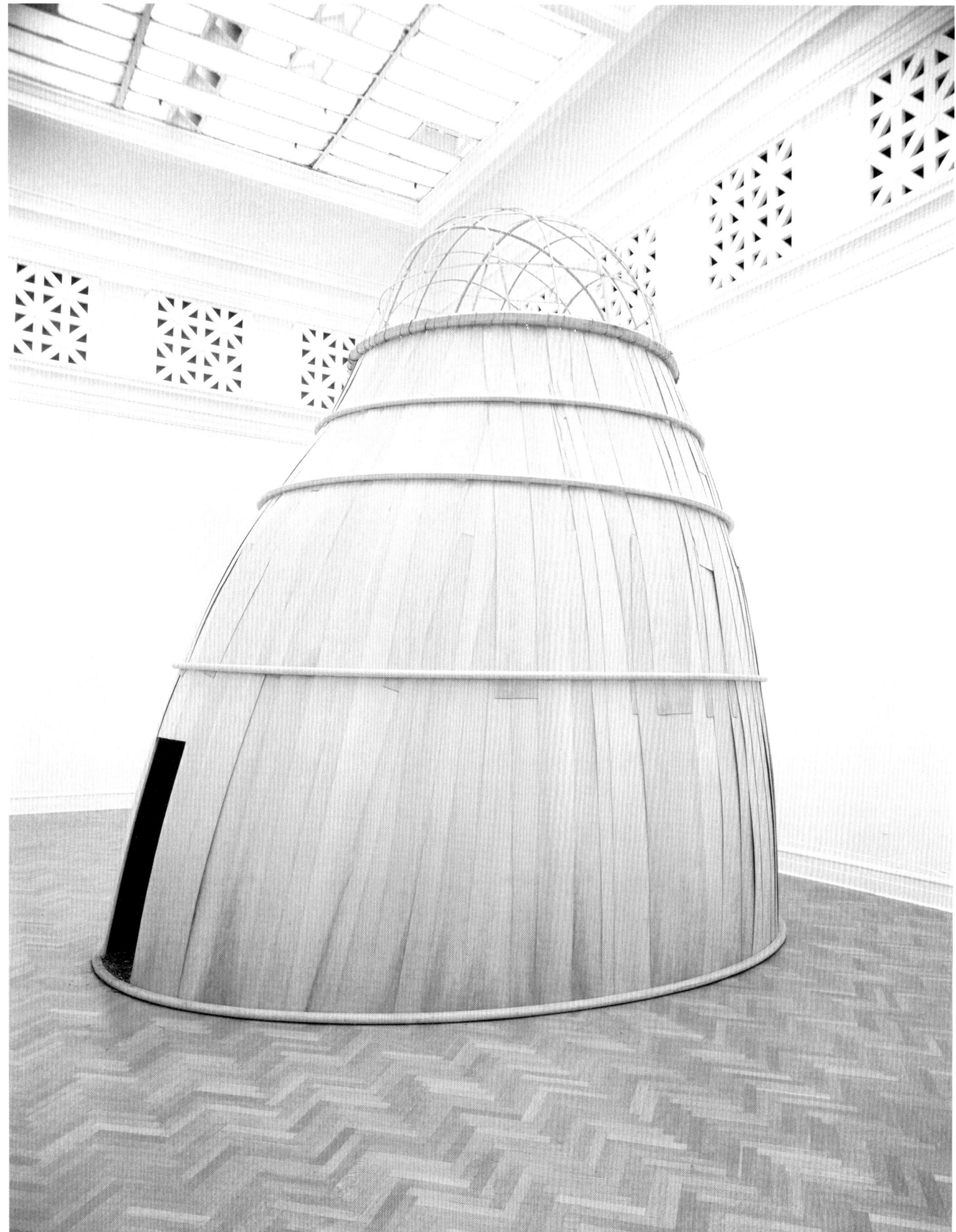

Fig. 7. Martin Puryear, *Cedar Lodge*, 1977. Red cedar, fir, and rawhide, 18 ft. × 16.5 ft. Installation at the Corcoran Gallery of Art, Washington, DC, 1977

In blocking entry to the Oliver Ranch piece, Puryear has invited a psychological reaction to that work: a viewer is made acutely aware of an indoor space, without being able to access it. Its interior is a dark, shadowed, and unknowable space; the contours of this interior can be assumed from its exterior appearance, but not confirmed. *Lookout*, on the other hand, invites the viewer in.

Perhaps none of Puryear's sculptures created for indoor display has served as more of a precedent for *Lookout* than a temporary work from 1977, *Cedar Lodge* (fig. 7). Soon after its completion, Puryear described this work as being "shaped like a haystack—about eighteen feet tall altogether. Like a barrel or canoe, it has ribs or stays, and sheath-like walls of red cedars which were fastened on the inside."[8] Across the ceiling was the dried skin of a cow stretched within a circular wooden frame, forming a translucent rawhide skylight. *Cedar Lodge* also had an entryway. To enter a sculpture, in Puryear's worldview, is to be able to learn more about the state of "sculpture," to envision the inside of something of which we are so often given only an outer skin. Puryear has said:

> *Cedar Lodge* . . . was a kind of strange, biomorphic, organic structure that had a door that you could enter. So I'm fascinated by that, and even in the things that aren't inherently about dwellings or about inhabitable spaces, there is the sense that if a thing is a certain size or a certain scale in relation to your body, and that you're conscious of the hollowness of it, I think there is a way to project yourself into it, to imagine what it would be like to experience that from the inside. This has given rise to a lot of my works which are not sealed off, unbroken skins, but are in fact various ways of articulating a space or a volume that's permeable, visually permeable, that you can penetrate, sense the inside as well as the outside. It's always been fascinating to me to have that dual sense.[9]

The unusual shape and structure of *Lookout* means that its interior is a perceptual experience. As Puryear has described, "You start with a tunnel, and it transitions into a dome. It's a cul-de-sac in space. *Cul-de-sac* means the 'bottom of the sack' in French. And this is in fact a brick pouch, with a domed roof, that the public is invited to go inside."[10] One is to gaze upon and enjoy the natural landscape outside *Lookout*'s cave by looking both forward through the entrance to Schunnemunk, but also up and out through the ninety cylindrical holes that punctuate the sculpture's surface. To be inside the sculpture provides an opportunity to look beyond it, out of it. According to the artist, "I wanted to penetrate the walls, so that it wasn't just inside and outside, but you're getting perforations, you're getting views of this amazing nature through these openings studded through the wall."[11]

The work's title has multiple meanings: it indicates a place from which to take in a beautiful view. Is it a warning? Is it a command? It is also a straightforward word that has connotations of hunting; of survivalist tactics; of someone in nature getting their bearings. It conjures a sense of fact-gathering rather than romantic ideals. Similarly, in its aesthetic, *Lookout* elevates a humble building material, the simple red brick. For Puryear, "It's an opportunity to work with a material that I've long been fascinated by, which is clay brick—red clay brick. A very common, very generic, very familiar material, but used in a completely different way."[12] Puryear has spoken of his love for this common material:

> The other part of it is the beauty of masonry. That's like tapestry, it's like weaving. All these little stitches of brick, these elements, these incremental elements, and the fact that the masonry is going through these changes, that reads as texture, that reads as evidence of workmanship, craftsmanship, care. . . . Not just the monolithic chunk of material, but something that was finessed at every single stage. Every single element was put in very carefully.[13]

This interest in the gradual, accumulative formation has resonances within Puryear's studio practice. The artist's sculptural work in wood tends to be additive: he brings pieces of wood together to construct sculpture, rather than carving into a solid mass.

Throughout his life and career, Puryear has sought occasions to learn building and craft techniques from artists and artisans around the world. He has taken opportunities to learn how to create objects in manners previously unknown to him, from virtuosos in their own mediums, as he is in his: wood. Puryear's commissions have provided some significant chances for engagement and learning. Puryear has consistently sought out tradespeople and craftspeople, and in so doing has brought to light deeply honed artistic skills that are often overlooked. For *Sentinel* and for his subsequent work at Oliver Ranch, Puryear labored alongside stonemasons, observing and learning their technique (fig. 8). For *Everything That Rises* (1997; pl. 20), commissioned by the University of Washington in Seattle, Puryear learned from artisans who make watertight liquor stills from hammered copper and bronze how to make a seamless work from hammered bronze sheets—forgoing the likely easier option of turning the work over to a foundry, to have it cast into a continuous bronze shell. For *Bearing Witness*, in Washington, DC, he collaborated with a company that specialized in creating domed shells of sheet metal for the hulls of sailing yachts. For an invitation to make a major work in Wanås, Sweden, he sought out a skilled thatcher to create an abstracted Buddha figure with a covering of reed straw for *Meditation in a Beech Wood* (1996; pl. 28)—thatching being a local tradition, but one rarely practiced by the time of the work's creation.[14] For *This Mortal Coil* (1999; pl. 36), a commission in the Chapelle Saint-Louis de la Salpêtrière in Paris, Puryear attempted to enlist Les Compagnons du Devoir, an ages-old organization of French craftspeople, to assist him, but he discovered that they would not work on a temporary structure. Instead, he engaged other local French experts: set builders helped him create the work, and alpinists scaled narrow chapel walls to install the work high above. Puryear's process has revealed a desire to collaborate, but never to assert himself as the expert, instead maintaining a deference to the deep knowledge of others.

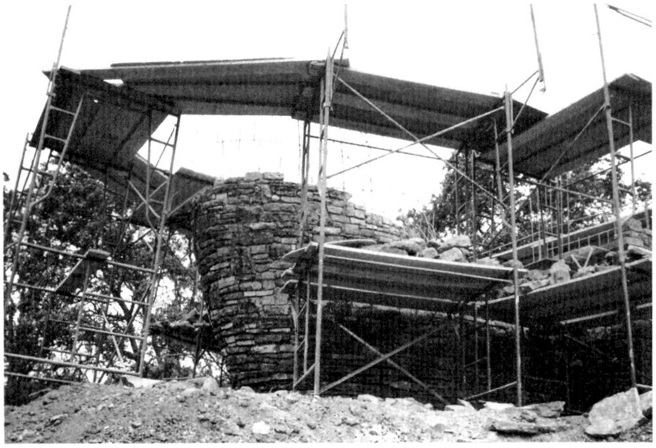

Fig. 8. Constructing *Untitled* (1994–95), Oliver Ranch, Geyserville, California

Puryear was met with much skepticism from engineers and masons when he first conceived of the contours of *Lookout*. The underlying structure required to create the work in brick is so complicated that finding the team that would execute it was challenging and, ultimately, invigorating:

> It's been a succession of encounters with different levels and different kinds of expertise. I was especially fortunate to meet people who could do more than say, "impossible." It takes a tremendous amount of effort to transmit ideas to another person so they can execute them faithfully. Particularly for an artist who doesn't like to repeat himself and who's always learning some new thing at every stage.[15]

Even when he asks these experts to help him create shapes that their materials rarely take, however, Puryear insists that his goal is not to stretch the limit of his material for the sake of such a feat; he is simply forming the enigmatic, organic forms to which he is drawn.

The planning and conceptualizing of most of his sculptures—and all of his public works—is accompanied by drawings, prints, and models along the way. While they are foremost planning documents, Puryear attends to them with a similar rigor and sense of aesthetic interest that he brings to his finished iterations. Some, such as a richly blackened print titled *Lean To*, represent works that would remain unrealized (fig. 9). (*Lean To* was an earlier conception for

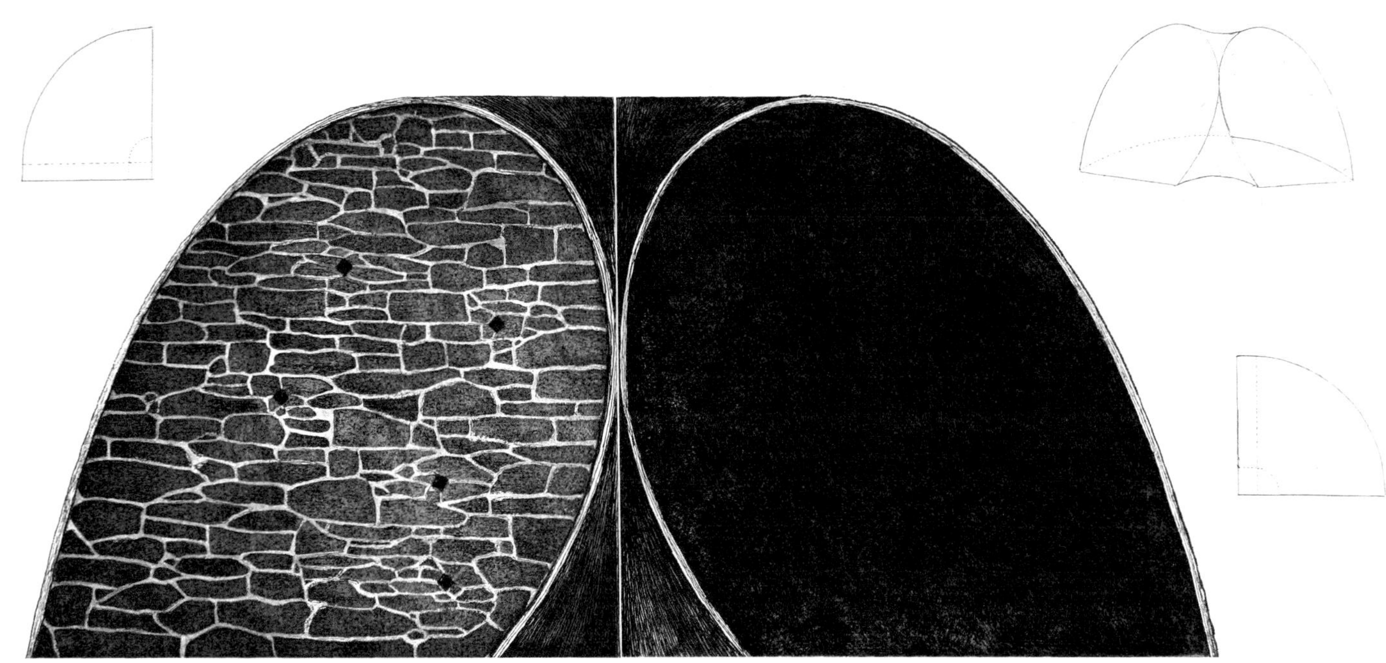

Fig. 9. Martin Puryear, *Lean To*, 2012. Aquatint and etching on paper, plate: 14 × 30 in. (35.6 × 76.2 cm); sheet: 23¾ × 39 in. (60.3 × 99.1 cm)

Puryear's Storm King commission; Puryear also made small sculptural models of it.) The print was designed with careful intricacy despite it being a preparatory work. A preliminary drawing and a maquette for an unrealized project at Tufts University show a similarly rigorous process of thought and meticulous planning (pls. 4, 5). For his maquette for an unrealized memorial for the United States Holocaust Memorial Museum in Washington, DC, Puryear charred the exterior of the wooden model (pl. 14). Puryear's models and drawings are created at many different points in the process of a work's creation. Early models help the artist describe and propose the work to a patron or institution; others help him understand how to create a certain shape, or to translate technical information to a partner or team of collaborators, enabling their next steps and parallel investigations. Resolving such details is critical prior to working on a larger scale, and also demonstrates Puryear's practical nature as he collaborates on projects too large and complicated for his studio to execute on its own. For *Meditation in a Beech Wood*, Puryear made one smooth wooden model to represent the completed contours of the work once covered by thatch, as well as another that demonstrated his proposal for how the underlying wooden structure could be created. Because this latter model was representing a layer underneath the thatched exterior (showing only structural beams), Puryear made it a slightly smaller size, so both models could complement each other at the same scale. With *Guardian Stone*, for which the artist desired to use contoured granite blocks to create a twenty-five-foot-tall seamless whole, Puryear determined the best manner in which to cut the blocks for the most streamlined impression, and was able to pass this model and information over to a team who then cut and hand-carved granite blocks to his exact specifications.

The structure of *Lookout* was puzzled through with the help of several clarifying drawings and sculptural models, created by Puryear along with his assistant Rob Horton and masonry specialist Lara Davis. Puryear created models from wood as well as high-density polyurethane foam, first representing a thirteen-segment brick laying, and then finally showing the work in nine segments (pls. 59, 61, 63). The second sculptural model also included a suggestion of paving for the base of the sculpture. Puryear finished the last model when the bricklaying for *Lookout* was well underway, but before it had been completed on top. Following the progression of these scaled-down bricks as they rose up the structure's nine segments allowed Puryear to visualize, understand, and plan for the manner in which the final bricks would join at the very top of the sculpture: he created the last brick in an oval shape.

While there are likely more expedient routes to create his desired forms, Puryear gravitates toward paths that lead him into deep research and provide platforms for knowledge acquisition. Ultimately, Puryear has seen each of his projects as an invitation to participate in a new type of creation:

> I'm just curious about how things are made, always have been. . . . There's creativity embedded in how things are made. Not just an idea, but how things are made. And the more deeply you get involved in how things are made, the more potential for a kind of richness is possible. That's been a big part of my life, and my work. How things are made, and what they're made from. And also the history of that, the history of whatever method it is that you're tapping into.[16]

Puryear's large-scale, outdoor commissions demonstrate that he is an artist who sees the process of creation and the intellectual and aesthetic pursuit of formal beauty as being inextricable. He finds—and elevates—the beauty in everyday life, and in the many craft practices that shape our world.

Notes

1. Martin Puryear, in conversation with Adela Goldsmith, Nora Lawrence, Jonathan Sanden, and Amy S. Weisser, August 22, 2023.
2. Ibid.
3. Schunnemunk itself is meaningful to Storm King's history: two thousand acres of the mountain were purchased by Storm King's founding family and given to New York State in order to keep the environs of Storm King green in perpetuity; since 2003 it has been Schunnemunk State Park.
4. Puryear, in conversation with Goldsmith, Lawrence, Sanden, and Weisser.
5. Puryear, quoted in "Museum Without Walls: *Pavilion in the Trees* (1993)," video produced by the Association for Public Art (formerly Fairmount Park Art Association), https://www.associationforpublicart.org/artwork/pavilion-in-the-trees/#mww--video.
6. Puryear, in conversation with the author, November 22, 2023.
7. Puryear, in conversation with Goldsmith, Lawrence, Sanden, and Weisser.
8. Martin Puryear, interview with Clarissa Wittenberg and Mary Swift (on air, WAMU-FM), July 1978.
9. David Levi Strauss, "Martin Puryear with David Levi Strauss," *Brooklyn Rail*, November 4, 2007.
10. Puryear, in conversation with Goldsmith, Lawrence, Sanden, and Weisser.
11. Ibid.
12. Ibid.
13. Ibid.
14. Many of the thatchers Puryear first contacted declined, unsure that they would be able to create the tight weave required over such an irregular form. Ultimately, he found one eager to take on the challenge. The sculpture's thatched roof has been replaced three times since it was built; when the thatcher retires, the work will be disassembled. Martin Puryear in conversation with the author, October 20, 2023.
15. Puryear, in conversation with Goldsmith, Lawrence, Sanden, and Weisser.
16. Ibid.

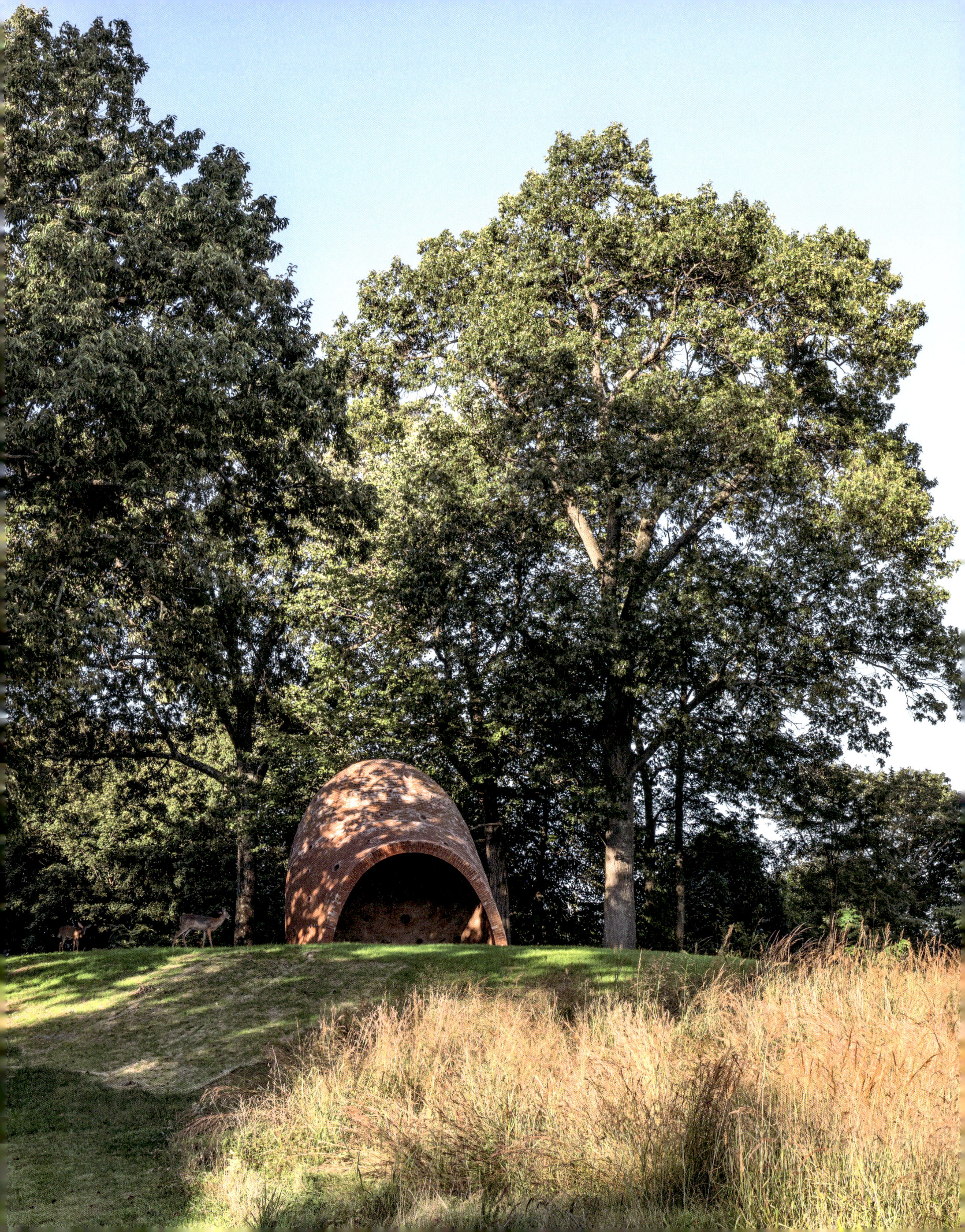

LOOKOUT
SEEING, CONSIDERING, FEELING

Amy S. Weisser

You say to brick, "What do you want, brick?"
Brick says to you, "I like an arch."

Louis Kahn, 1973

The more deeply you get involved
in how things are made, the greater the potential
for a different kind of richness.

Martin Puryear, 2023

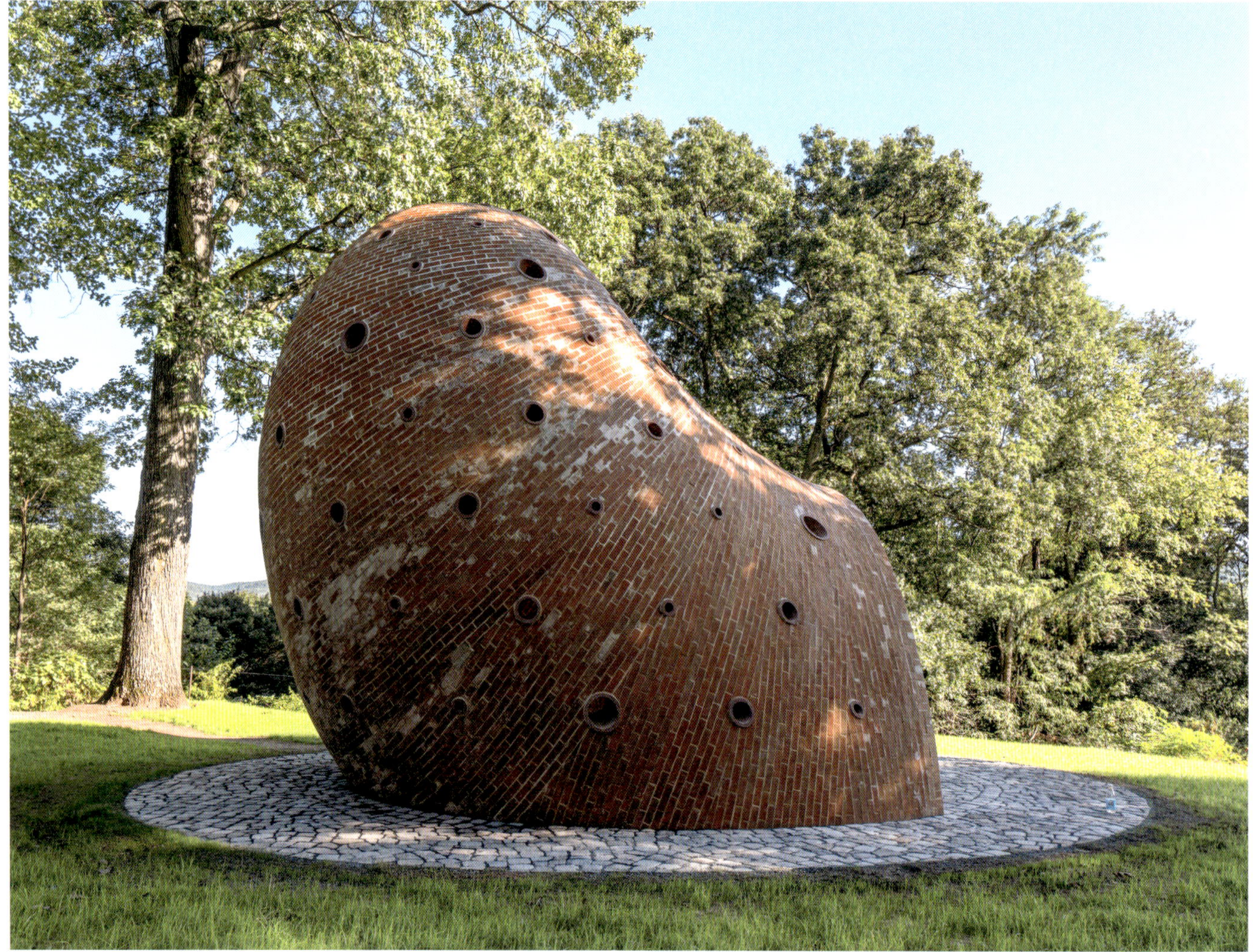

Fig. 1. View of *Lookout* looking east, September 2023

Seeing

We first notice Martin Puryear's *Lookout* (2023) from a distance. As we face north on Storm King Art Center's Museum Hill, a rounded form, with an opening, beckons. It extends the height of a distant hill in an act of homage or hubris. Coming around a corner as we climb the hill from the west, we glimpse an unnameable outline: the large form curves up and back and then reverses itself and slopes down (fig. 1). Or, approaching from the north, the shape seems to turn its back on us, drawing attention to the sunlight toward which it opens (fig. 2). A gaping mouth, a profile, a seed.

As we stand on the gently domed ground on which the object sits, our attention is called to the details of its construction. *Lookout* is built of bricks. These bricks create, at the open end of the work, an arch. At the artwork's highest point, they encircle a dome. In the transition from opening to covering, the bricks balloon out and upward. An arch, a vault, a dome.

As our observations shift from shape to surface, we discover that the methodical laying of the bricks—creating a grid of orange-red rectangles bordered by off-white mortar—is

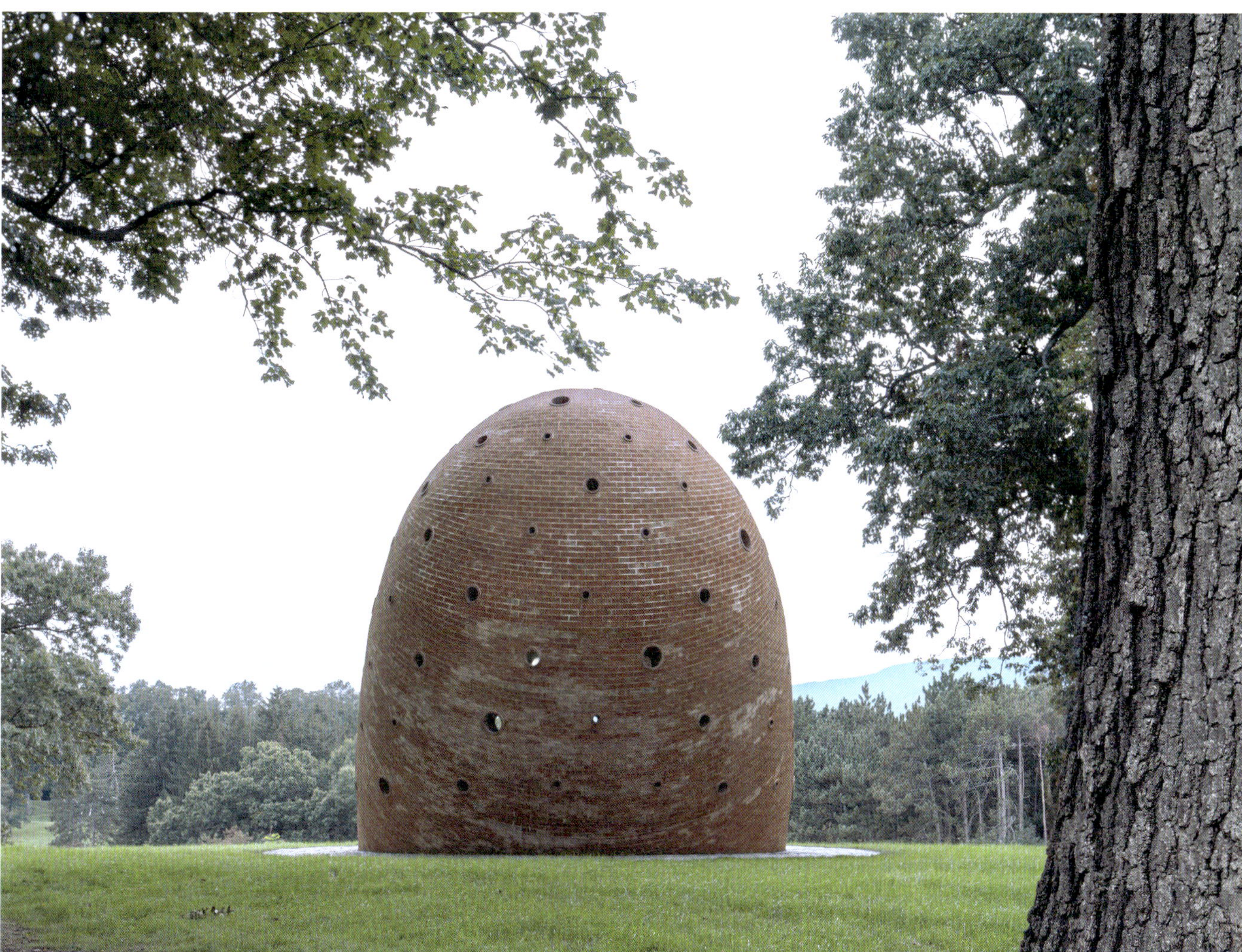

Fig. 2. View of *Lookout* looking south, September 2023

interrupted by bricks abruptly cut on a slant.[1] These cuts form sharp lines that follow the form's overall curves. On the upper side of these cut lines, rows of uncut bricks again march across the surface, now at a slight angle from the bricks before them. Eight times the level of brick adjusts so that gradually but methodically the vertical form of the arch transitions to the horizontal baseline of the dome. With each segment set ten to thirteen degrees off from its neighbor, the bricks move from perpendicularity in relationship to the ground plane to coplanar with the ground. The lines that mark the borders between segments are the only straight lines in the artwork. A surface, a cut, a change of direction.

Punctures also lace the brick surface. These apertures are in three sizes and rimmed with brick-colored tubes: the smallest allows a view but not an arm; the middle accepts a hand as a tool for exploration; the largest simultaneously welcomes arm and eye. The openings are arranged in a loose grid, even enough to avoid a distracting logic puzzle yet irregular enough to briefly stay the glance. The edges of

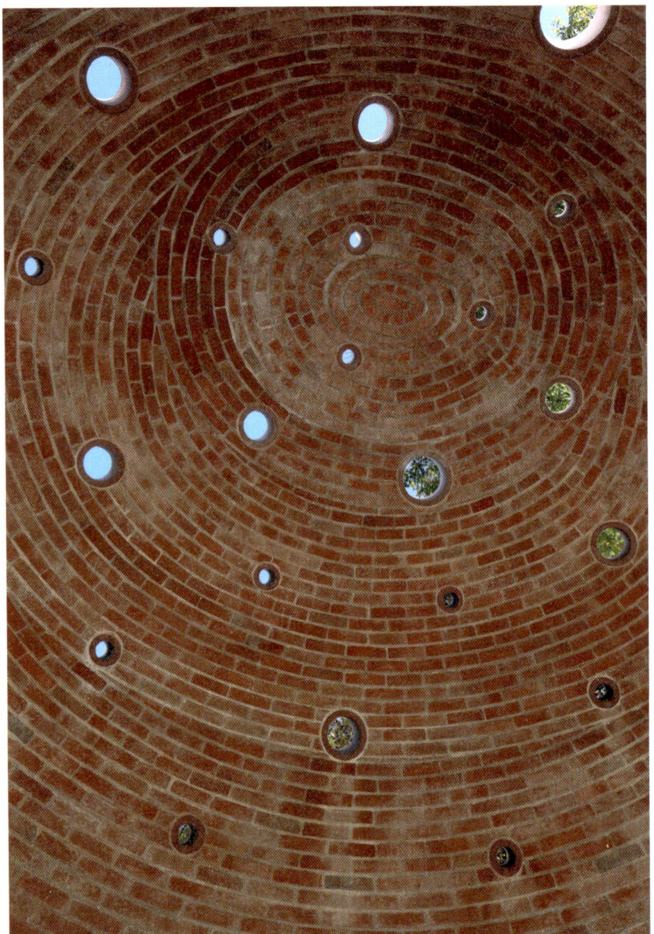

Fig. 3. View from inside *Lookout* looking up, September 2023

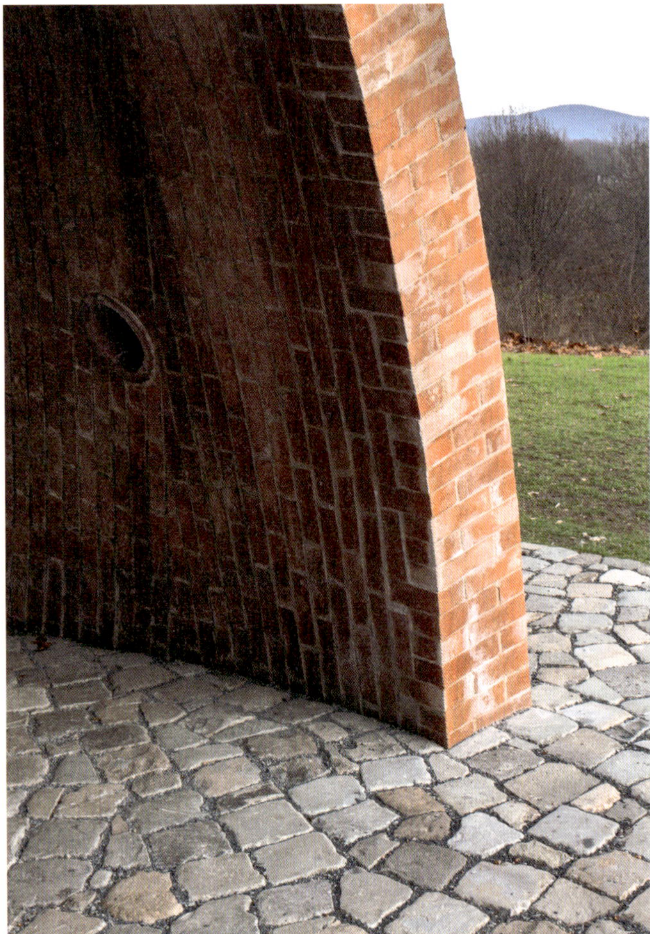

Fig. 4. View of the thickness of *Lookout*'s masonry wall, December 2023

the tubes extend slightly beyond the exterior surface of the sculpture, creating a soft staccato. From the outside, apertures provide seemingly accidental views. We glimpse the inner shell, other people exploring the sculpture, and the landscape beyond the artwork. A beehive, a penetration, an invitation.

Stepping inside, we are now enveloped on three sides. The space, measuring at the widest point of the base seventeen feet, or several arm lengths, is intimate at eye level. The brick courses seem to swell, drawing our gaze upward. As we take in the full interior height of eighteen feet, the conceptual understanding that the interior is the negative of the exterior is disrupted empirically. While the interior transitions remain graceful, the pace of alteration accelerates, astounding with the rapidity of the progression toward the vault, the complexity of the undulations that lead to the apex, and the rapid-fire interruption of the openings. Compression, tension, release.

The arch opens to a view of the valleys and hills of Storm King and the Hudson Valley landscape beyond. In the foreground, artworks sit among figural areas of lawn and tall grass. Museum Hill, Storm King's historical center, holds the middle ground, with the double crest of Schunnemunk Mountain filling the backdrop. The sculpture's matrix of portholes directs the gaze forward to the view and upward to the sky. While fragmenting the surrounds, the openings imbue the faraway landscape with import and wonder, specific and general. We trace the time of day and year by the dots of light the apertures cast on the inner brick surface. Proscenium, planetarium, sundial.

Within *Lookout*, the ground plane slightly mounds toward a point in the center back. We confirm that the tubes align to our eye level at this spot. Here, the image through the apertures is direct, unimpeded. Elsewhere crescents of tube and sunlight interlace the interior and exterior, the physical and the ephemeral. Summit, telescope, temple.

As we focus on the details, we realize that the arch forms half of an ellipse, not a semicircle. This sparks a second look at the bricks that form the dome. They too outline an ellipse, with the final brick at the apex carved at the corners into an elliptical form (fig. 3). The pavement inscribes an oval. Connected, dynamic, baroque.

Close looking awakens other senses. Our bodies move from the soft padding of grass to the uneven surface of stone pavement. As we traverse the cobblestone and bluestone pavers, we might hear the tapping of locomotion. We might perceive the echo of our voices against the curves of the form or the whistle of the wind through the tubes. Perhaps we smell moisture in the interior. On a hot day, our skin feels cooler inside; on a cold day, we sense heat radiating from the brick. Shelter, shell, cave.

Back to our eyes: we note that the paving stones that create the artwork's base and encircle it are rough-cut squares against the rectangles of the brick, gray-blue against orange-red, dark mortar against light. The loose relationship of the stones one to the other amalgamates into a circular stone at the sweet spot indicating the focal point of the view through the tubes. The pavement surrounding the sculpture makes an oval, slightly wider than a body at the sides, while billowing to an apron in front of the opening and stepping away from the swollen form at the rear. The distinct edge between dark pavement and green grass sets a specific zone of the sculpture. A podium, a pedestal, a place setting.

Considering

Close observation of *Lookout* reveals clues on how it was engineered and built. The arm's-length depth of the tubes makes evident an enclosure of some thickness. At the opening, the bricks that line the arch allow measurement. They say: this edge is as thick as two layers of brick surrounding a cavity (figs. 4, 5).

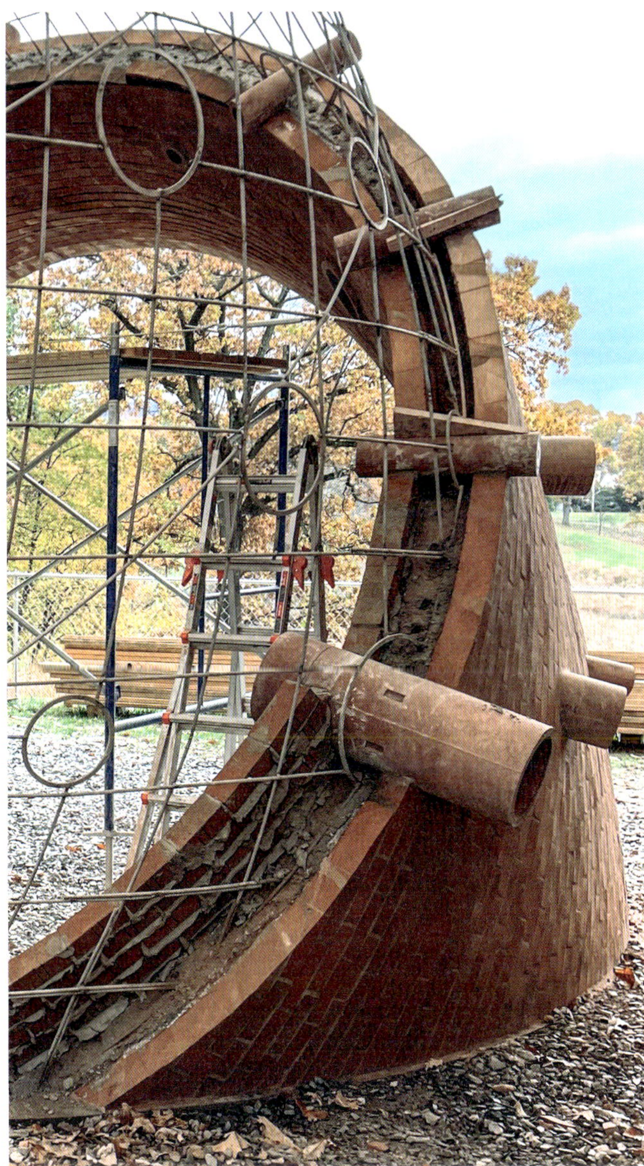

Fig. 5. View of rebar frame and tubes during *Lookout* construction, November 2022

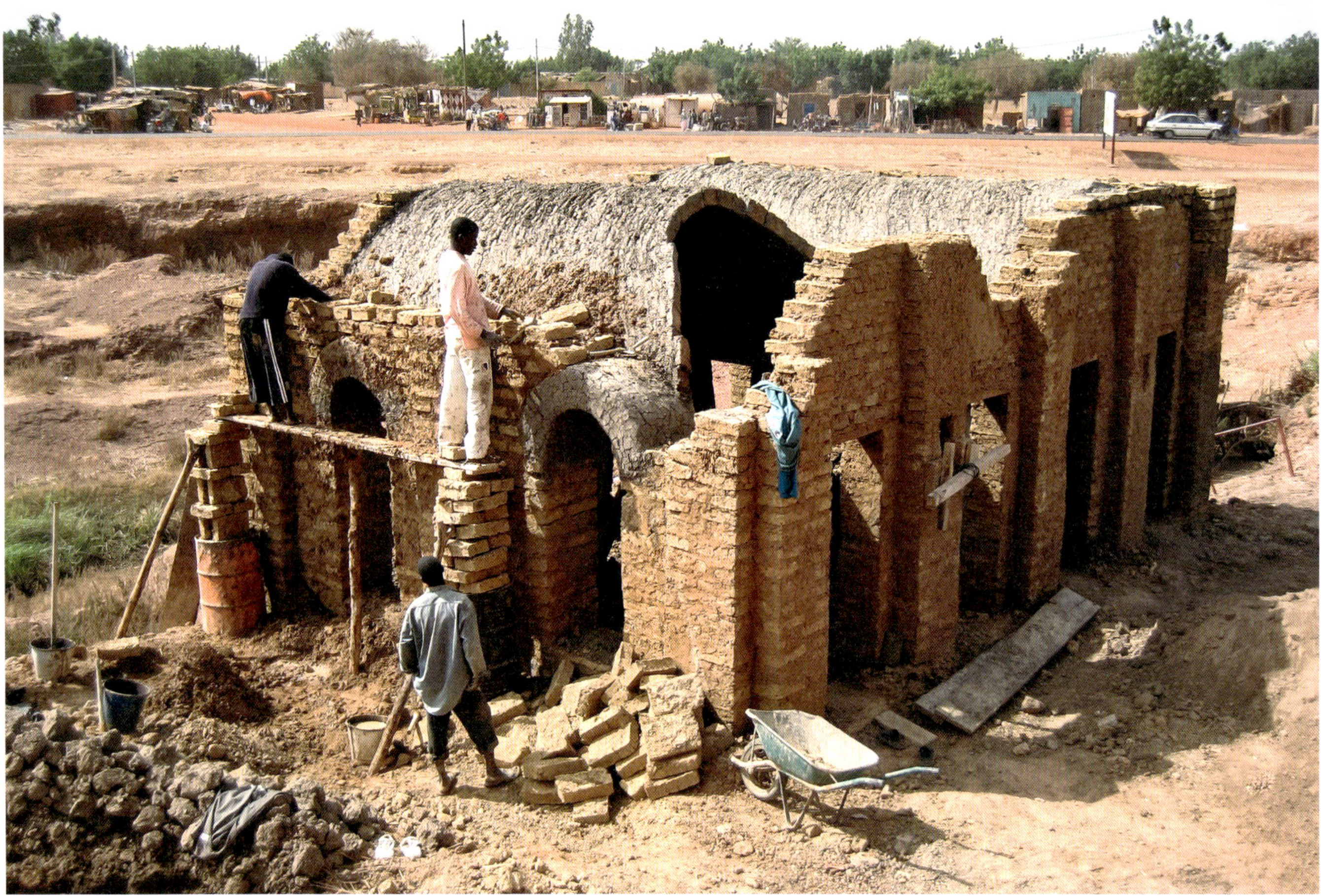

Fig. 6. Construction of a mud brick house, photographed by Martin Puryear during a trip to Mali, 2009

Puryear describes *Lookout* as beginning with a tunnel and moving upward toward a dome. Tunnel (an elongated arch) and dome are both conventional and historical architectural forms, deployed across global cultures. These forms efficiently span large openings or spaces and manage structural forces in compression and tension. The structure of the form is dependent on each row of bricks, after those of the first segment of the arch, being supported by rows laid earlier. The radial shift of each segment progressively decreases the angle to the ground at which the bricks lay. Still, the angle to the ground is only one marker of the placement of the bricks in space. To trace the bulging form, each brick twists slightly in relationship to the bricks around it.

This methodology of building, less commonly known in the West than the arch and dome, is Nubian vaulting. It is the oldest arch technology in the world, developed two thousand years before the Romans.[2] Because building blocks are placed against modules already laid, structures can be built without the use of formwork. Puryear witnessed a house being built with a Nubian vault on a trip to Mali in early 2009, organized by the former Museum of African Art in New York, and the memory of that experience encouraged the artist to use the technology with *Lookout* (fig. 6).

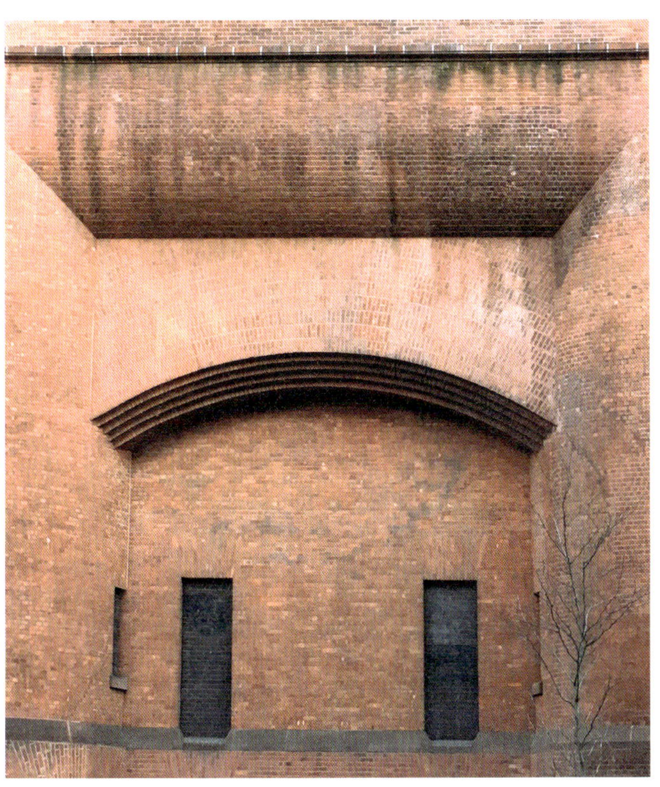

Fig. 7. Detail of Squadron A Armory (1895), New York

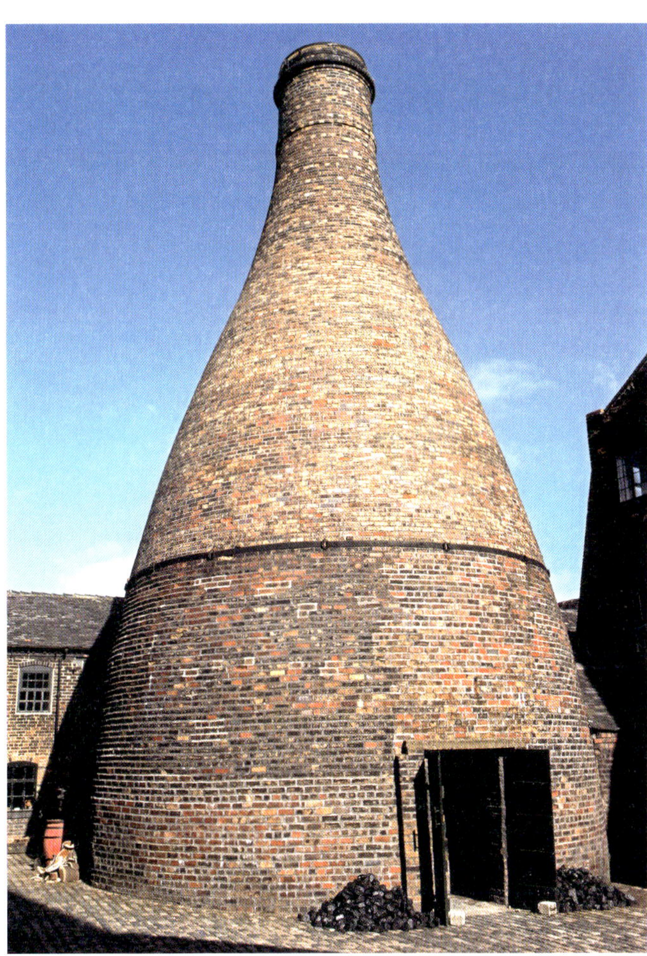

Fig. 8. Bottle kiln at a former ceramics factory (now the Gladstone Pottery Museum), late eighteenth century, Stoke-on-Trent, Staffordshire, England

In developing *Lookout*'s form, materials, and colors, Puryear also looked at vernacular brick structures across the local Hudson Valley landscape, where he has made his home for more than thirty years. The artist cites, as well, the former Squadron A Armory on the Upper East Side of Manhattan (fig. 7), particularly its heavy, curved entablature that seems to defy gravity, and the curved and tapered forms of bottle kilns at the ceramics factories of Stoke-on-Trent, England (seventeenth century to twentieth century) (fig. 8). About the kilns' bulbous swelling, Puryear has said, "They're very beautiful shapes. And it's partly what got me interested in wanting to mold bricks into a shape of my own."[3]

In reality and metaphorically, Puryear builds sculptures piece by piece, or brick by brick, using additive processes rather than subtractive ones. An additive exploration of site, structure, material, and collaborators directed the way *Lookout* was made manifest.

The topography of Storm King Art Center was Puryear's first collaborator for the sculpture that would become *Lookout*. The idea grew out of an initial invitation by Storm King in late 2010 and progressed through site visits and dialogues.[4] Puryear had approached his commission for Storm King with a concept of conjoined open curved forms, reminiscent of bandshells, that would gradually reveal themselves on a visitor's approach on intersecting paths (fig. 9). He referred to this proposal as a lean-to. A tour of the grounds to find such a site yielded instead a hill at the edge of the North Woods. After extensive consideration of his first concept in this location, Puryear embraced the opportunity of the prospect—the view from the hill—and began to reconsider the form of the artwork.

Travels in 2016 in Iran, where Puryear saw artisan bricklayers at work, led to the artist adjusting his initial concept of using bluestone from the Hudson Valley and fieldstone from Storm King's site to exploring the possibilities of brick, a material he had not used before. He pursued constructing his plastic form by applying gunite, a sprayable form of concrete, over a mold and then facing the outer surface with brick. Puryear engaged in extensive dialogue with Mark Mendel of Monterey Masonry, an artist and mason who was then restoring a historic home in Hudson, New York; Chris Hoppe, a structural engineer; and Tod Williams and Billie Tsien, architects. With Mendel and Hoppe, a mock-up to test the coherence of concrete and brick was attempted but failed when the bricks pulled away from the overhang.

At the suggestion of Williams and Tsien, Puryear reached out to John Ochsendorf, the Class of 1942 Professor of Architecture and Engineering at Massachusetts Institute of Technology who was then serving as the director of the

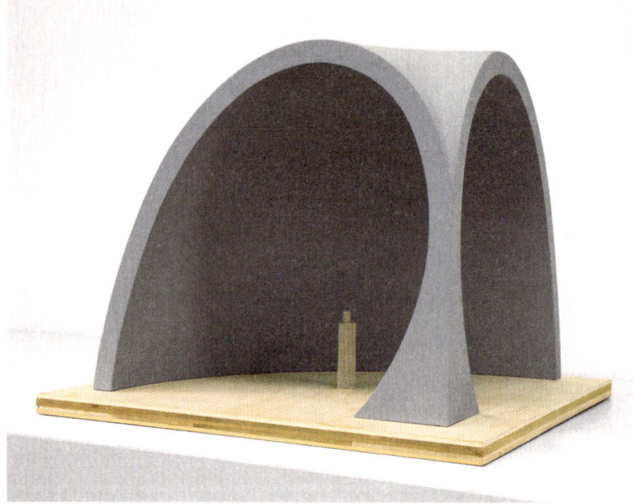

Fig. 9. Martin Puryear, *Maquette for "Untitled,"* 2016 (unrealized). Fiberglass and paint, 12¼ × 14½ × 14½ in. (30.5 × 35.6 × 35.6 cm)

American Academy in Rome. Puryear knew Ochsendorf's work on thin-shell vaults and his book *Guastavino Vaulting: The Art of Structural Tile* (2010). In late 2019, meeting in Rome, Ochsendorf encouraged Puryear to pursue brick as both structure and surface, with Nubian vaulting construction techniques as the key to making that possible. Together, artist and engineer also reduced the number of proposed segments from thirteen to the nine used in the final work (fig. 10). Over time, Ochsendorf and his students would go on to create digital models of the work, calculating the forces and estimating the number of bricks (eighteen thousand) required to fabricate it.[5]

But who would build the artwork? Several months later, Ochsendorf introduced Puryear to Lara Davis, who had earned a master of architecture degree from MIT in 2010 and had spent most the next decade at Auroville Earth Institute in India teaching about and building earthen structures. Davis, who had serendipitously relocated to the Hudson Valley when the COVID-19 pandemic hit, joined Puryear and his longtime studio manager Rob Horton, a sculptor, in planning the construction, testing techniques and materials, and documenting the project.

A half-scale mock-up of segments four and five of the sculpture proved the viability of construction in general and the Nubian vaulting technique specifically (fig. 11). It also introduced a structural innovation. Typically, brick ties would be used to literally tie the outer and inner layer of bricks of a cavity wall to each other, fortifying against their tendency to bulge outward or slump inward. The team worried that the atypical placement of bricks would conflict with the required regular distribution of ties. Rebecca Buntrock, an engineer at Silman, performed an analysis of the structural system and verified that the concrete tubes would connect the inner and outer layers of brick, serving the function of brick ties.[6] Progressively, the relationship between form and construction was tightening.

Lookout is built with a double wall of brick (an inside face and an outside face) that encases a cavity filled with concrete and is reinforced by a cage of stainless steel rebar at its center. The rebar cage was built by Kurt Wulfmeyer and Christopher Powers using digital coordinates scaled from Puryear's handmade model.[7] It served two purposes: structural and positional. Structurally, within the sandwich of brick, the steel counters the forces of tension while the brick and concrete resist the forces of compression. The second, positional, function of the rebar cage was to control the shape during construction.

For the first three segments of the sculpture, where the bricks are perpendicular or nearly perpendicular to the ground, a form was built as is typical for the fabrication of an arch. Here, the bricks were supported in the desired position by the formwork as the mortar dried (fig. 12). For the remaining segments, formwork was no longer necessary for support during brick laying. For these segments, the welded cage facilitated the masons' ability to build the form Puryear had developed through modeling (fig. 13). The

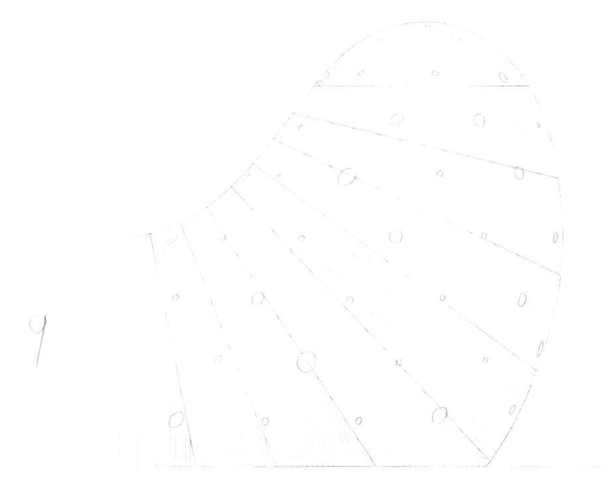

Fig. 10. Martin Puryear, *Brick Sculpture for Storm King Art Center (Nine Segments)*, 2021. Graphite on vellum, 23 × 29 in. (58.4 × 73.7 cm)

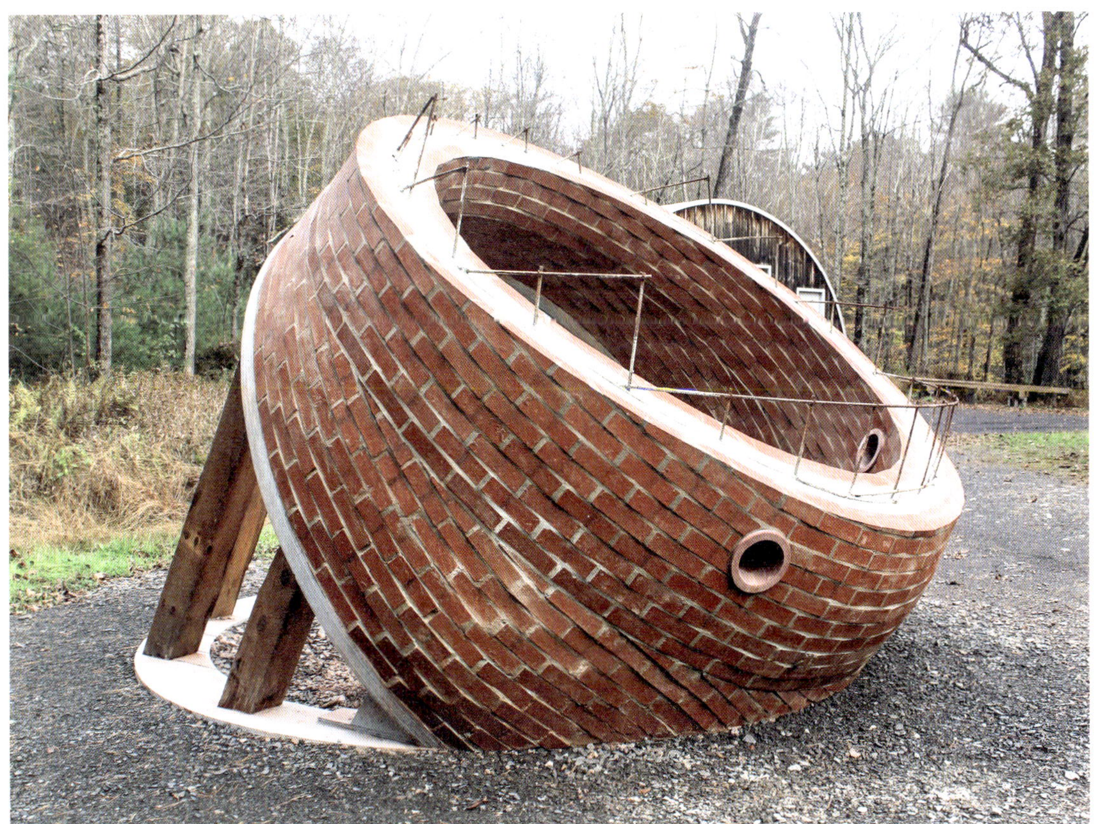

Fig. 11. Half-scale mock-up of *Lookout* constructed at Martin Puryear's studio, Hudson Valley, New York, early 2022

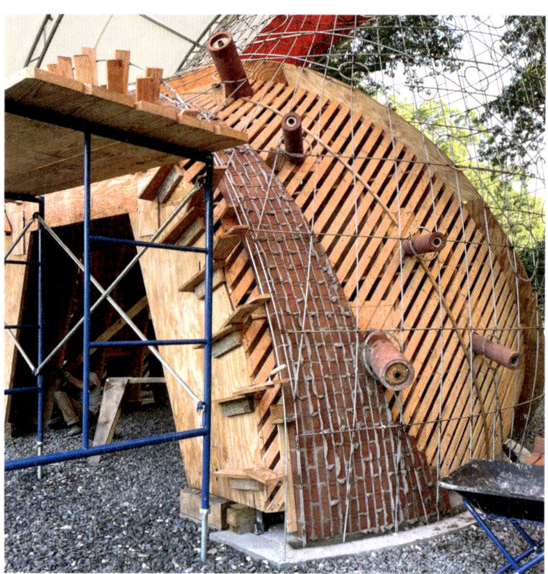

Fig. 12. *Lookout* in progress, showing arch construction over wooden formwork, September 2022

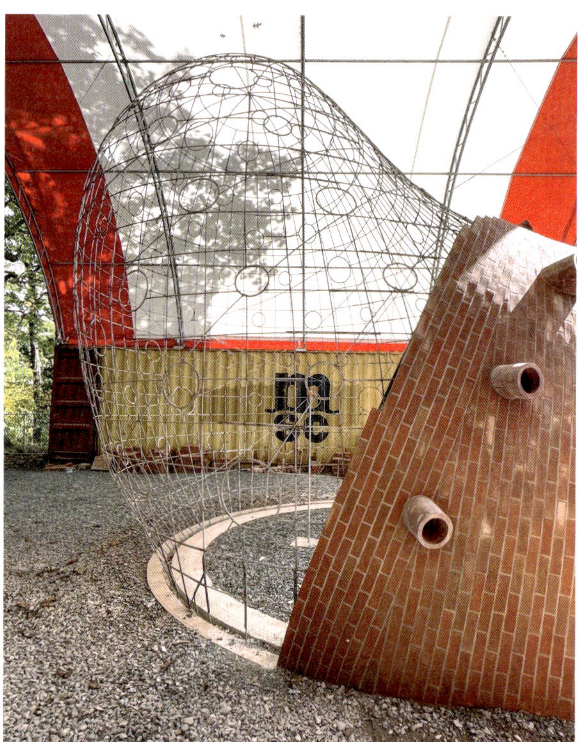

Fig. 13. *Lookout* in progress, showing vault construction over rebar cage, September 2022

masons replicated the desired form by placing the bricks in relationship to the rebar. In wondrous contrast to the sophisticated digital technology used to set the rebar, the tool used in the field to place the bricks was a stick of wood marked in ink with three lines: a mason would align the center line with the center of the rebar and place a brick against an outer line, which marked the placement of the inner face of one of the two walls of brick.

In addition to engaging in intense discussions about and experiments with fabrication methodologies, Puryear dug into material considerations. For him, the origin and history of materials is integral to the creation of an artwork. While the mock-up used bricks available locally, for the artwork Puryear specified material from a Danish manufacturer whose bricks are individually molded, have a nonuniform look, and are made of clay resilient to freeze/thaw conditions, aided by a process of molding that allows the bricks to absorb and release moisture.[8] While a vertical brick wall efficiently sheds water and snow, *Lookout*'s horizontal surfaces would absorb and hold them. With a custom mold, Puryear had the opportunity to order the bricks of the outer layer to be made with a slight radius across their front face. From the available thirty-three colors, Puryear selected a red brick with relatively even coloration, similar to the bricks used in houses and schools in the Hudson Valley region for several centuries.

Seeking a mortar that would be fast-setting and long-lasting, the team identified natural hydraulic cement, a type of cement that was first produced in nearby Rosendale around 1825.[9] A fast-setting mortar was essential given the way bricks were being laid on a slope, and long-lasting was a requirement Puryear established; he has said that the sculpture will outlast all of those who have worked on it, and perhaps even Storm King itself. Rosendale cement has its own history, which intrigued Puryear. It was instrumental in the construction of key nineteenth-century buildings, including the Washington Monument, the Brooklyn Bridge, and parts of the United States Capitol.[10] Compared to the now more commonly used Portland cement, Rosendale-like cement does not utilize chemical additives, has a faster set time, and hardens over time to exceed the durability of Portland cement. Edison Coatings, based in Connecticut, produced a custom mix of natural hydraulic cement for *Lookout*.[11]

With an ample foundation crafted by Storm King's staff—its substantiality and sophistication affirming the goal of permanence[12]—the stainless steel reinforcing cage in place, and materials on-site, bricklaying began with Davis, Horton, Scott Cafarella, Mario Magana, and Aaron Getman-Pickering.[13] A serious challenge quickly emerged: the well-crafted bricks and the storied mortar had conflicting properties. The bricks, with their ability to absorb water, pulled so much moisture from the fast-drying cement that the mortar became fragile, prevented from reaching its full strength and undermining the structure of the artwork. Davis reached out to Steve Blankenbeker, a longtime colleague in North Carolina, and within days Puryear, Davis, and Horton were in a car driving to North Carolina to troubleshoot with Blankenbeker at Taylor Clay Products.

Blankenbeker and Charles Taylor, the owner of Taylor Clay Products, were taken by Puryear's project and wanted to help. Blankenbeker, a material scientist at Taylor, tested the mortar, the bricks, and Taylor's own clay bricks. Taylor's bricks formed a strong bond with the necessary fast-setting mortar, and the factory expedited the required quantity of bricks, meeting Puryear's color specification, to Storm King in an astonishing two weeks. Taylor's bricks are extruded rather than molded. Those for *Lookout* are composed of four clays, or shales, and wire-cut to create a textured surface. The primary clay is red shale, dating back in excess of three hundred million years, from the Carolina Slate Belt, an area of ancient volcanic deposits. This composition was then mixed with kaolin, to lighten the color. The final two clays, fireclay from a deposit west of Birmingham, Alabama, and Catawba clay, from western North Carolina, toughen the brick and make it easier to handle.[14] With the switch from Danish bricks to North Carolinian ones, the artwork now contains not only veins of geologic history but strands of the history of American industrialization as well as the spirit of generosity that emerged from Taylor Clay's commitment to Puryear and his commission for Storm King.

Laying the brick for *Lookout* took about six months. Even with the extensive planning, construction continued to be a process of discovery. To align the ninety fiberglass-reinforced concrete tubes with the sweet spot that allows a visitor to see out of each tube simultaneously, the crew sighted the centerline of each of the three-, six-, and nine-inch tubes with a fluorescent orange tennis ball skewered on a metal rod marking five feet six inches off the final ground plan.[15] Puryear and the crew explored how to cut the bricks around the tubes, how to saw-cut the lines between the segments, and how to angle the bricks for the smaller diameter of the later sections. As the sculpture neared completion, Puryear decided to cut the tubes to about a half-inch beyond the brick form. Trimming the tubes so that they protrude slightly above the surface routes precipitation down the wall rather than through to the inside; on an aesthetic level, these small rises create punctuation marks—interrupting the seductive smooth surface and suggesting a dialogue between surface and depth, between inside and out.

With construction of the brick structure complete, the team installed the pavement to Puryear's specifications. Here, Puryear referenced a centuries-old building he had seen on a visit to Denmark, where the brick wall met cobblestone pavement directly—brick against stone (fig. 14).

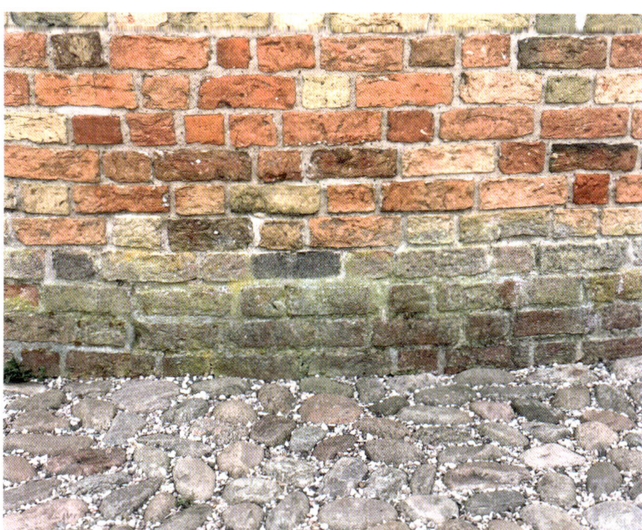

Fig. 14. Building photographed by Martin Puryear during a trip to Denmark, 2019, showing a brick wall meeting cobblestone paving

At Storm King, the pavement defines a zone of the sculpture distinct from the surrounding landscape.

Puryear has called *Lookout*'s surface a tapestry. That elaborate weaving emerges from deep and wide-ranging collaboration that elevated technical solutions to an aesthetic experience. In the artist's words, the artwork celebrates "the kind of dignity in labor."[16]

Feeling

The artist who has given us *Ladder for Booker T. Washington* (fig. 15), *Bearing Witness* (1994–98; pl. 26), and *A Column for Sally Hemings* (fig. 16) chose with *Lookout* to honor the dying art of brick masonry, a once thriving industry in the Hudson Valley that profited from the labor of those without other economic opportunities, including recent immigrants

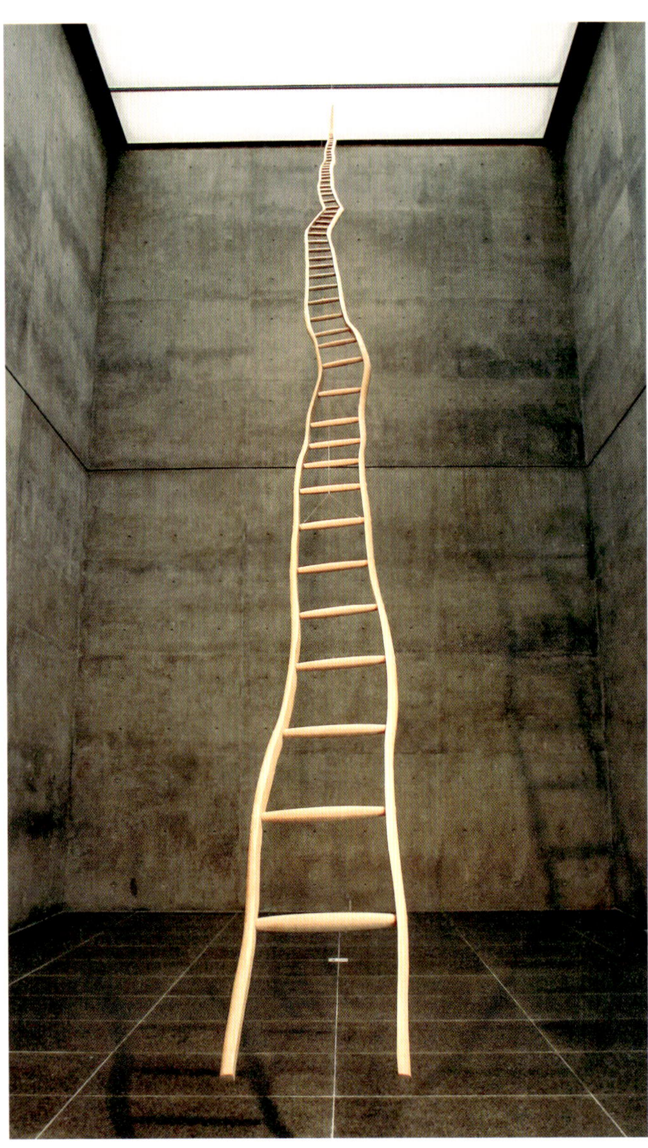

Fig. 15. Martin Puryear, *Ladder for Booker T. Washington*, 1996. Ash and maple, 36 ft. × 22¾ in. × 3 in. (1097.3 × 57.8 × 7.6 cm). Collection of the Modern Art Museum of Fort Worth, Gift of Ruth Carter Stevenson, by exchange

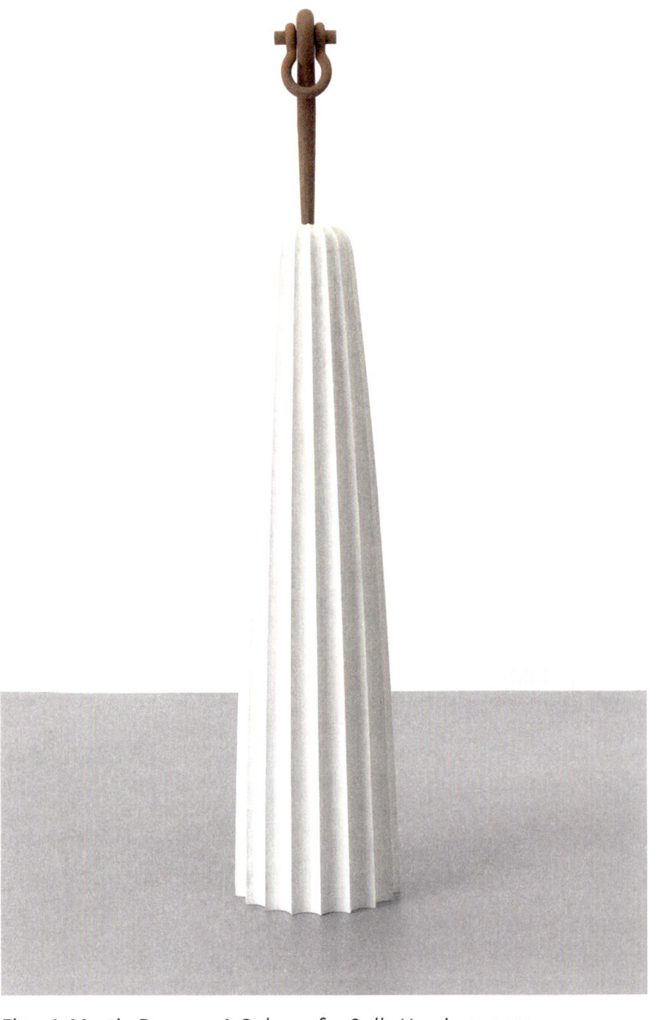

Fig. 16. Martin Puryear, *A Column for Sally Hemings*, 2019. Cast iron and painted tulip poplar, 6 ft. 8 in. × 15¾ in. × 15¾ in. (203 × 40 × 40 cm)

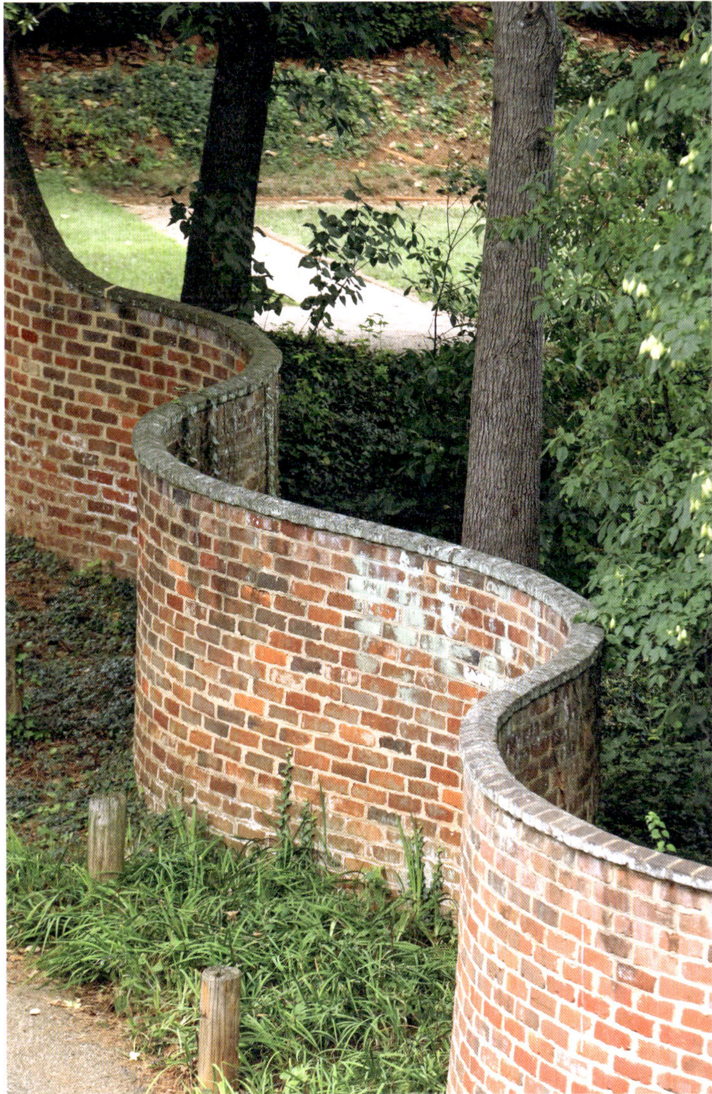

Fig. 17. Serpentine brick wall at the University of Virginia, Charlottesville, between 1817 and 1823

and Southern Blacks who migrated north for the season. The Hudson Valley became known as "the brickmaking capital of the world" between 1880 and 1920 as New York City grew into a major metropolis. When the construction of tall buildings left bricks aside in favor of steel, this industry, a brutal one for its workers, collapsed.[17]

The history of bricks in America also includes the extensive use of masonry for prominent buildings in the South, especially before the end of slavery. Thomas Jefferson's serpentine brick walls at the University of Virginia are celebrated for their inventive form and construction methodology, yet recognition of these formal achievements comes with the understanding that they were made possible by Jefferson's enslavement of the masons who built them (fig. 17). Recalling this historical example of inventive brickwork in association with *Lookout* highlights Puryear's greater formal ambitions as he bends his form on the y and z axes as well as the x axis. More critically, it punctuates the generosity of Puryear's creative exploration with respected project partners and of the resultant form, which invites congregation rather than delineates boundaries.

With the open, enveloping, and exalting space of *Lookout*, Puryear presents optimism and uplift, tinged with a provocation about the future. The artist celebrates manufacturers and laborers. In titling the artwork, Puryear highlighted the view of Storm King and beyond, including Schunnemunk Mountain, to which he oriented the arched opening. He also offers a second way of seeing from the inside: Puryear has said, "It's like a strange kind of diurnal observatory providing many separate and distinct views of the surrounding landscape."[18] Puryear puts the viewer at the center of his artwork, reminiscent of Leonardo da Vinci's *Vitruvian Man* (fig. 18), but he flips the Renaissance humanistic narrative by creating a place where occupying the center means looking out at the cosmos, at what humans have created, and at the precious world we have not yet touched. Even more, Puryear turns our gaze from the artwork itself. He is indeed asking us to look out.

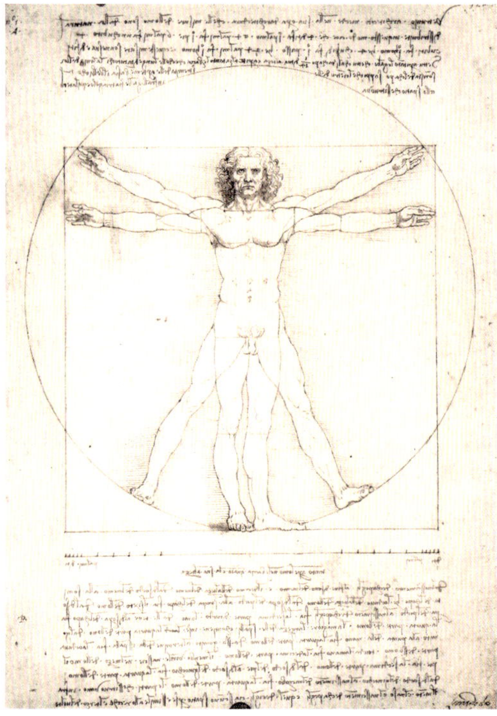

Fig. 18. Leonardo da Vinci, *Vitruvian Man*, c. 1490. Pen, brown ink, and watercolor over metalpoint on paper, 13½ × 9⅝ in. (34.4 × 24.5 cm). Galleria dell'Accademia, Venice

That inversion from one way of looking to another is the nucleus of *Lookout*. Like much of Puryear's work, *Lookout* holds contradictions, playing out the metaphor of change in perspective that is physically realized in the transition from arch to dome. Myriad meticulous details vibrate with economy of form. While *Lookout* uses classical forms, the basis of both the arch and the dome is not a static circle but an empowered ellipse. While it draws on traditions of craft, Puryear's sculpture unsettles historical, cultural, and psychological assumptions. Though it incorporates techniques of architecture, it has no functional program. *Lookout* is not a primitive hut, a sukkah, or a garden folly, but it is all of these. It shelters us, gathers us together, and astonishes us. And then it sends us out into the land with eyes tuned to see without preconception.

As Louis Kahn enjoined, "You say to brick, 'What do you want, brick?'"

For *Lookout*, Martin Puryear's brick answers,

I want to dance.
I like to come from deep in the earth,
I like to reach the sky.
I like to be an object,
I like to shelter experience,
I like to command.
I like to open to the world,
I like to inscribe hallowed space.
I like that I am an ordinary unit,
I like to weave complexity.
I like to be seen,
I like to be considered,
I like to be felt.

Notes

I am grateful to David R. Collens and Nora Lawrence for the invitation to join the *Lookout* project team, Martin Puryear for his generosity and trust, and the entire fabrication team for their wisdom and craft.

For the epigraphs, see Louis Kahn, quoted in John Lobell, *Between Silence and Light: Spirit in the Architecture of Louis I. Kahn* (Boston: Shambhala Publications, 1979), 40; and Martin Puryear, in conversation with Adela Goldsmith, Nora Lawrence, Jonathan Sanden, and Amy Weisser, August 22, 2023.

1. The bricks are standardly sized American bricks, measuring two and one-quarter inches high by seven and five-eighths inches wide by three and five-eighths inches deep. Three-eighths of an inch of mortar borders the bricks on the sculpture's surface.
2. John Ochsendorf, "Engineering of a Brick Sculpture," *A+U* 627 (December 2022): 86.
3. Martin Puryear in correspondence with the author, November 20, 2023.
4. Storm King's President, John P. Stern, and then Director and Chief Curator, David R. Collens, initially invited Puryear to propose a permanent work of art at Storm King. Shortly thereafter Nora Lawrence, now Artistic Director and Chief Curator, joined Storm King and the Puryear project as Associate Curator. Director of Facilities and Conservation Mike Seaman; Curatorial Assistant Adela Goldsmith; Administrative Assistant, Curatorial Department, Hanna Washburn; and the author completed the team for Storm King.
5. Ochsendorf, "Engineering of a Brick Sculpture," 86.
6. Indents, or depressions, were molded into the sides of the tubes so that, when set in concrete, the tubes would lock into place.
7. Wulfmeyer and Powers, of KC Fabrications, based in Gardiner, New York, previously worked with Puryear on *Connecting* (2018) and *Swallowed Sun (Monstrance and Volute)* (2019).
8. Petersen Tegl, "Facts on Bricks and Frost," https://en.petersen-tegl.dk/media/401420/gb_fact_on_bricks_and_frost.pdf.
9. Production of the material in Rosendale ceased in 1970. In 2004 Edison Coatings, based in Connecticut, resumed production of this type of cement.
10. Edison Coatings, Inc., "History of Rosendale Natural Cement," https://www.rosendalecement.net/html/history_of_rosendale_cement.html.
11. Mixing this cement with Marfil, another natural cement, shortens hardening and curing times.
12. Storm King's Facilities and Conservation team built the artwork's foundation, and, at the project's conclusion, graded and landscaped the hill. Reed Hilderbrand Landscape Architecture collaborated with Puryear and Storm King to design a drainage and reinforcement system under the grassy hilltop that would facilitate visitors who require mobility assistance to approach and enter the sculpture. Josh Safdie of KMA consulted on these efforts.
13. The masonry team included Lara Davis; Rob Horton; Aaron Getman-Pickering, a woodworker, who worked on the mock-up at Puryear's studio; Scott Cafarella, owner of Hudson Valley Mason Works; and Cafarella's associate Mario Magana. Donovan Palmquist, who builds brick kilns at Master Kiln Builders, traveled from Minnesota to join the team in the early weeks.
14. Steve Blankenbeker, "Brick Materials Used in Making Bricks for the Puryear Storm King Project," received August 26, 2022; Taylor Clay Products, "Brick composition—Puryear Storm King Project," October 24, 2023. Taylor added Catawba clay to the mixture because of its history, since the early nineteenth century, as the clay traditionally used in Catawba Valley pottery.
15. The tubes were fabricated by David Kucera, whose studio abuts KC Fabrications in Gardiner, New York. They are made of glass fiber reinforced concrete, colloquially referred to as GFRC; the fiberglass in the thin wall of the tubes serves the same purpose as the rebar in the thick wall of the sculpture.
16. Puryear, in conversation with Goldsmith, Lawrence, Sanden, and Weisser.
17. Julie O'Connor, "Feat of Clay: Looking Back at the Once-Mighty Hudson Valley Brick Industry," *HV1*, March 27, 2020, https://hudsonvalleyone.com/2018/01/11/feat-of-clay-looking-back-at-the-once-mighty-hudson-valley-brick-industry/. Between 1880 and 1920, coincident with extraordinary growth of New York City, "the Hudson Valley was the brickmaking capital of the world, producing more than a billion bricks a year and employing nearly 10,000 people in more than 120 brickyards. By the late 1970s, the once-mighty molded-brick industry was no more." These brickyards were staffed by recent immigrants and Southern Black laborers who came north for the warmer months when bricks were produced. The job was arduous and poorly compensated: "At the turn of the 20th century, brickwork was avoided by anyone who could find any other employment." Among the books Puryear has been looking at "forever" is George V. Hutton's *The Great Hudson River Brick Industry: Commemorating Three and a Half Centuries of Brickmaking* (Bovina Center, NY: Purple Mountain Press, 2003).
18. Puryear in correspondence with the author, November 20, 2023.

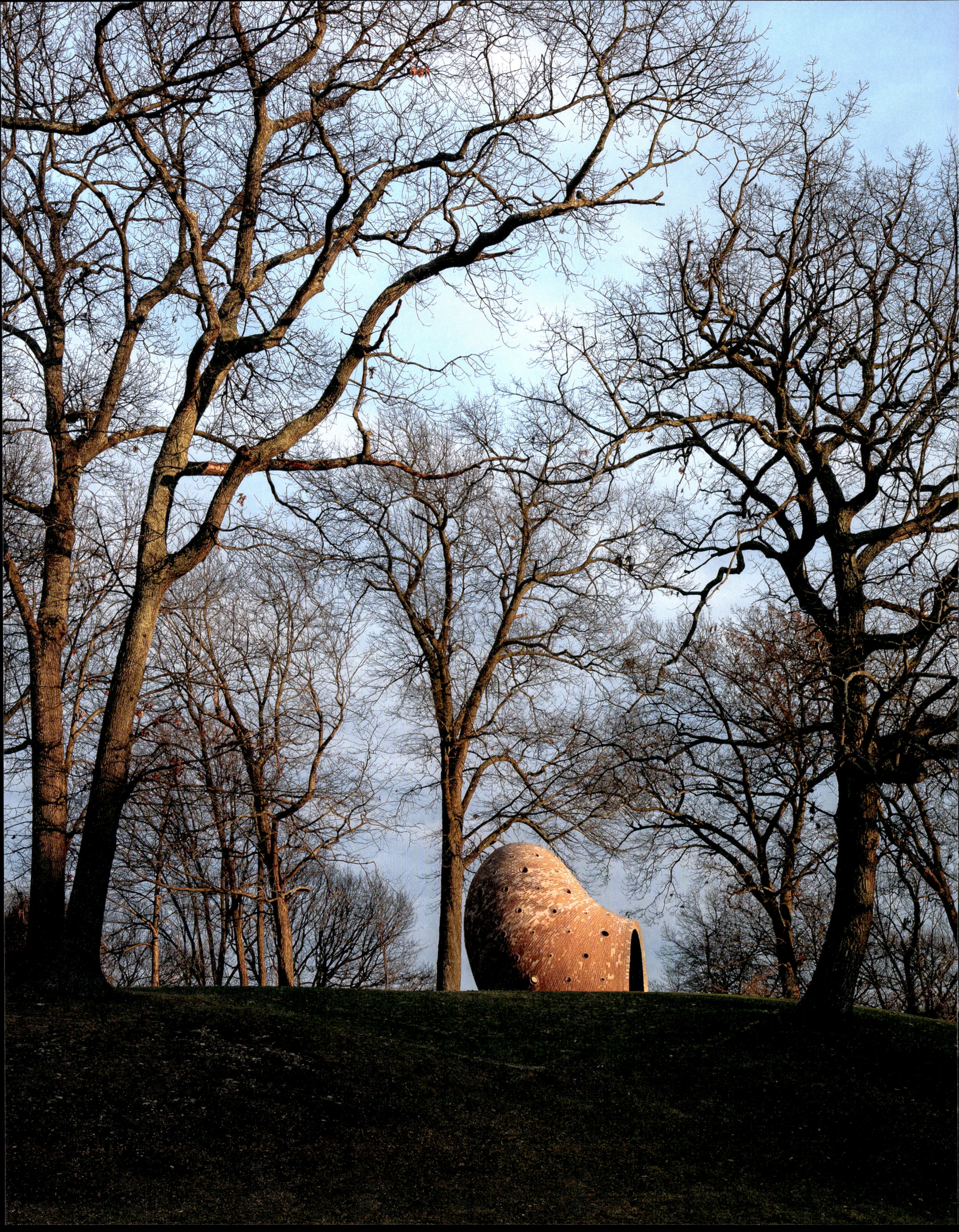

MARTIN PURYEAR IN CONVERSATION

with Glenn Adamson

This past fall, Storm King Art Center was crowned by *Lookout*, a monumental new sculpture in red brick by Martin Puryear. Working from his Hudson Valley home and studio, Puryear devised a form that—like all his work—is at once powerful and multivalent, open to numerous interpretations. A pocket of space rising from the ground, punctuated by apertures, it is a permeable envelope in which one can stand, see, and simply be. The work describes a progression from an arched vertical opening to a horizontal dome. In the transit between these two simple shapes—from one point of view, purely mathematical—a wondrous, sensuous complexity unfolds.

The project was developed through collaboration with engineer John Ochsendorf and masonry specialist Lara Davis. The first step was to construct an armature of stainless steel rebar welded together over a temporary plywood formwork. (The armature provides structural reinforcement and also controls the shape.) Tubes were incorporated through the brickwork as the masonry progressed, each one aimed at a single interior viewpoint five feet off the ground—these would become the piece's portholes, or oculi. Finally, two layers of brickwork, the space between them filled with concrete, were constructed around the armature, in nine segments. This was done using an ancient method called Nubian vaulting, in which bricks are laid at an angle, each course resting on the previous one. No interior formwork was needed for the upper tiers of the sculpture.

In the following interview, conducted on May 3, 2023, Puryear talked about his monumental undertaking with curator and critic Glenn Adamson.

I think it was almost ten years ago that Storm King first approached me, and I began to visit with an eye toward finding a site. At some point David Collens, the director at the time, said, "I want to show you a spot." It was spectacular: a rise that came out of the woods. And that's when I came up with the idea.

We are creating a work that frames a spectacular view from the hilltop over Storm King's fields and the mountains beyond, but because of all the circular openings—oculi, I guess you'd call them—you will also see a constellation of different views, glimpses of the surrounding woods and sky. It's a form that you can see from a distance, but you don't just experience it from the outside. It's a sculpture that you can enter. It marks a location, and it provides a view from that location, in many different directions.

It's also a celebration of masonry. I've been fascinated with brick for a long time. It goes along with my interest in incremental making of all kinds. Masonry is probably the most commonplace permanent building method on the planet, but it's also capable of being used in very innovative, surprising ways. There's a brick building that I've always enjoyed on Madison Avenue in New York, the Squadron A Armory at Ninety-Fourth Street (see p. 27, fig. 7). It has massive rounded forms that seem carved, rather than made from bricks laid one-by-one, by hand. And then, of course, there's the history of brick in this area. Kingston, New York, was a major brickmaking center.

You have said that you were interested in bricks partly because they're a universal technique.

Masonry is universal. Building something big and substantial by stacking little units is something that nearly every culture has done from the beginning of time.

This is something I'm very interested in, Martin. And I think it's true of all of your work. It's big, it's monumental. In this case, it's going to be on one of the highest points in Storm King. And yet it seems utterly without ego.

That's a fascinating observation. This project depends on the skill and expertise of so many people beyond myself. We were fortunate to have been able to pull together a team of very skilled brickmasons and people with highly specialized engineering expertise. It's a true collaboration. Anyway, Soetsu Yanagi said, "The thing shines, not the maker." And I think that is a beautiful idea.

Was there a moment when you committed to the three different sizes for the openings, or oculi?

The first model had all the holes the same size, but then I decided it needed to have some variety. I decided on three different sizes, and to distribute the holes on a loose diagonal grid rather than vertically and horizontally.

To make it more dynamic?

And to break up the strict linearity of where the holes are punched through. You get a feeling that there's a grid, but it's not rigid.

Like a system that you can't quite grasp, which is very characteristic of traditional architecture. You can tell there's a logic, but you can't necessarily pin it down.

This whole thing has been one long succession of problems solved. Meeting the engineer John Ochsendorf was a game changer. He was the first one to believe that the bricks could be used structurally and not just as a veneer or skin. As we developed the idea further it actually became a hybrid structure, because it does incorporate reinforced concrete between the inner and outer walls of brick.

Your structure feels simple, though, after all the complexity.

That's good fortune when it happens. I generally arrive at my forms by hand. I don't use a computer as a design tool at all. I may draw, but when it comes to the third dimension, typically I will actually carve it or build it somehow with the tools in my shop.

The first wood model that you showed me . . .

That's carved out of a block of pine.

Do you have any theory as to why it's so generative for you to use your hands in that way?

I don't have a theory, I just know where my creativity flows from. From my brain through my hands to the work. I think like a craftsperson or an artisan, in the sense that I have always worked with my hands, worked through my hands. A lot of artists today don't need to do that because of advances in technology.

And complexity too, I suppose?

Yes. But when I came into my maturity as an artist, Minimalism was ascendant. I don't consider myself a Minimalist, but I do feel like there's always been a drive in my work to reduce things to something really essential. Not always simple, but essential. And not even always, because the pendulum swings, and sometimes I really need to elaborate, but generally I tend to want to hone things down to their essentials.

Do you think there's also something about wanting to stay in touch with the human scale—by using your hands, and coming up with forms that relate to the body?

Certainly that's one of the things that you get with masonry. Because a brick—no matter what culture uses it—is something you can pick up with one hand. That's what defines the size of a brick, the module. You can pick it up with one hand, and put it into place in the wall.

The Storm King piece is articulated according to those modules, too, because it has very defined mortar lines.

Right, and the seams between the nine segments. I could give you a litany of all of the solutions that we came up with as we worked it all out. For example, we had realized from making the model that we were going to have to make a diagonal seam through the masonry at an angle for each segment, which would result in lots of little wedge-shaped pieces. If you cut through a grid at an angle, you get triangles. And at first we thought, well, we could just cut a bunch of wedge-shaped slivers, and lay them in place along the transition line. But instead we decided to lay the bricks past the transition line, then use a laser to mark the line and finally make the diagonal cut using a masonry saw. So we got a perfectly clean seam between one segment and the next.

So that gives you another datum to lay onto?

Exactly. And that was the solution.

And the changing angles of the masonry courses create a shape that moves from a ninety-degree vertical at the opening, to a dome whose base is exactly parallel to the ground. Can you talk a little bit about that movement?

Right. That's the key thing for the work. It expresses, or illustrates, a transition from a tunnel—at the opening, at the mouth—to a dome, through a succession of different angles. That's what's taking place within the form.

From the upright to the level. So it's basically about two planes.

Well, it's what happens between those planes.

Going from A to Z, and seeing what happens along the route.

Yes, it's been a puzzle to solve.

One last question. Have you thought about what it might be like at different times of day and night?

I've thought about it. But I mean, it's all guesswork at this point. The portholes could be thought of as a constellation of light, like stars. But they'll be large, and along with the view out, they'll deliver light in separate units, maybe shafts or beams of light, at various times. I don't like to predict what's going to happen before it's finished, because I haven't done it in a predictive way. It's been all very intuitive.

There will be a feeling that the sculpture is embracing you, given that all the holes converge on one point; when you stand there, they are all in your sight line. Underneath the night sky, and all the stars sending their light to you, from all that time ago and across all that distance. . . . I feel like it might allow you to feel tuned into something quite vast.

If that's the reaction people have to it I'll feel fortunate. Now, it's going to have a certain reality from the outside—it will have this stitched-together character because of the way the masonry segments will lean into one another, with bricks encircling the form, and climbing at steeper and steeper angles.

When it's completed, I hope the transition from tunnel curving upward into dome is what hits the viewer, along with the realization that they're seeing bricks used in a completely new way. And I'll be especially pleased if a heightened awareness of place results, not only from seeing the sculpture in nature, from the outside, but also from experiencing the work and the view it provides from the inside, looking out.

It bridges back to a time before there were professional engineers and there was a more intuitive style of building.

In September there will be an exhibition at Storm King presenting a number of my past projects for sculpture in public places. We've been collecting models and documentation going back almost fifty years. And a lot of the work has been about how things have been made, and the trades involved in the making of them. I like my work to have some aspect of acknowledgment, because I think there's a potential for entry into the work, that is approaching something universal.

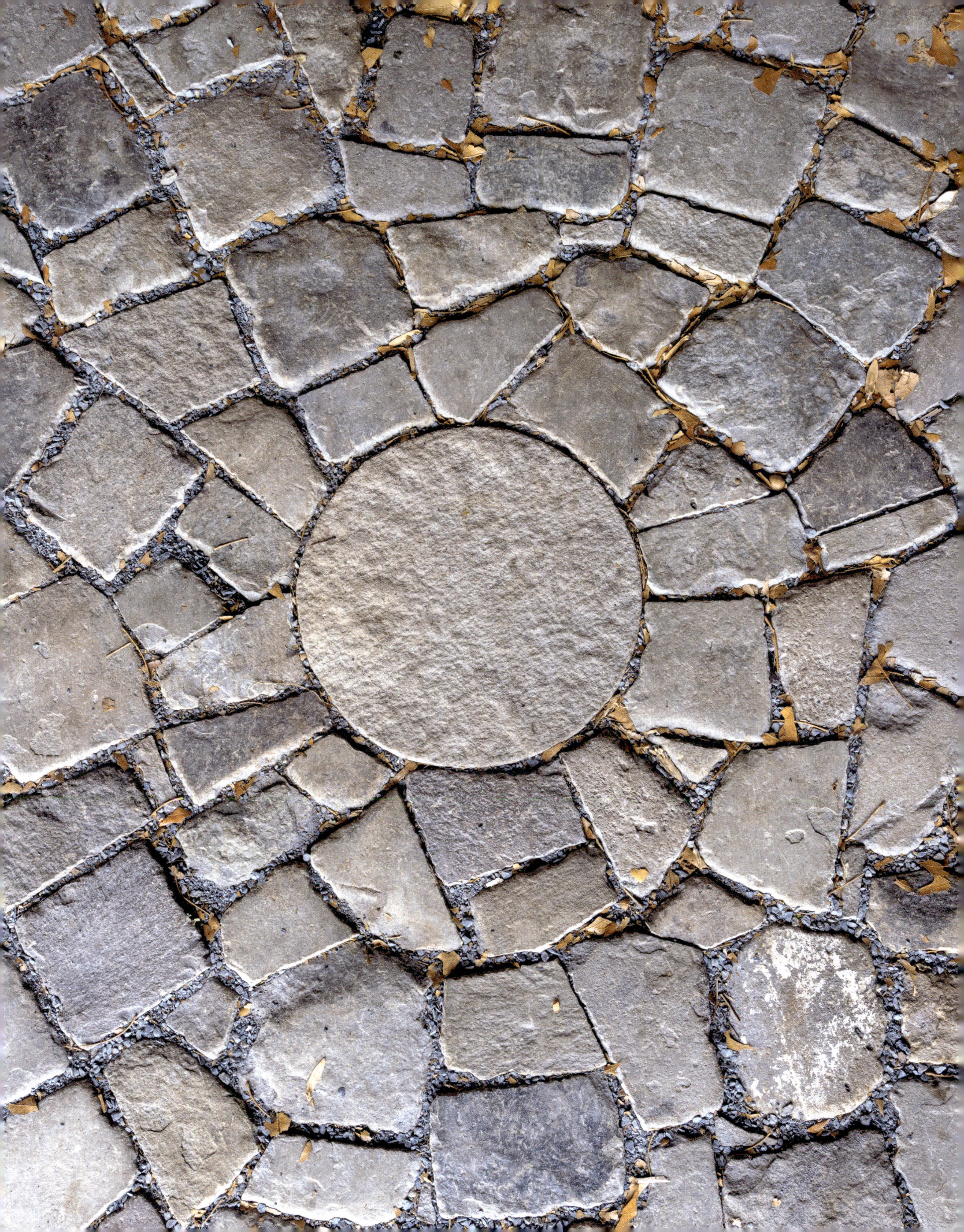

MAKING *LOOKOUT*

Photographs by Carlton Davis

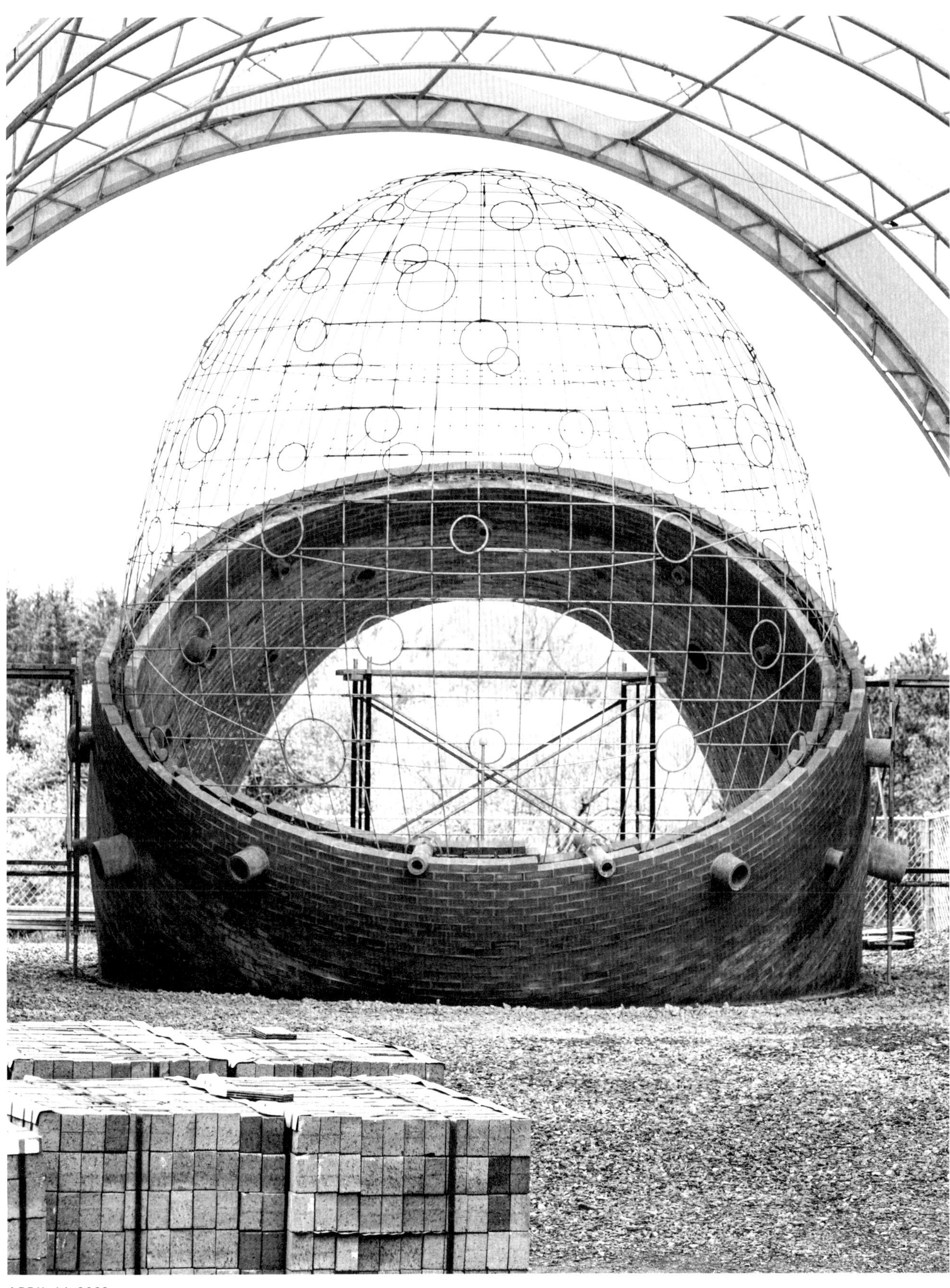

APRIL 16, 2023

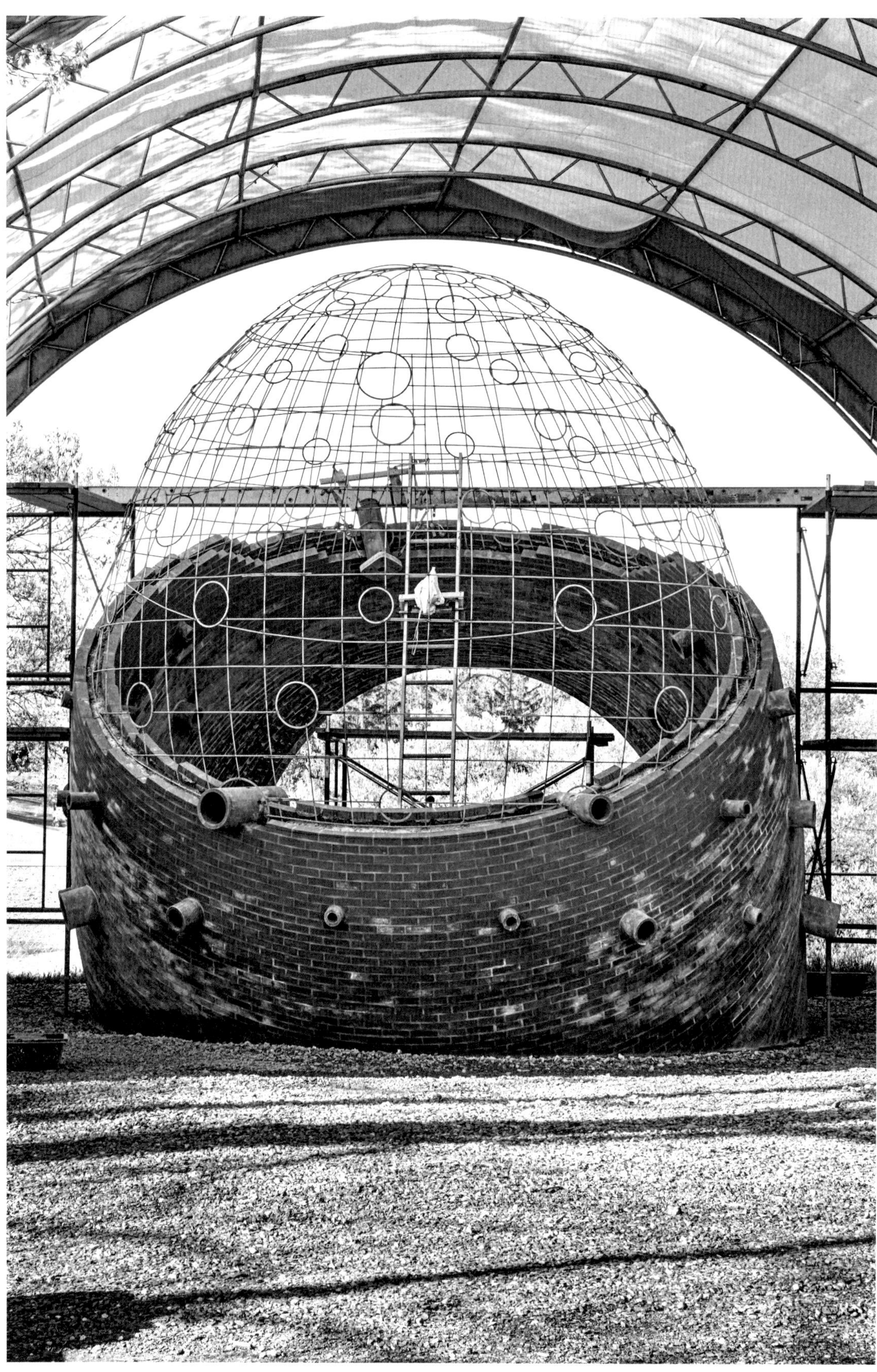

MAY 1, 2023

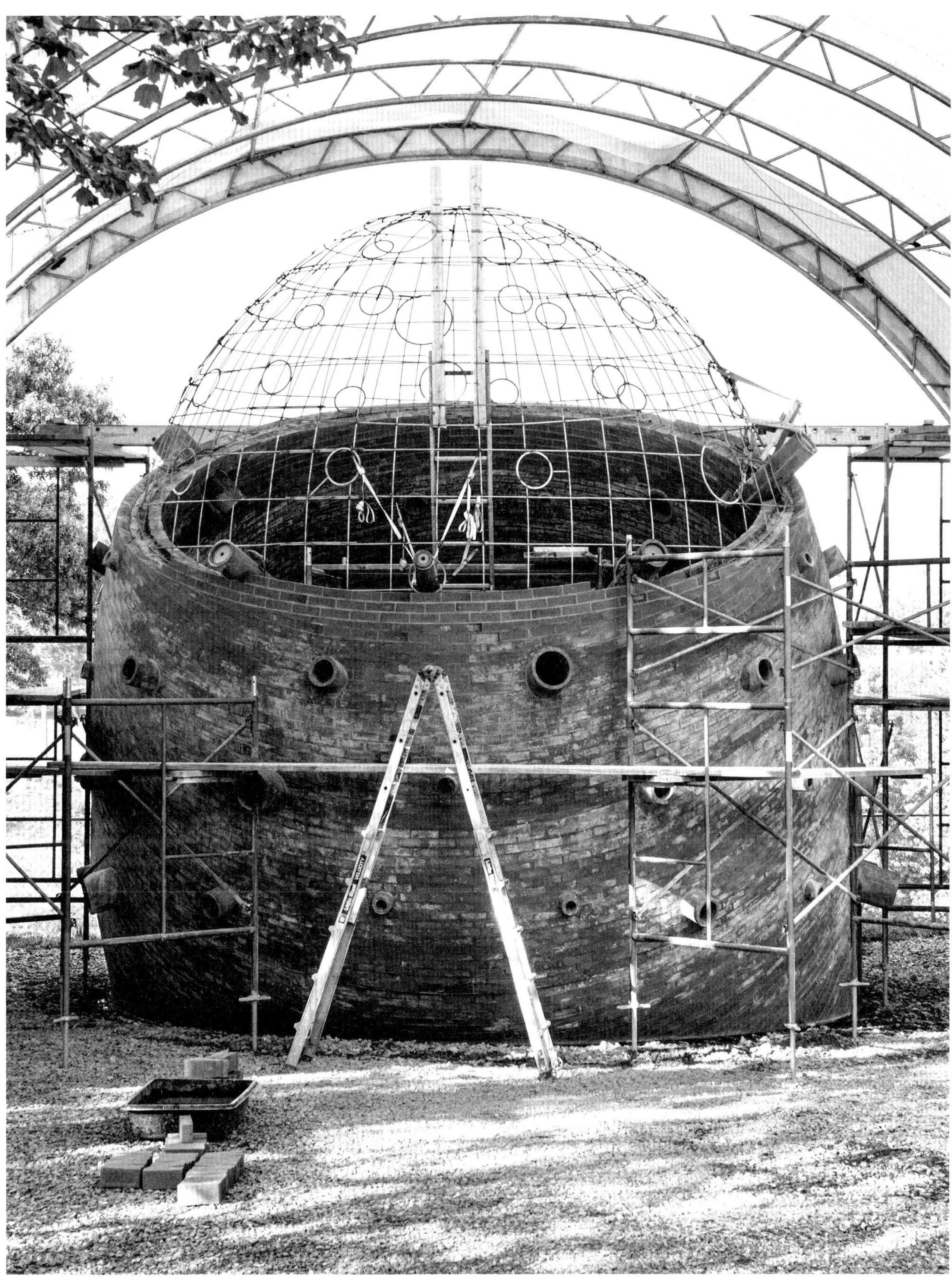

JUNE 1, 2023

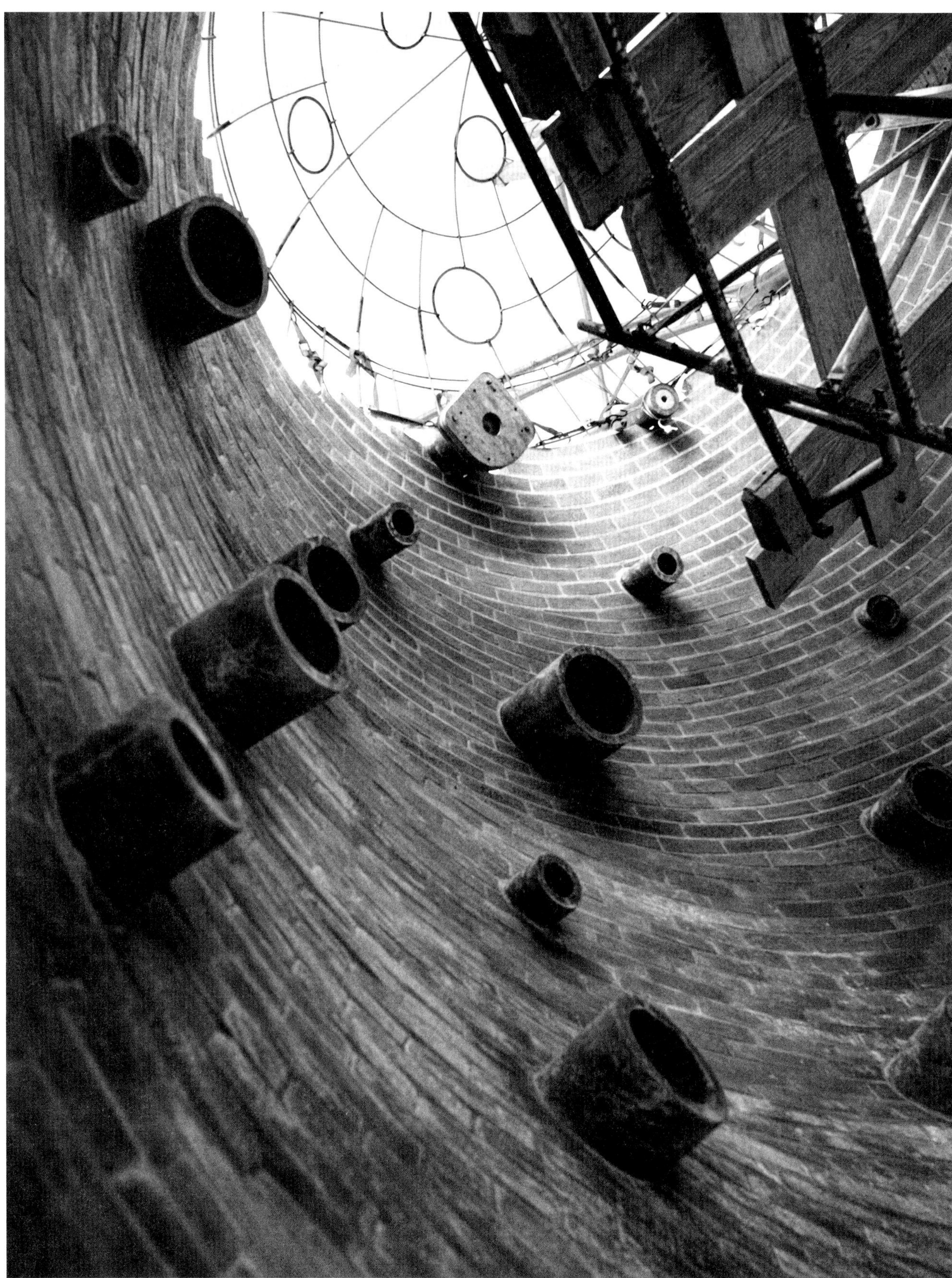

JULY 6, 2023

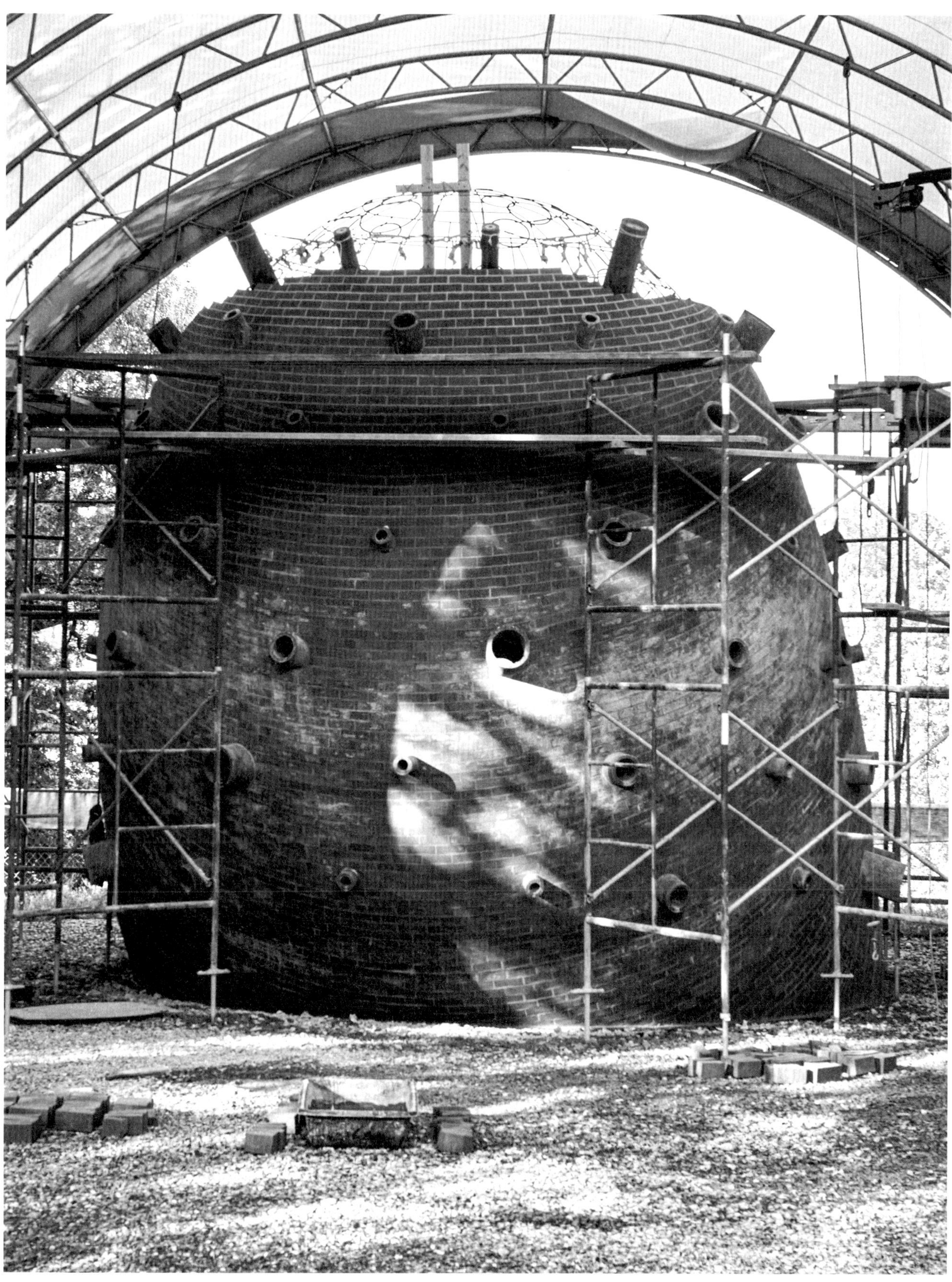
JULY 6, 2023

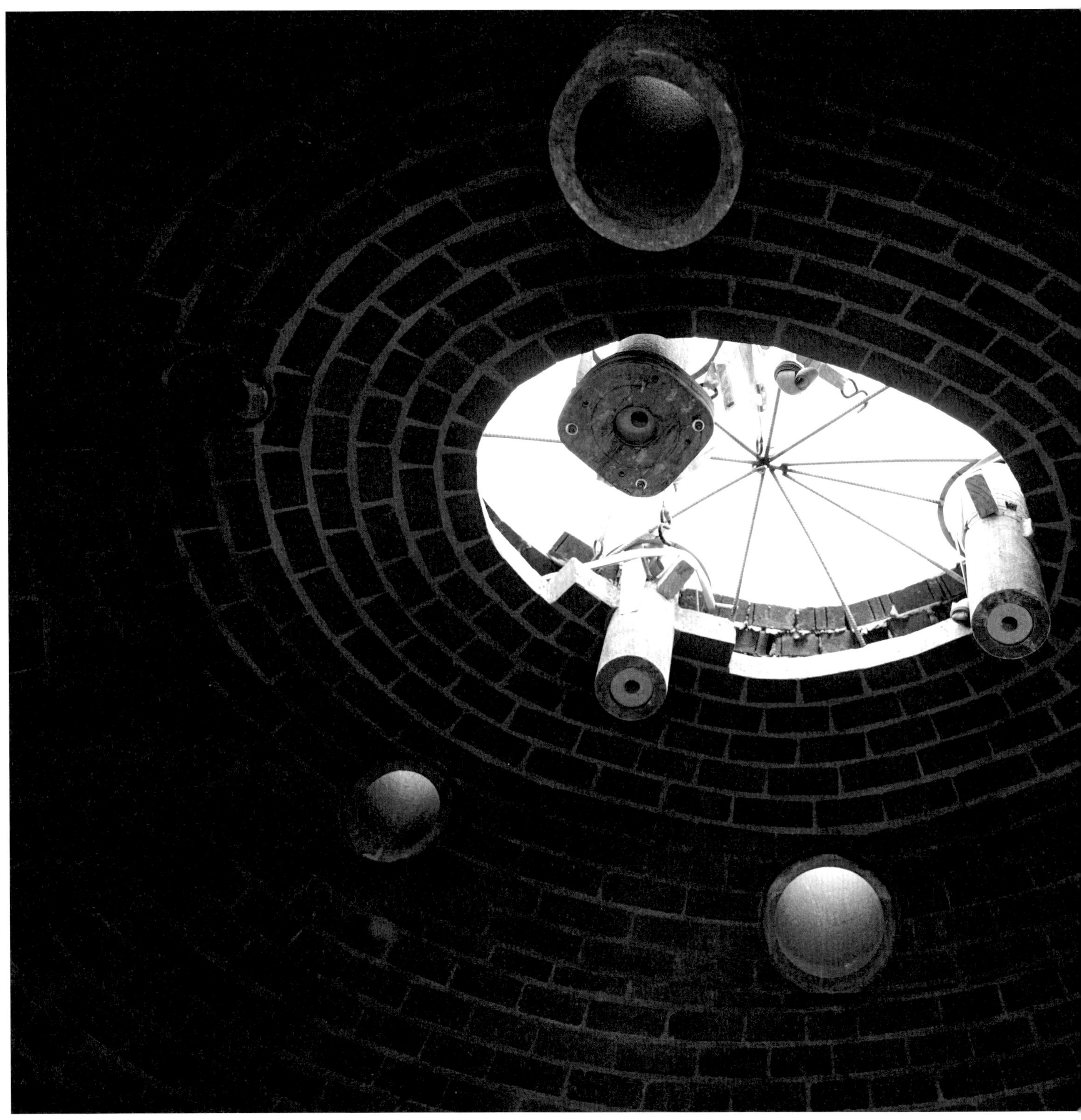

AUGUST 1, 2023

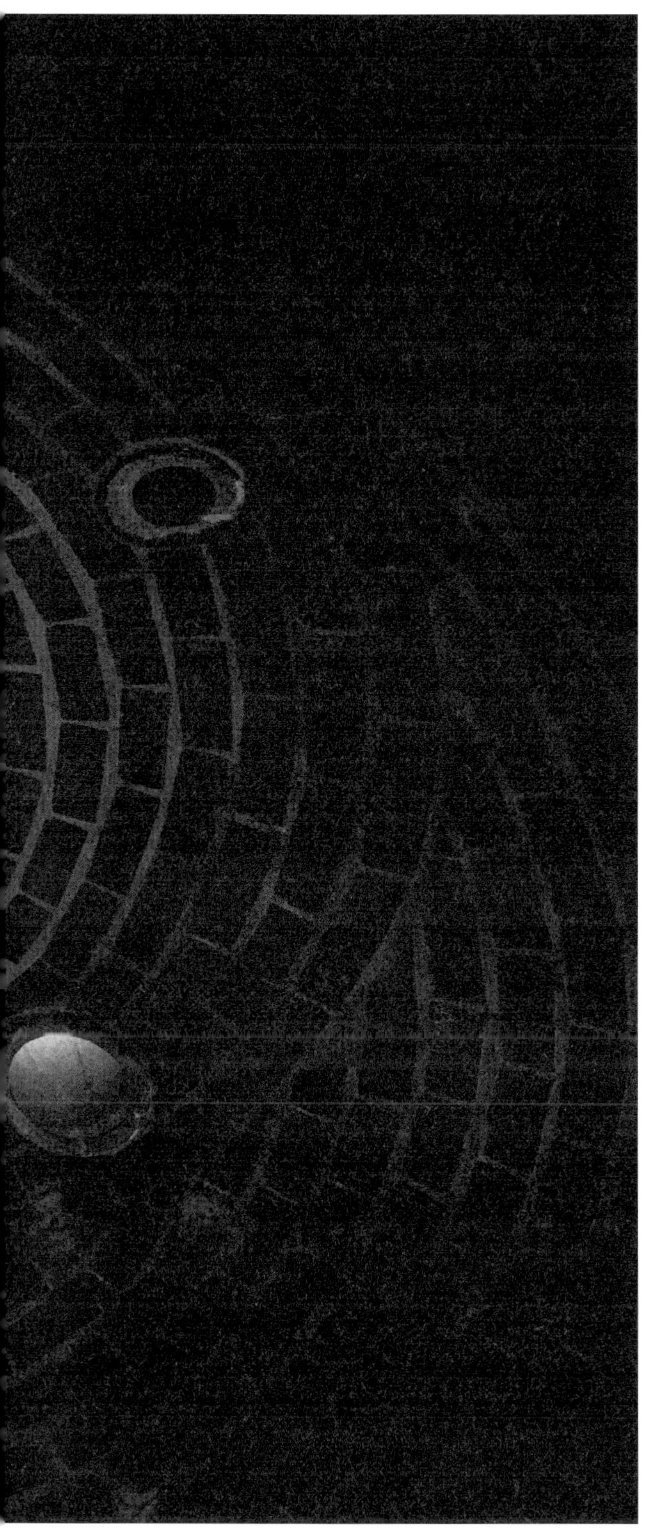

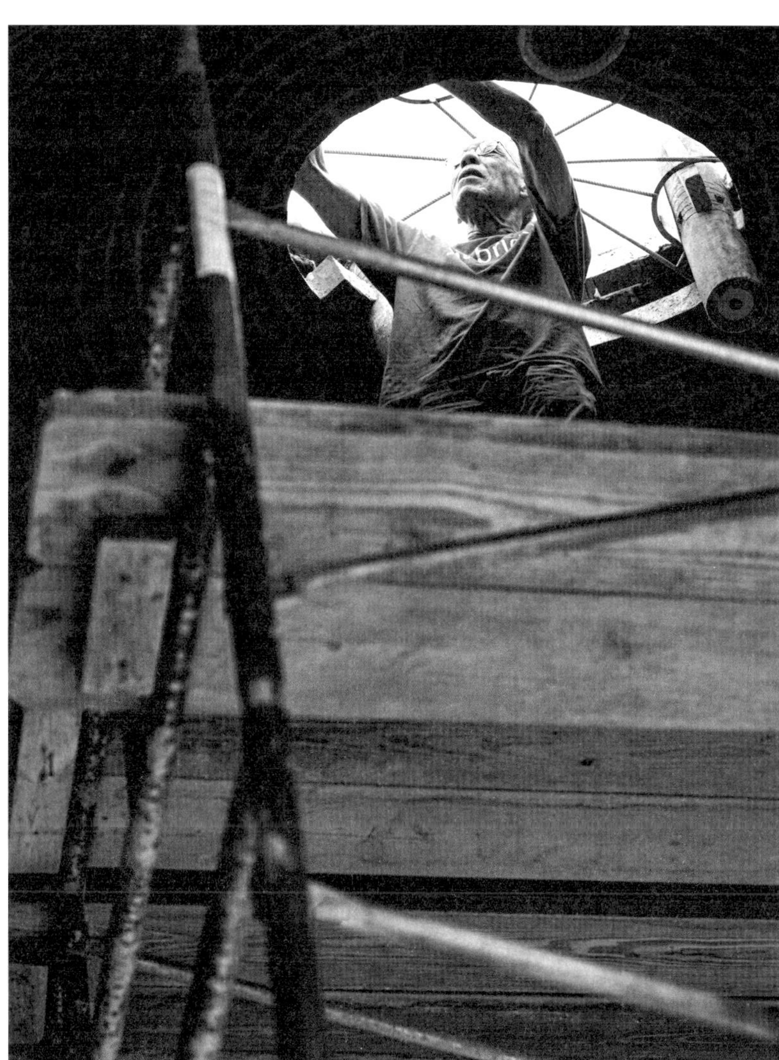

AUGUST 1, 2023

50

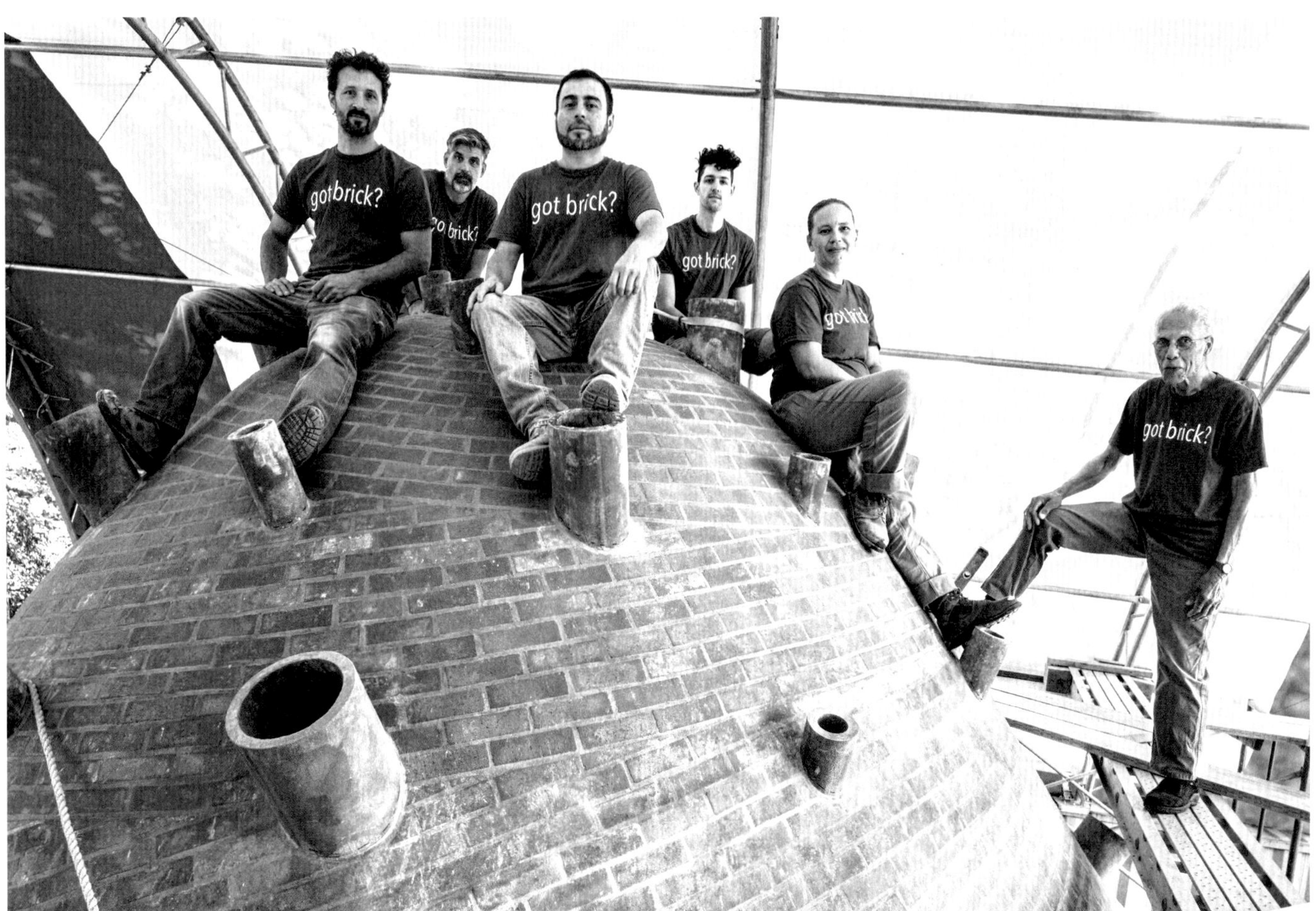

AUGUST 1, 2023

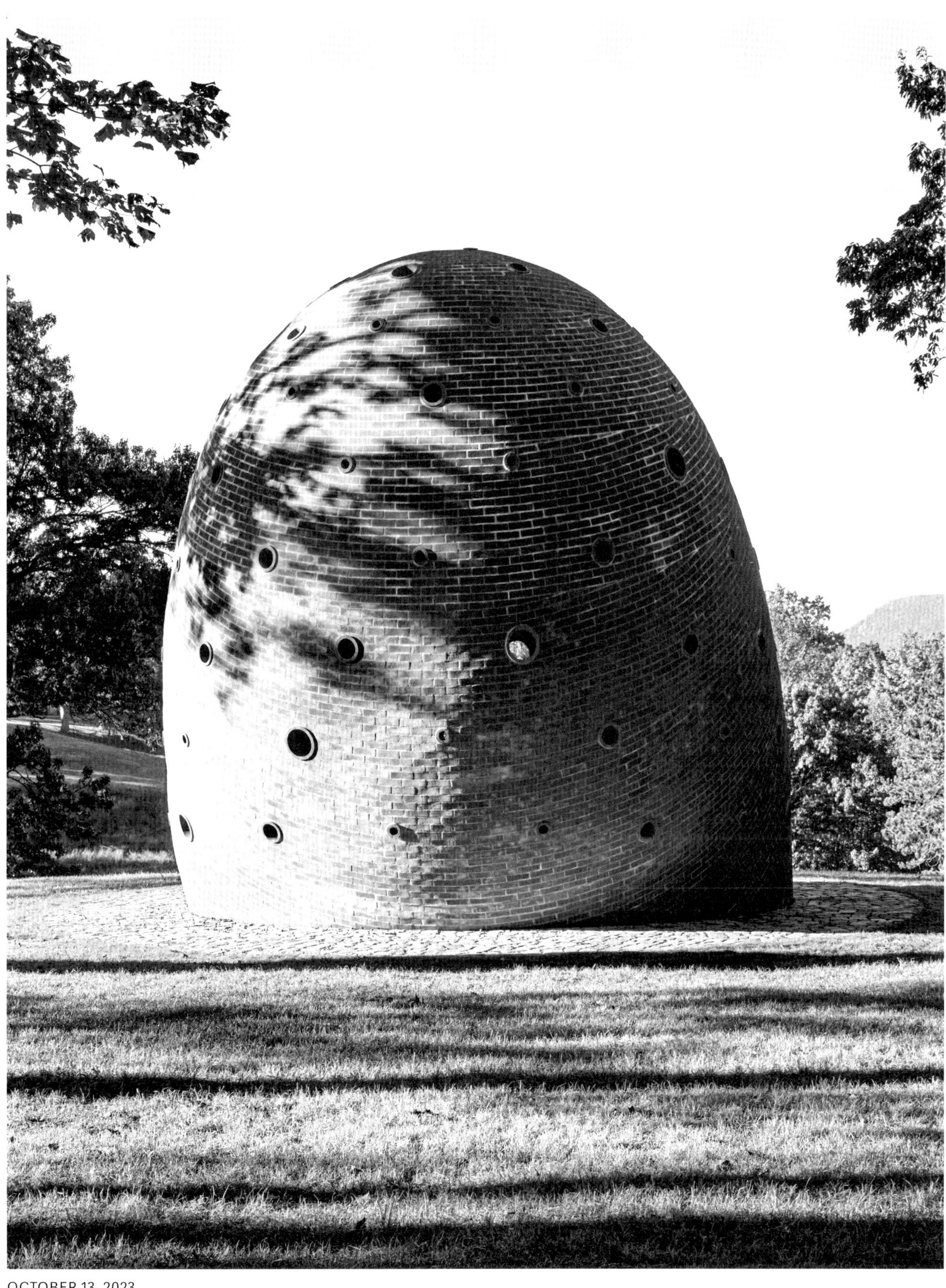

OCTOBER 13, 2023

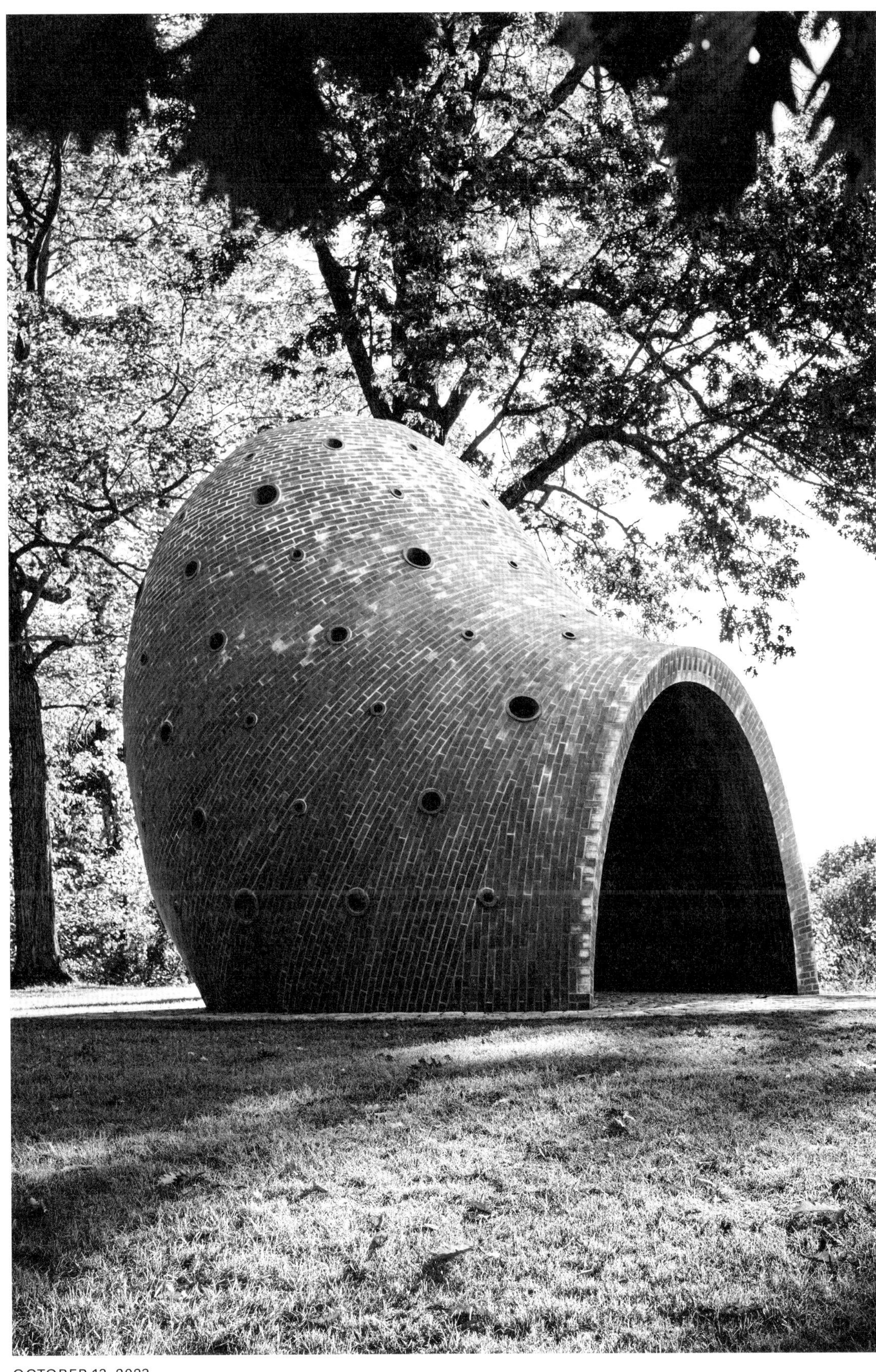

OCTOBER 13, 2023

LOOKOUT

Photographs by Jeffrey Jenkins

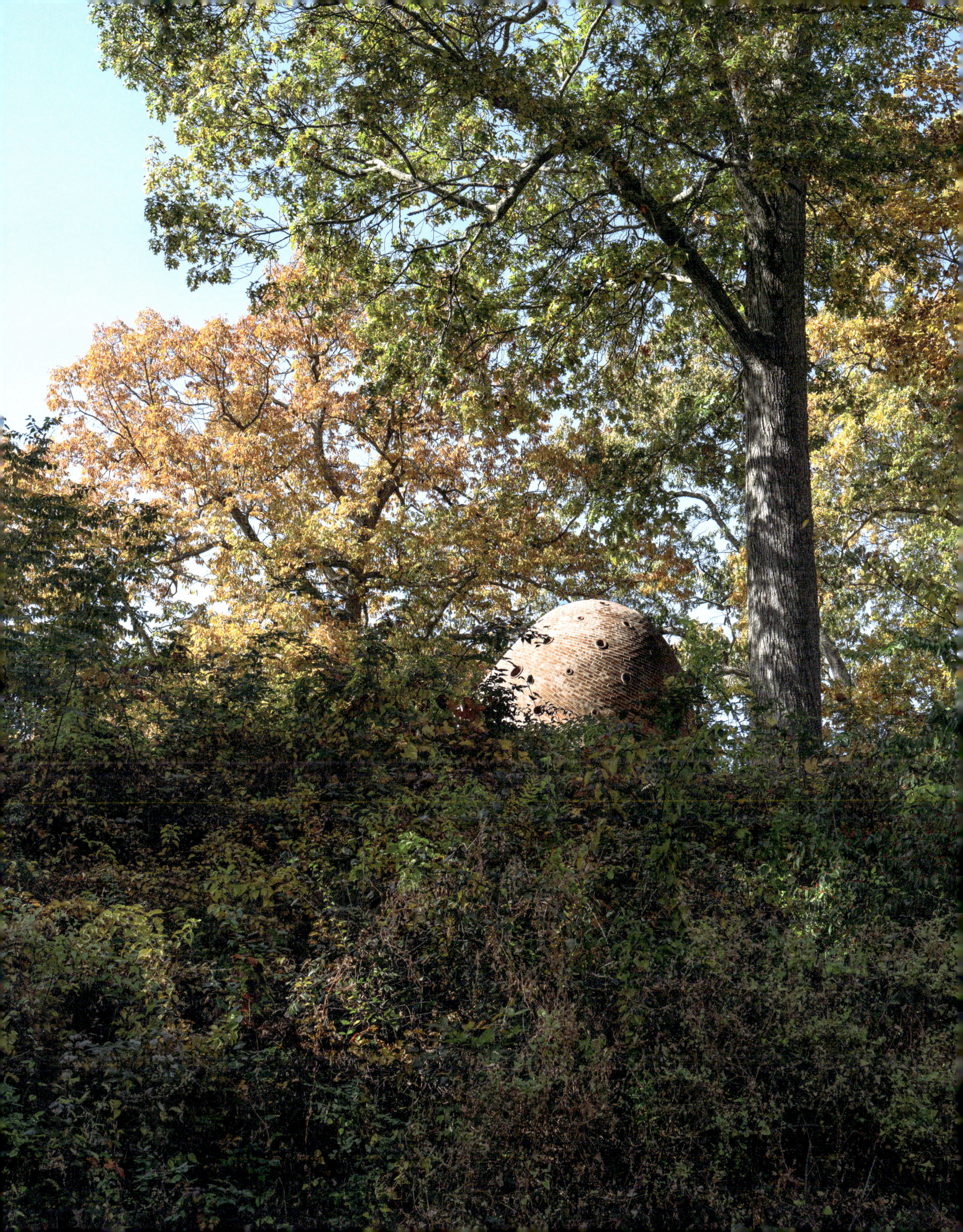

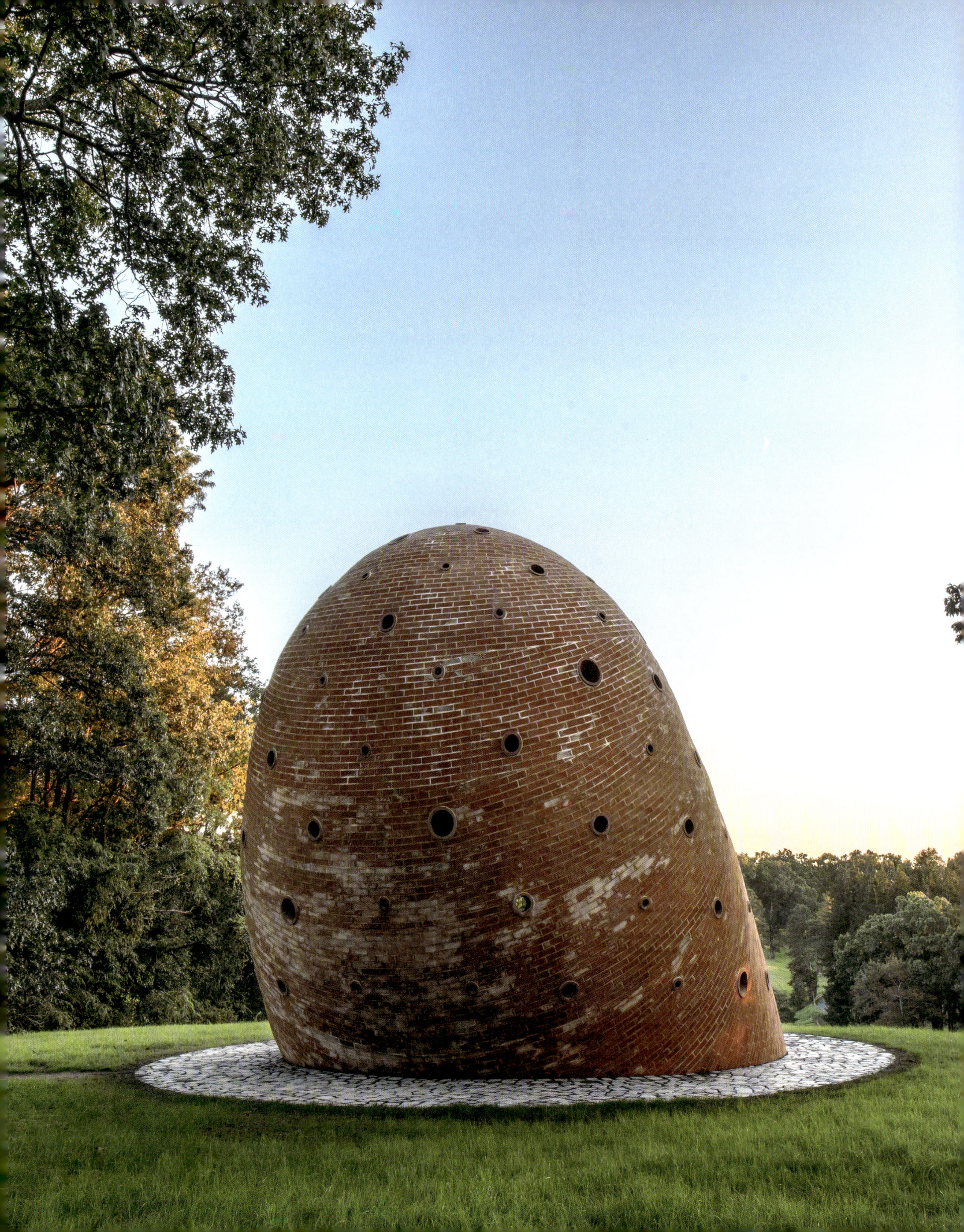

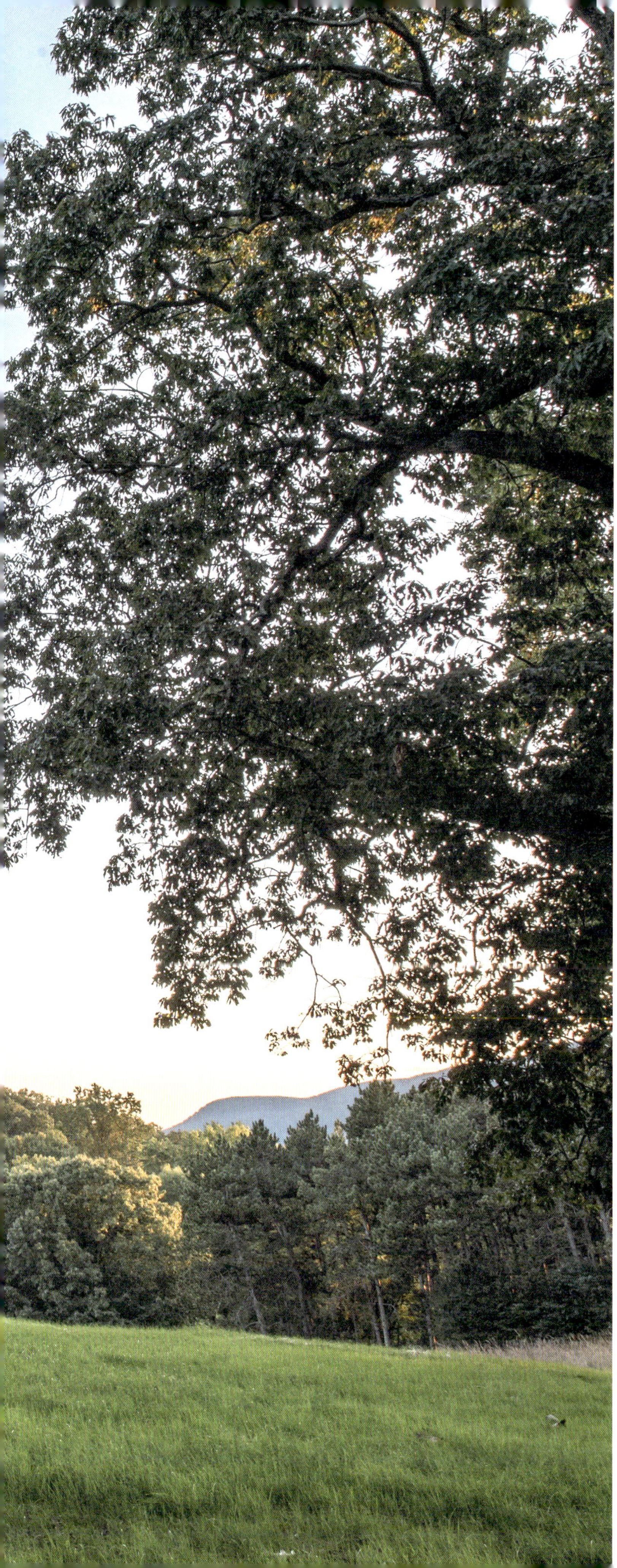

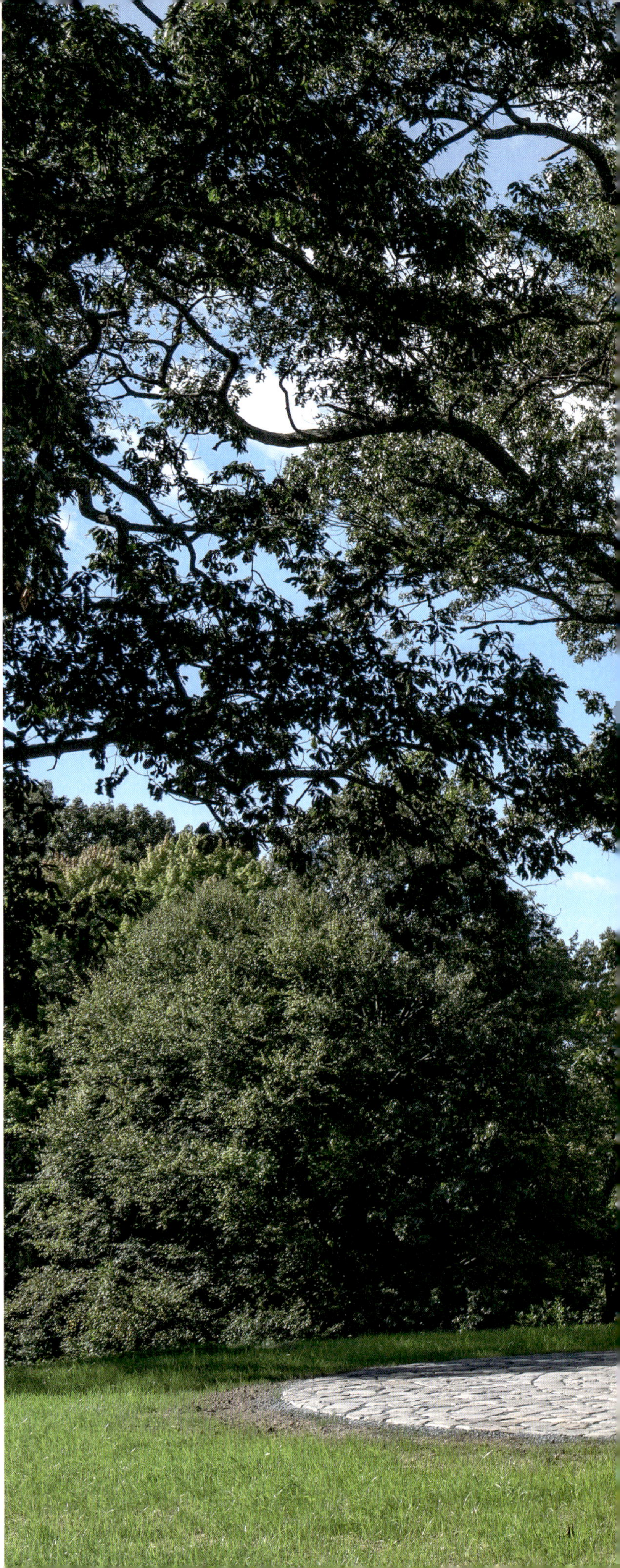

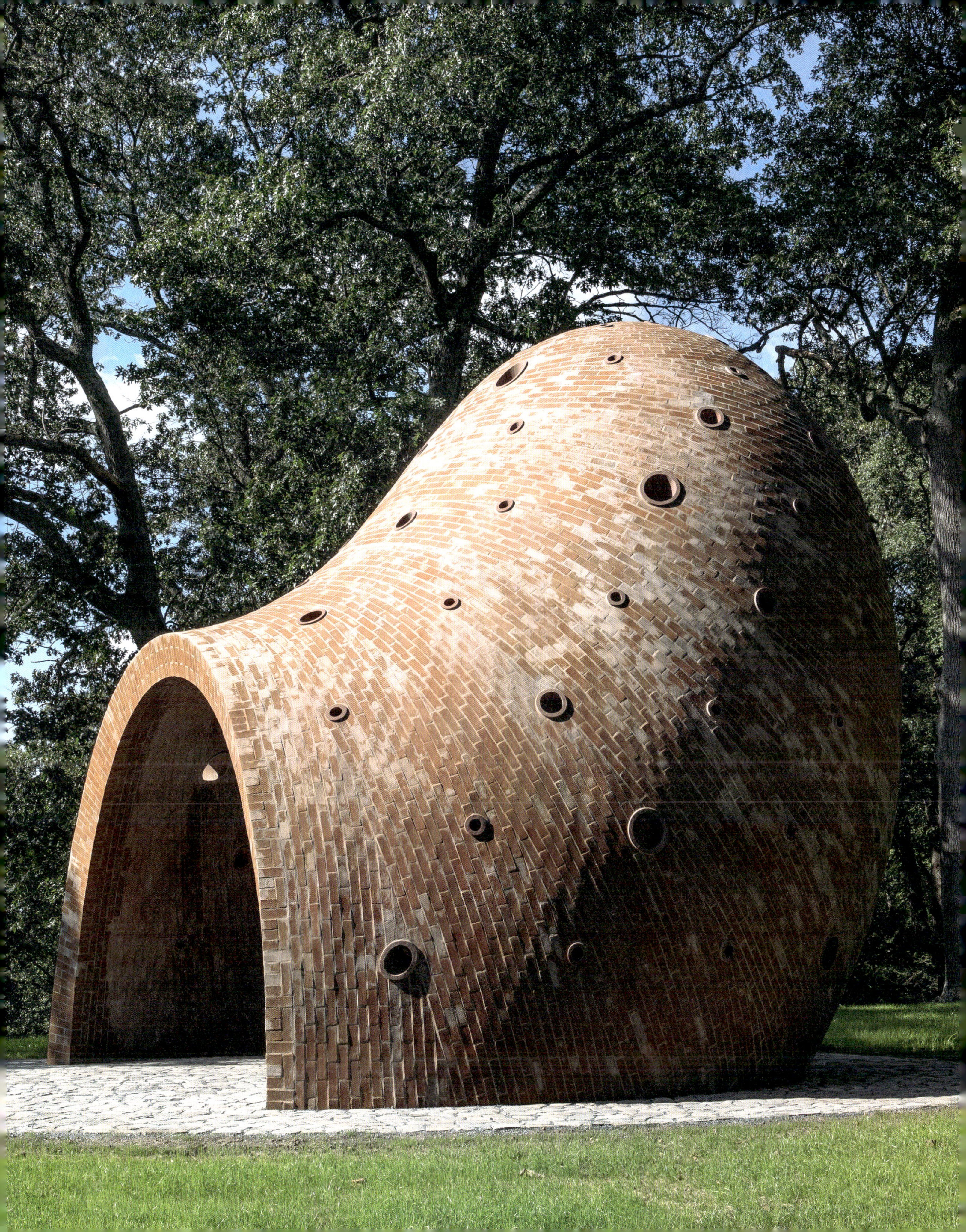

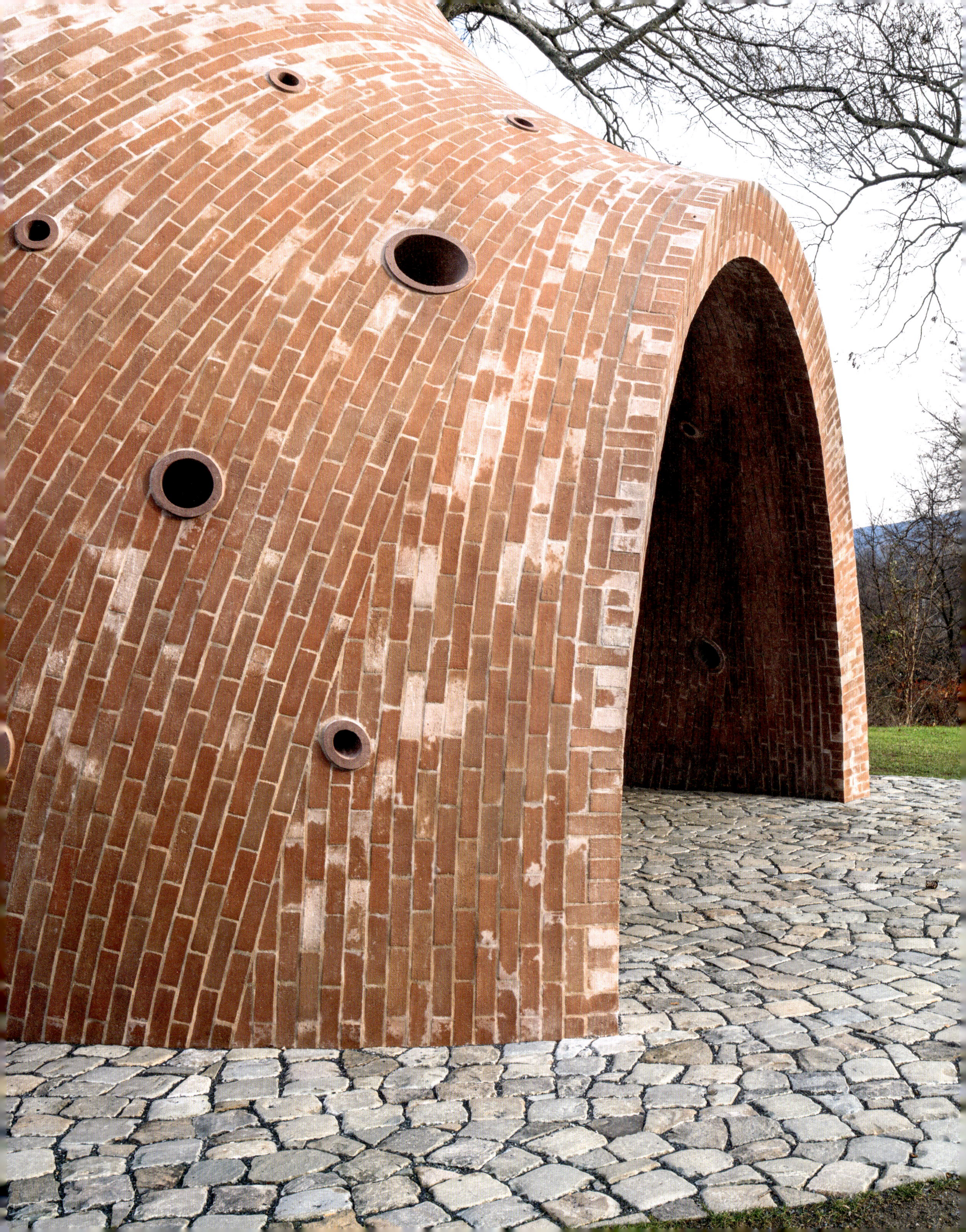

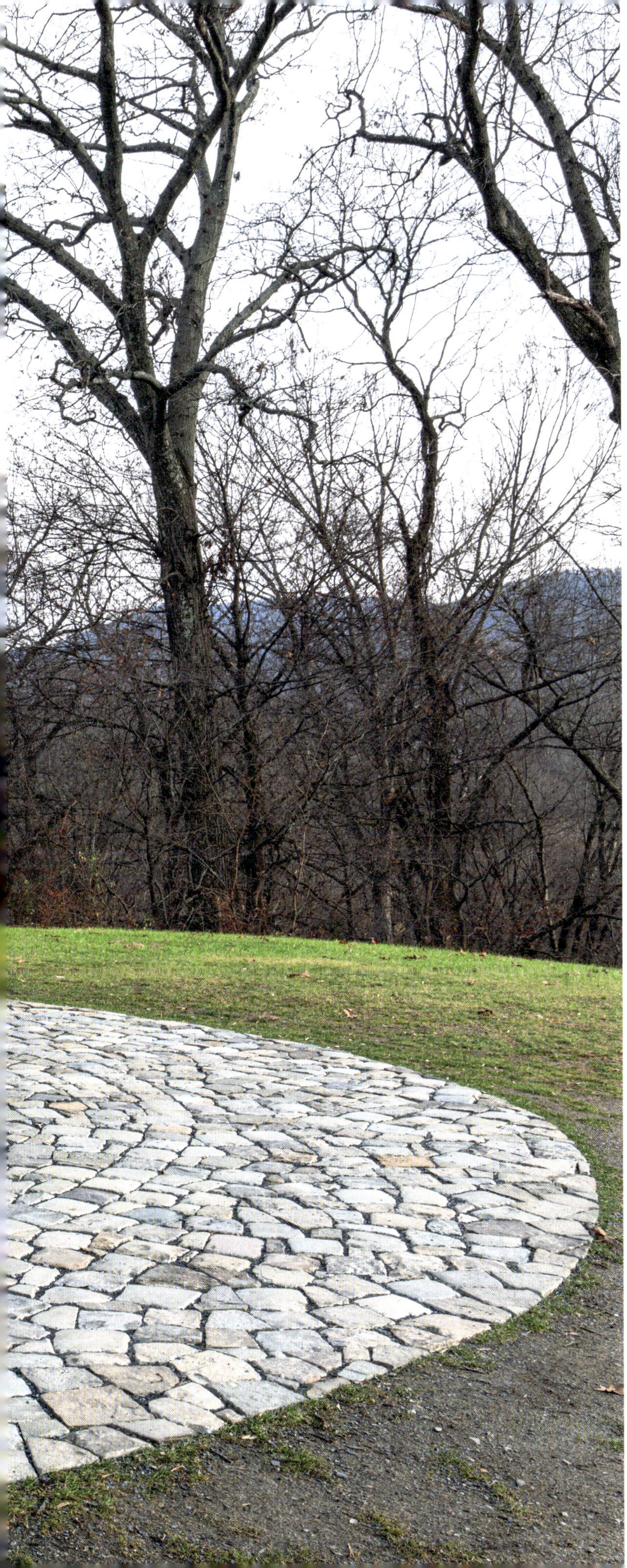

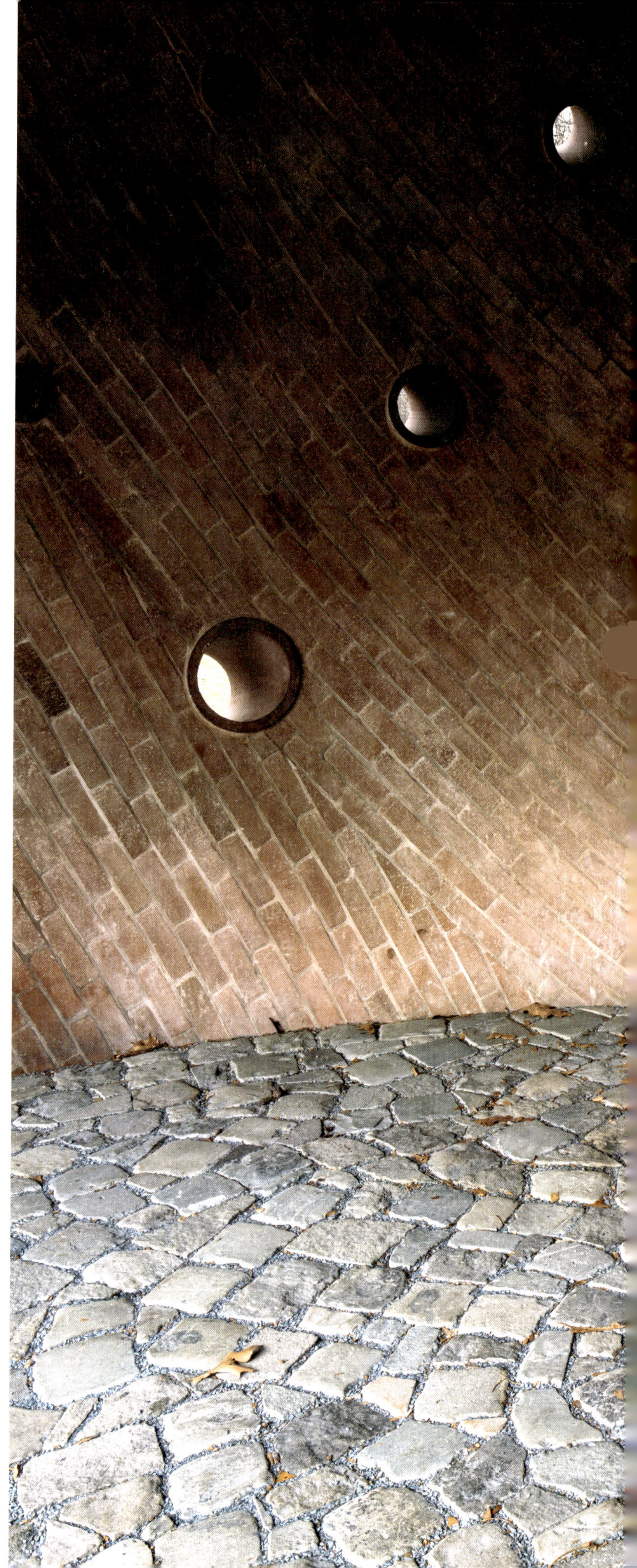

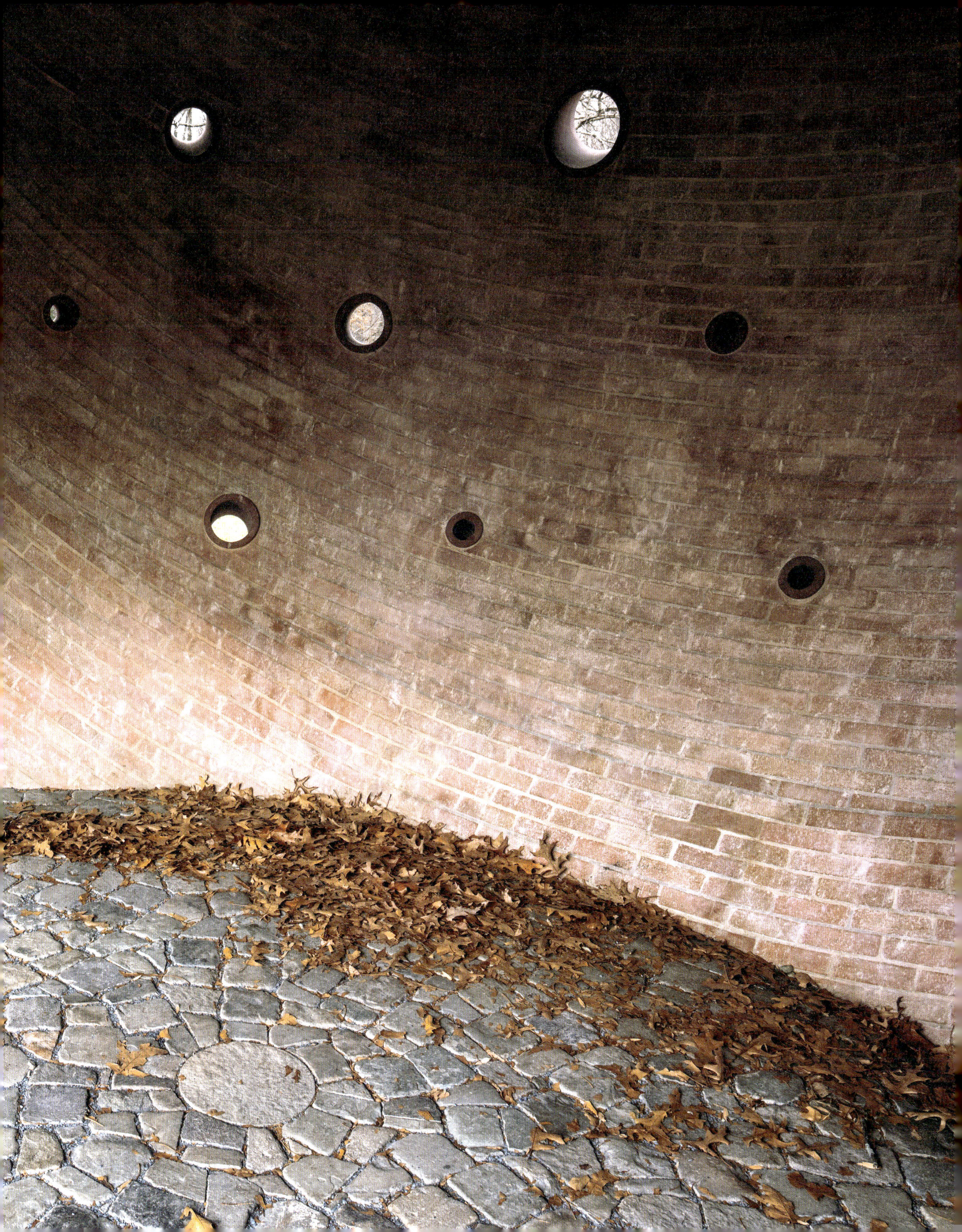

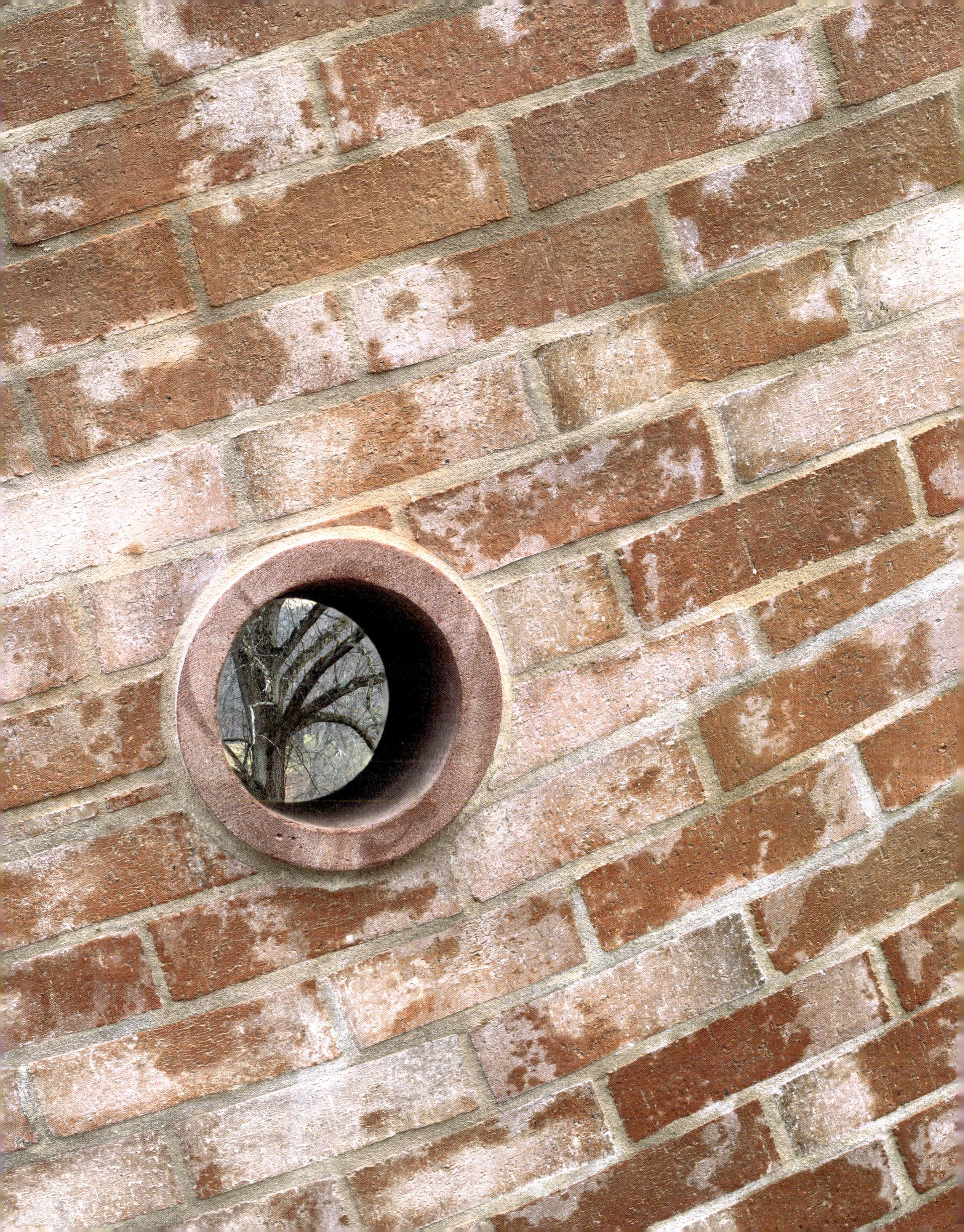

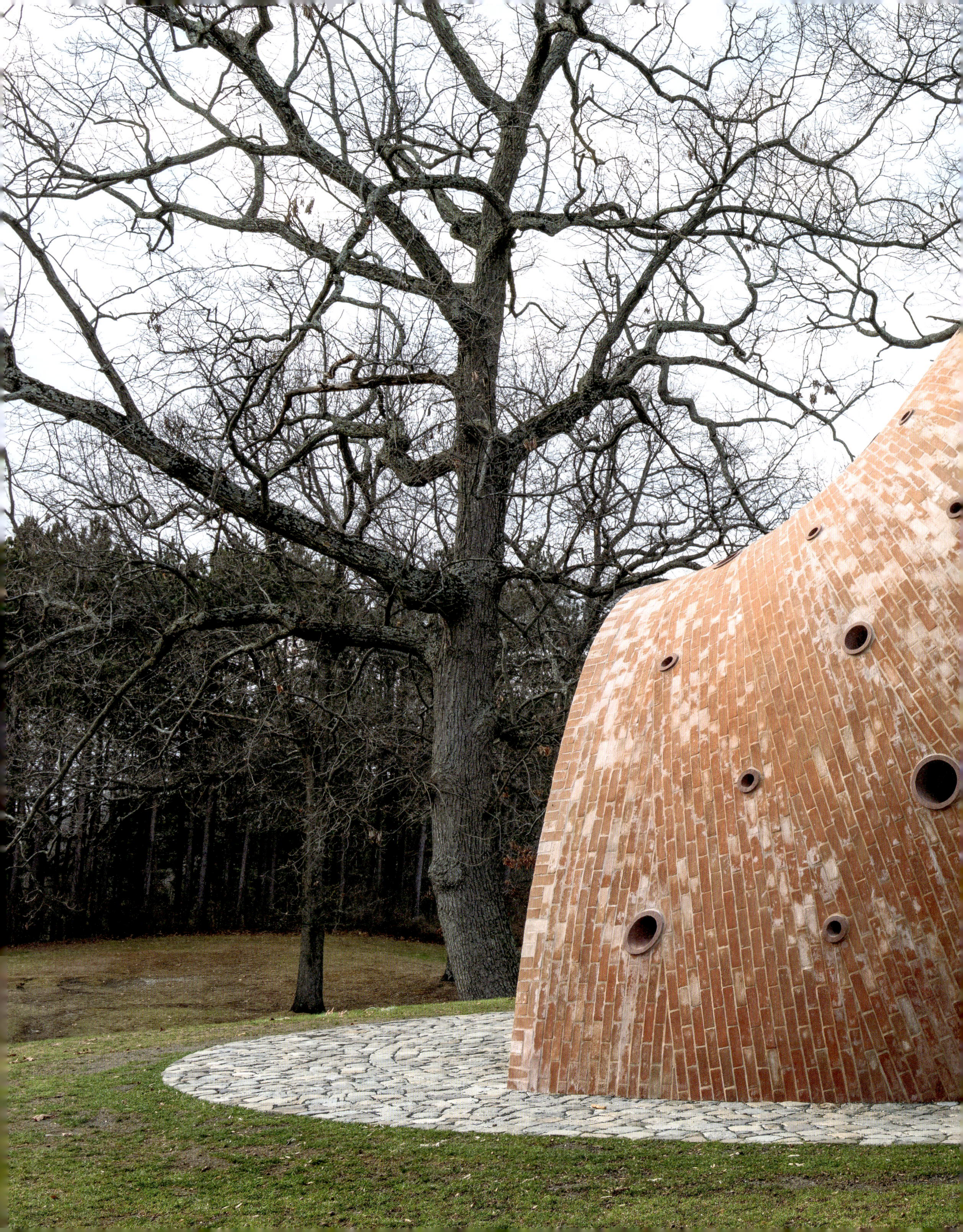

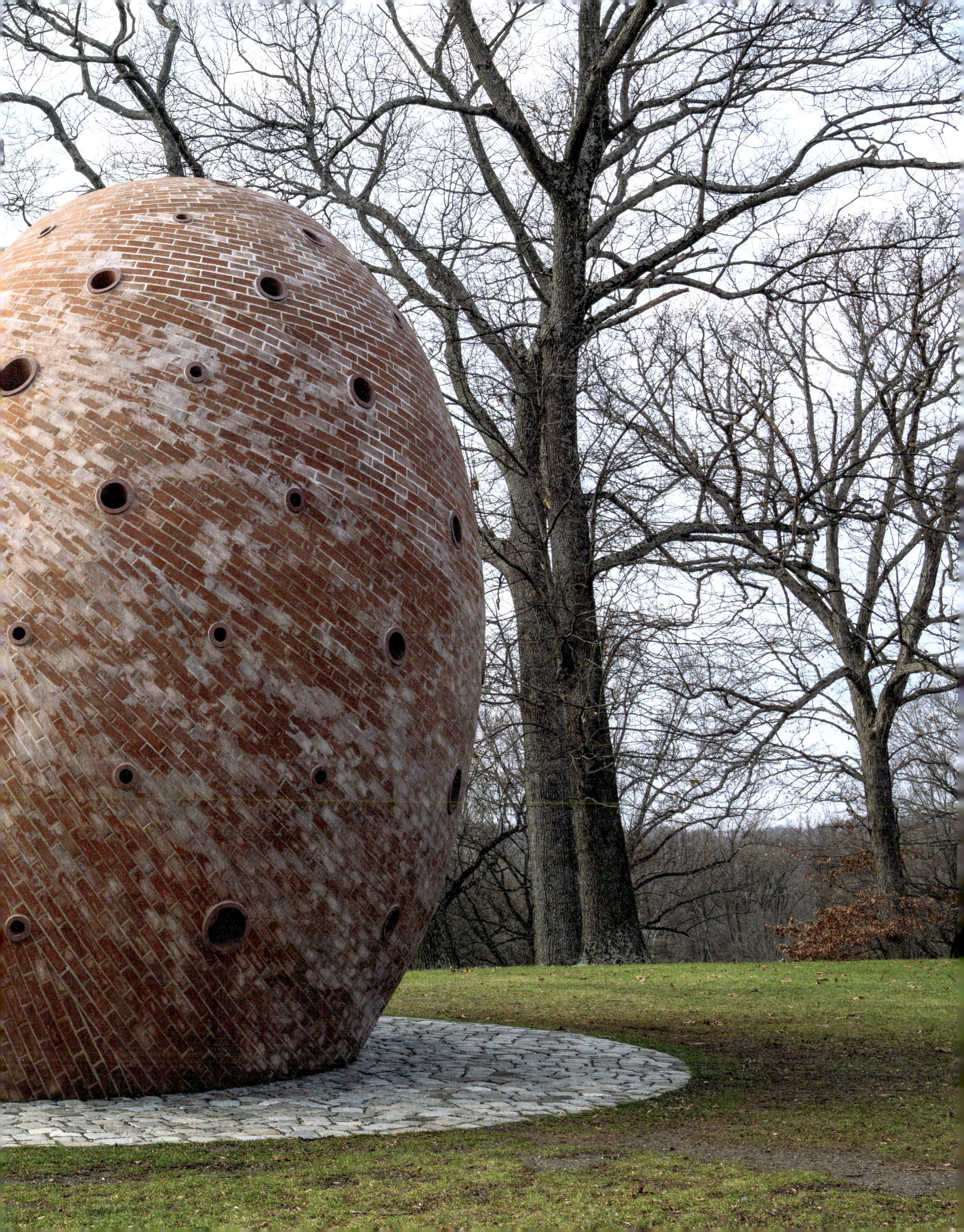

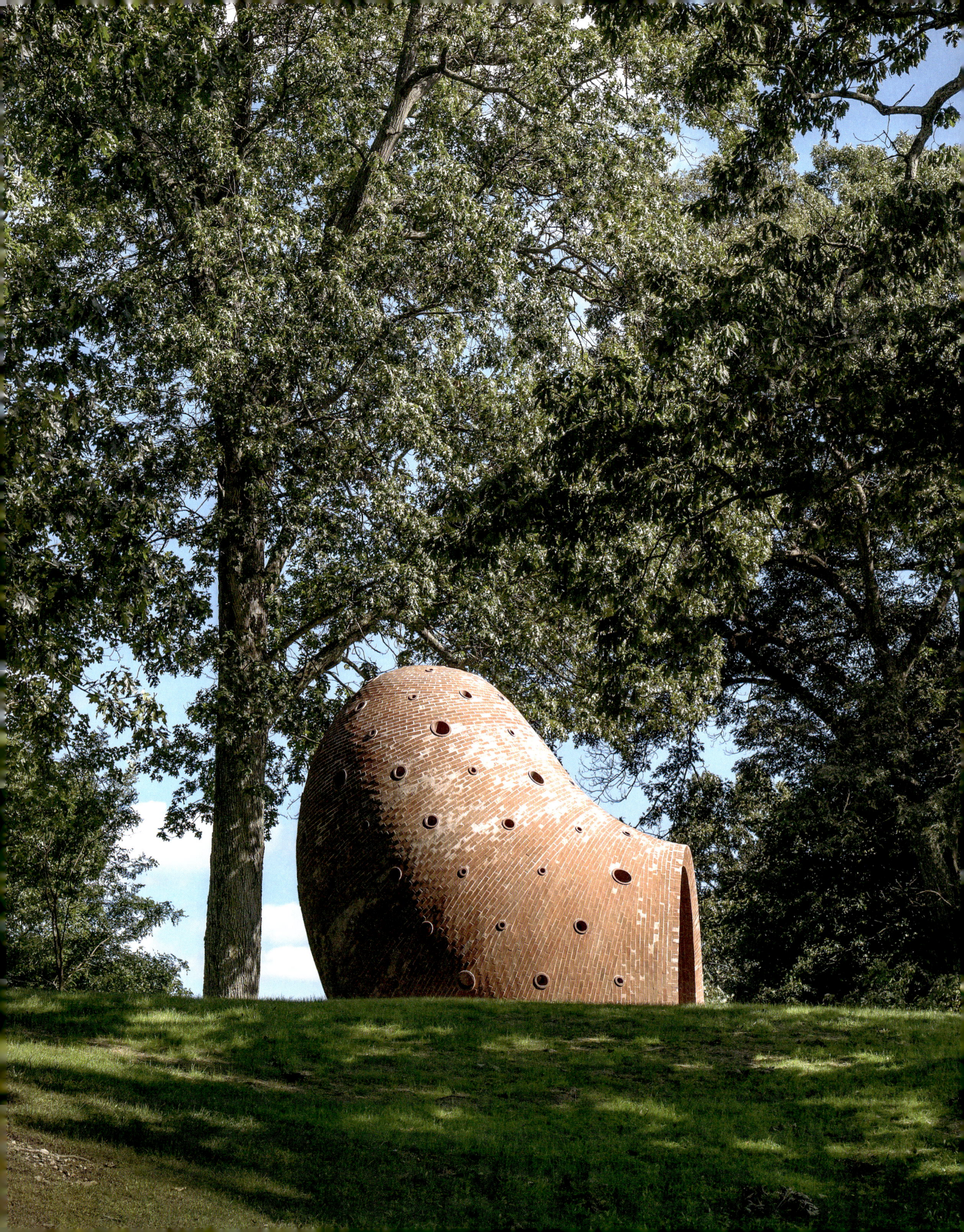

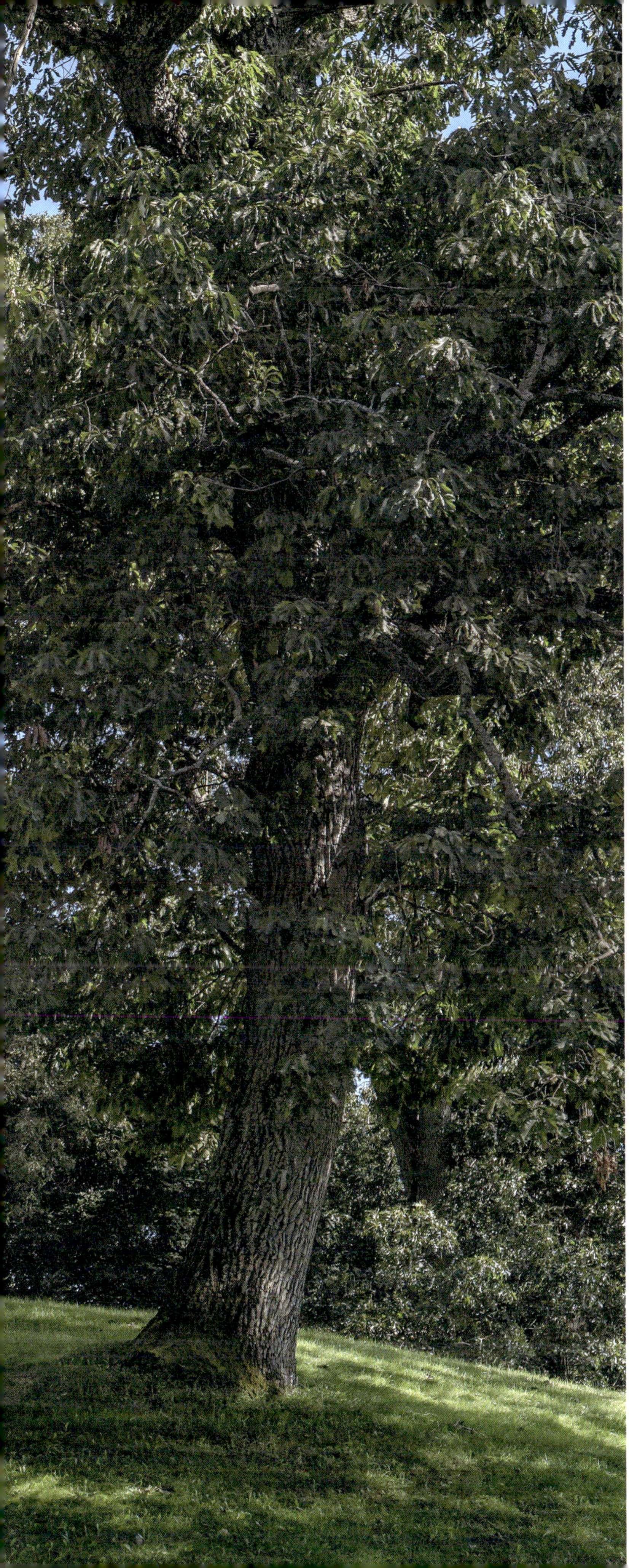

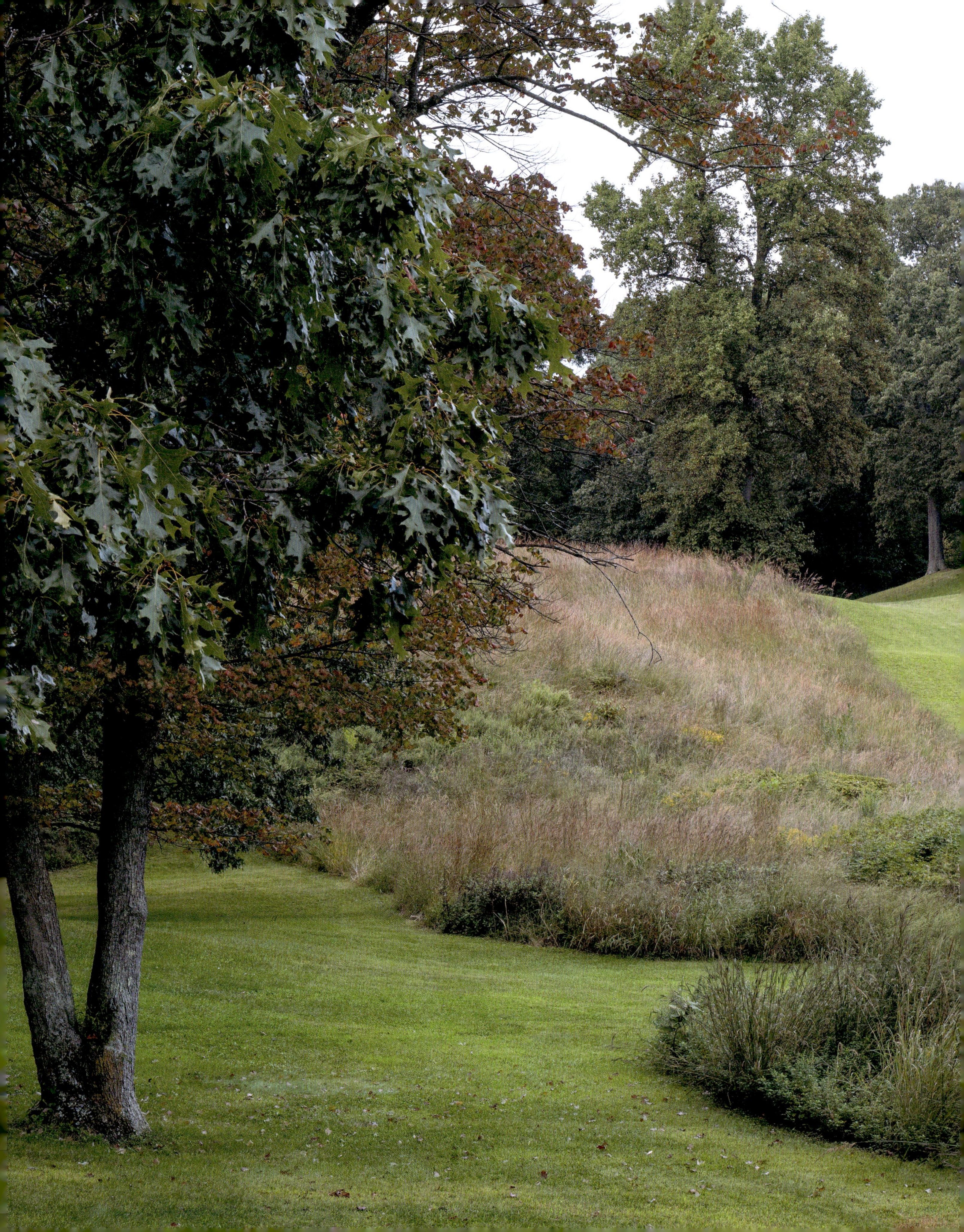

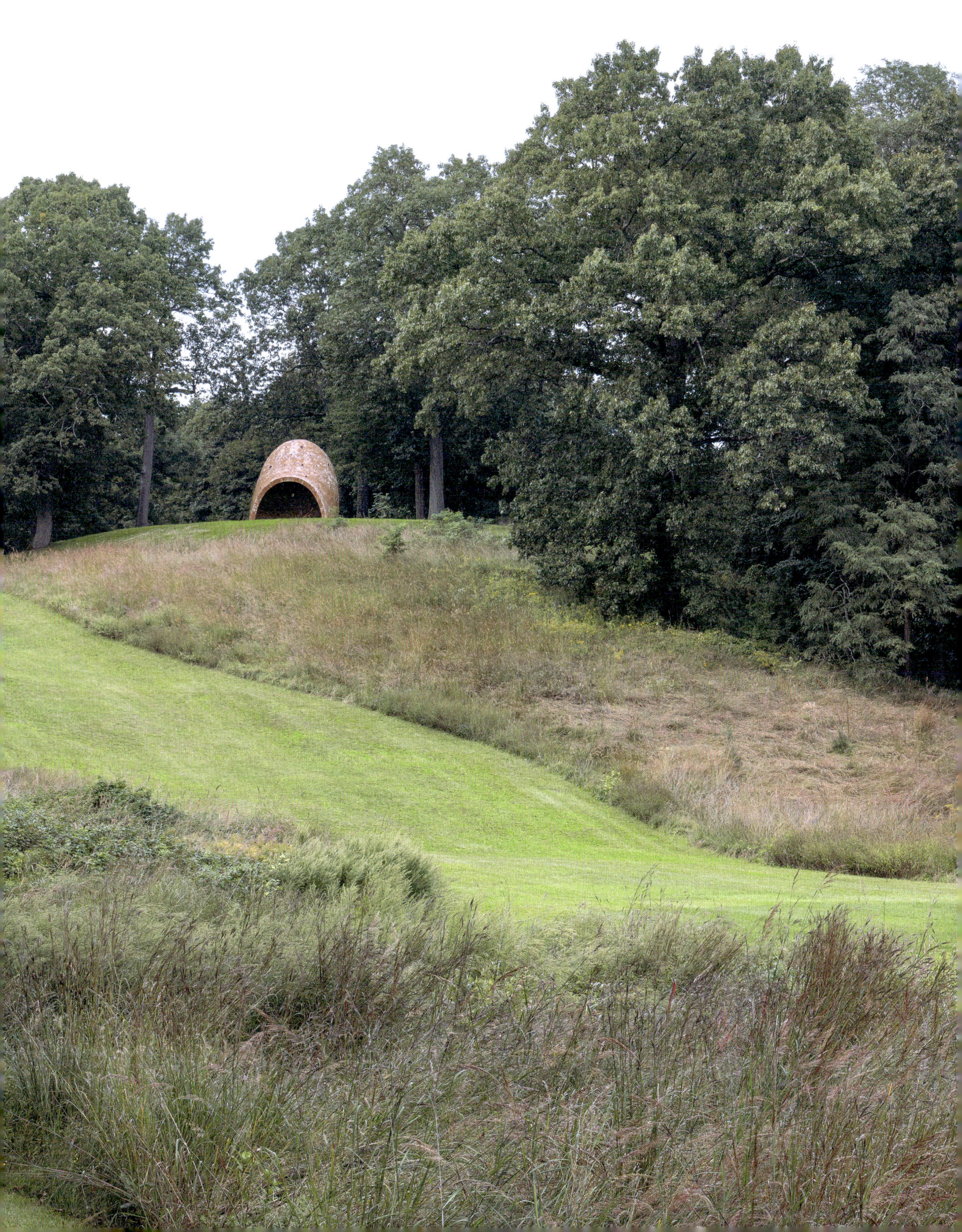

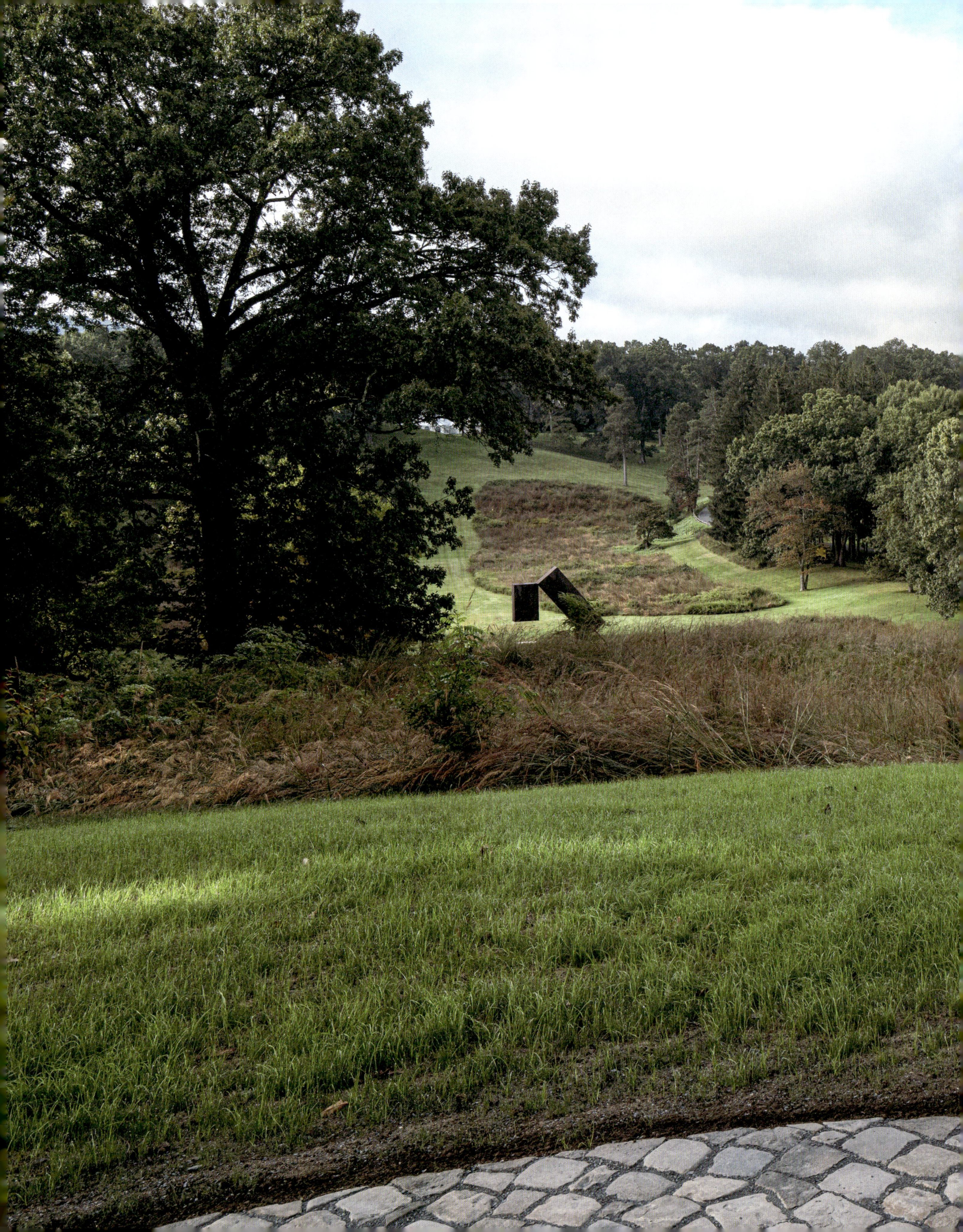

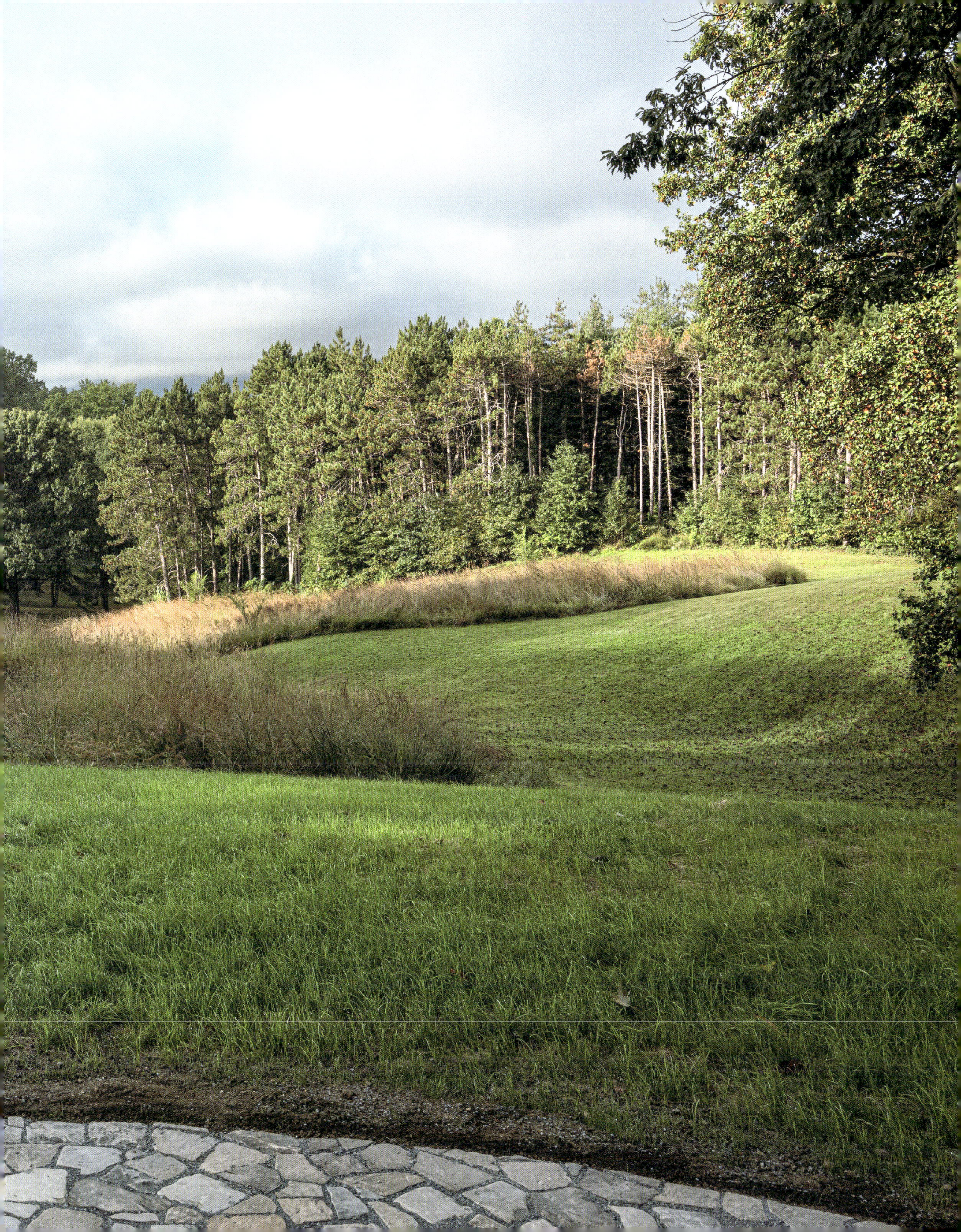

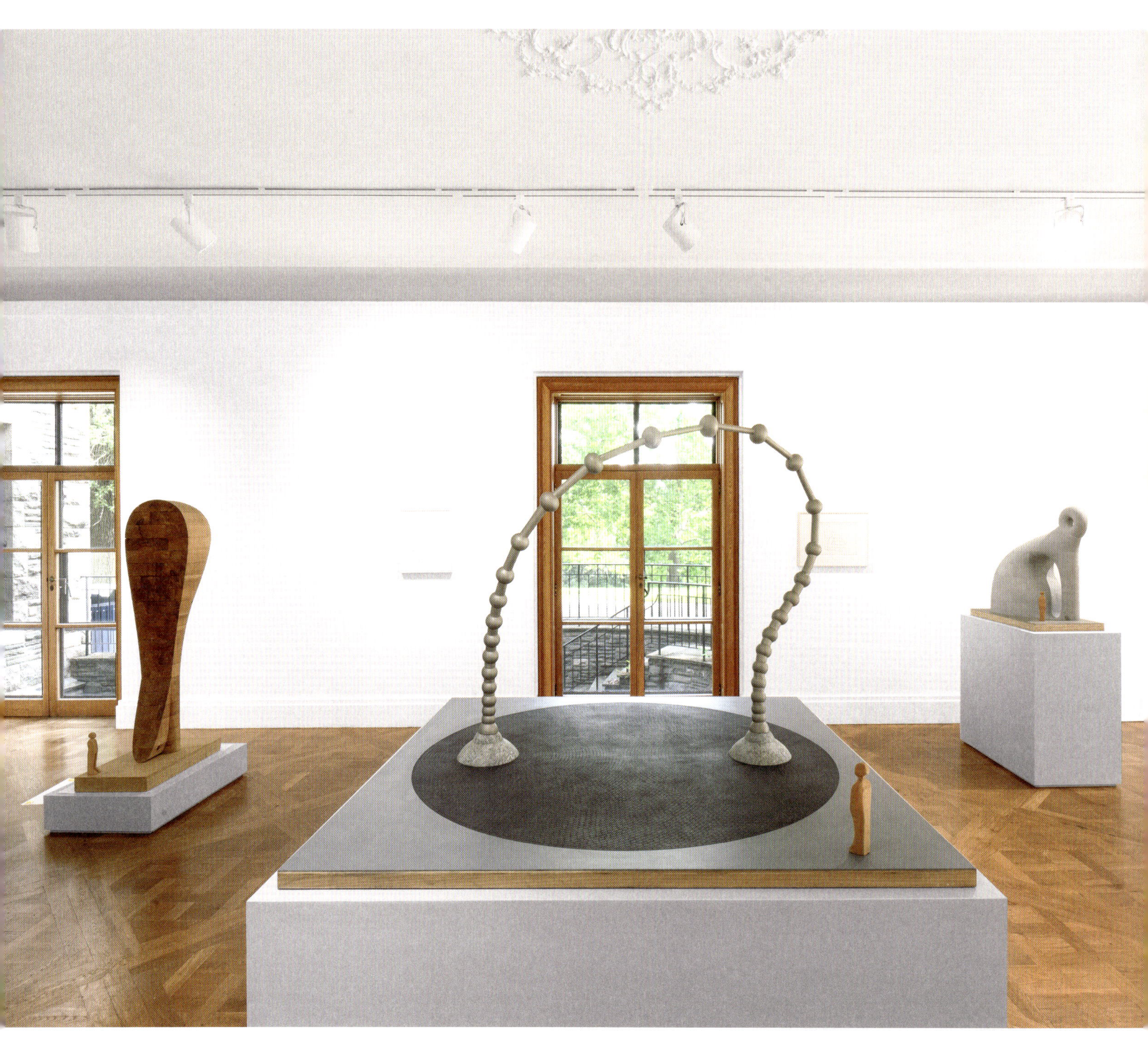

PROCESS AND SCALE

Adela Goldsmith, Nora Lawrence, and Martin Puryear

In the summer of 1977 Martin Puryear was invited to create a temporary site-specific work for Artpark, in western New York State, his first project to be exhibited outdoors. For this work, the artist made a wooden box by hand from twelve-inch-by-twelve-inch hemlock timbers with dovetail corners, constructed over the course of a summer. Puryear paired this box—which he has described as "very much a woodworker's expression"—with the longest utility pole he was able to find. Onto this he spliced another pole, which tapered gradually upward until reaching a thin tip at nearly one hundred feet tall, noting, "I wanted to pierce the sky; I wanted to engage the space by pointing to the sky."

While one preparatory drawing for *Box and Pole* conveys the modeled forms of the work's two elements, the other is more diagrammatic, showing a cross section of where the work intersects with the ground and the point where the artist fused two segments of pole together. Written in Puryear's own hand are notes about dimensions, types of wood, and construction details. Puryear even used hand-drawn wood grain to distinguish the box's tongue-and-groove corners. Together, the two drawings illustrate the artist's process of imagining a sculpture for a particular setting, and then working through the practical logistics of its construction.

After its temporary installation, Puryear reused the wooden box, pairing it with an inverted wooden cone in an outdoor installation titled *Equivalents* at Wave Hill, in the Bronx, in 1979. For this work, he attempted to achieve the same cubic volume in two disparate geometric forms.

PLATE 1. *Box and Pole*, 1977
Graphite on paper, 29 × 21 in.
(73.7 × 53.3 cm)

PLATE 2. *Box and Pole*, 1977
Graphite on paper, 29 × 21 in.
(73.7 × 53.3 cm)

PLATE 3. *Box and Pole*, 1977
Canadian hemlock and southern yellow pine, box: 54 × 54 × 54 in. (137.2 × 137.2 × 137.2 cm); pole: 100 ft. (3,048 cm) tall
Temporary installation, Artpark, Lewistown, New York

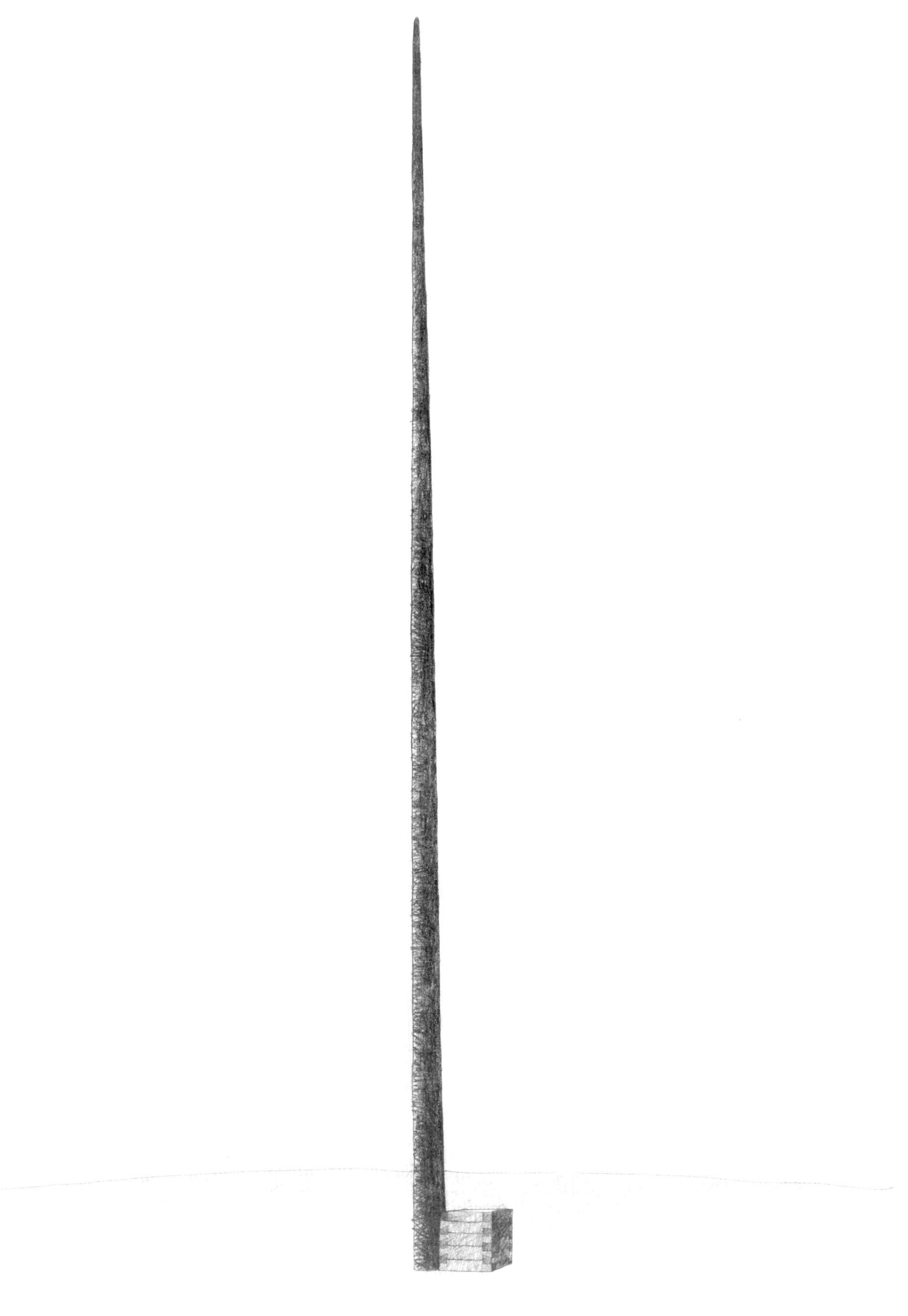

PL. 1

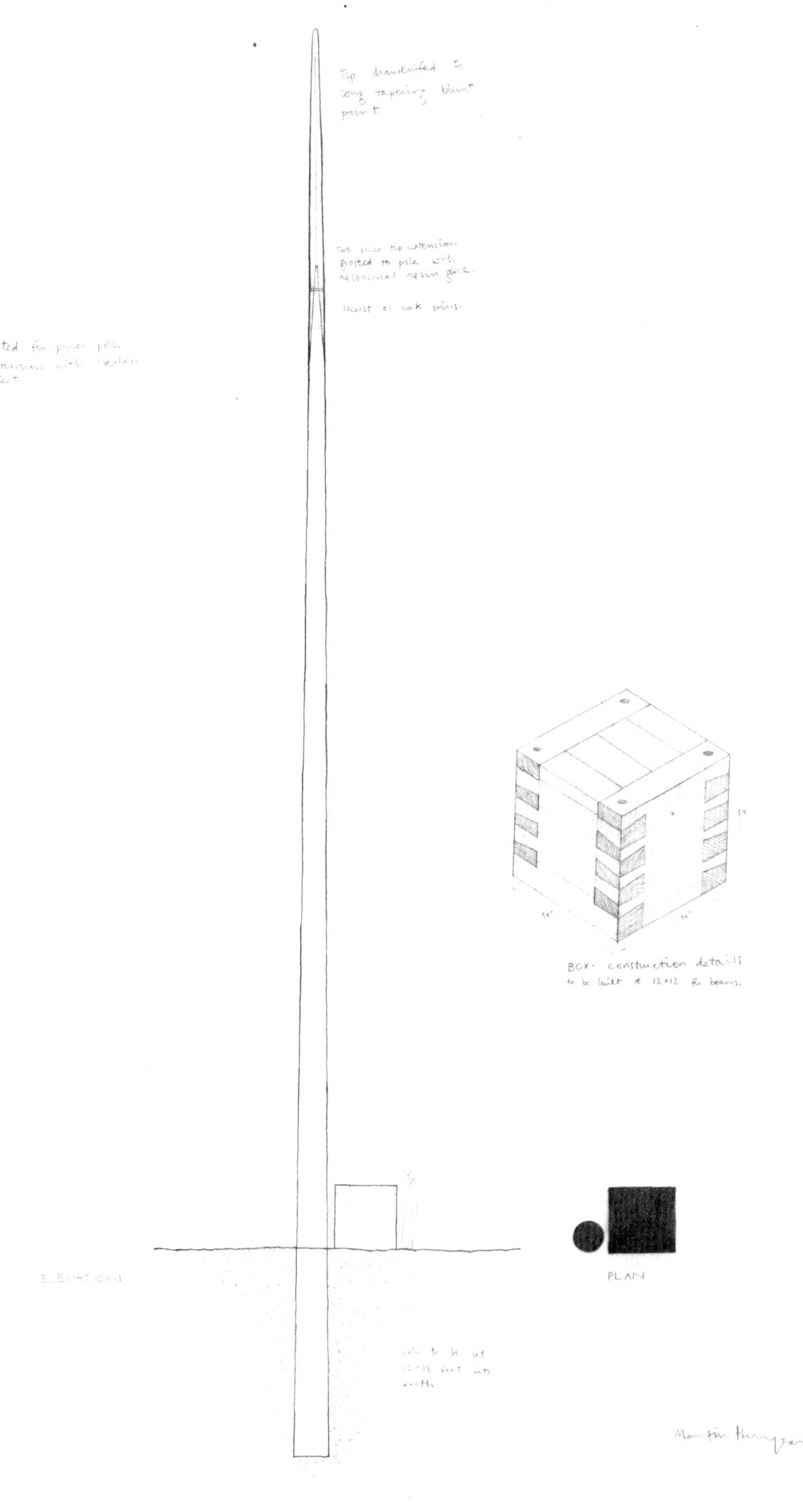

Two piece tip extension
grafted to pole with
resorcinal resin glue.
locust or oak pins.
54"
54"
BOX- construction details
to be built of 12×12 fir beams.
ELEVATION
PLAN

PL. 2

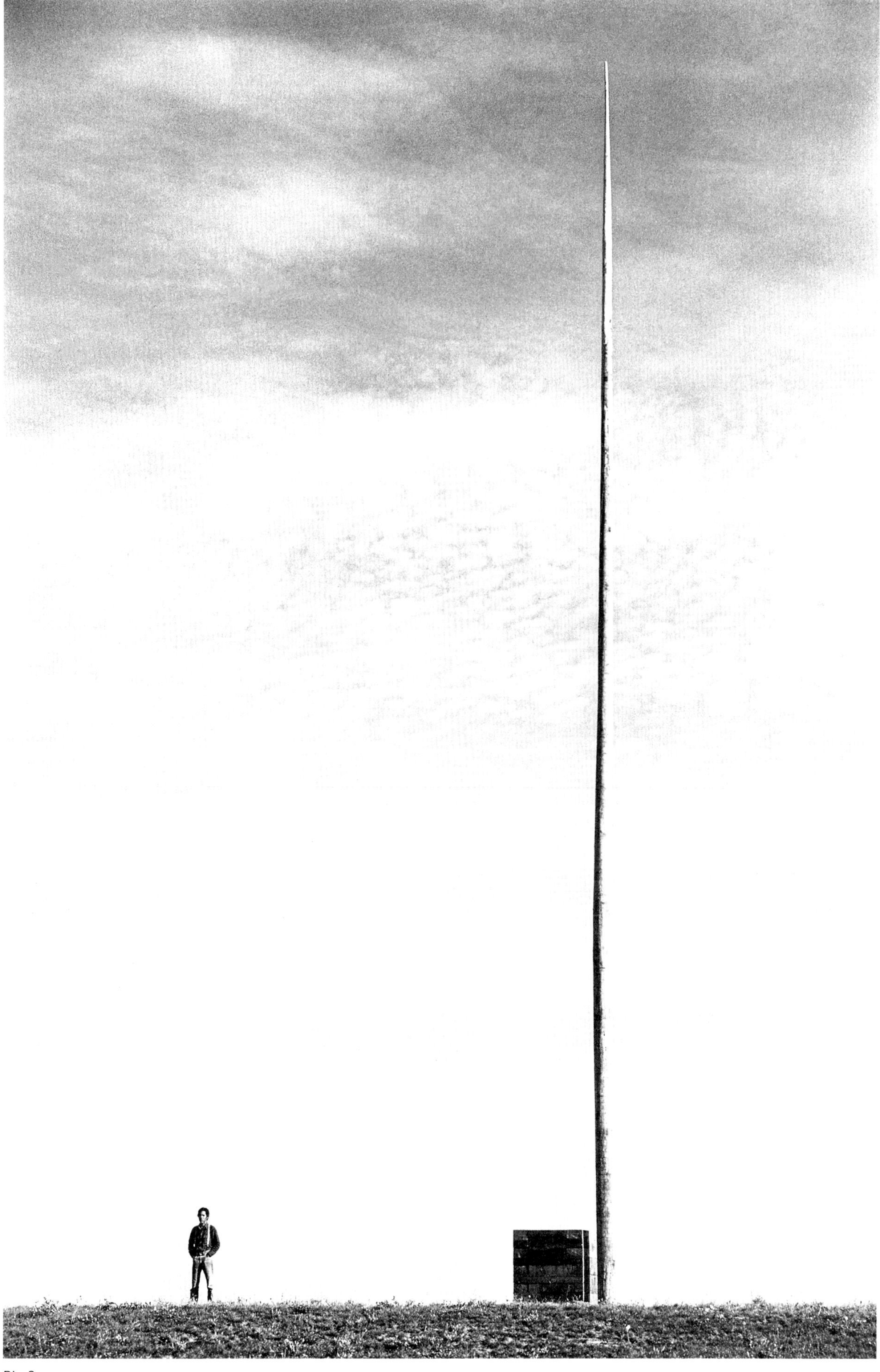

PL. 3

Stone Bow was a public sculpture proposal solicited by Tufts University in the early 1980s. It was the second of two options that Puryear envisioned for the school; the first took the form of a large installation that would cut across a lawn, while *Stone Bow* was suitable for a smaller site. Puryear wanted to make an arch out of stone. The work was designed to have a stainless steel cable running through consecutive curved granite cylinders, themselves cut at a slight angle (larger on top than bottom) to form the arch. The steel cable would hold the cylinders taut, while another cable would pull the two sides of the work together underground. This would have been Puryear's first work created in stone, and he wanted to work both within and outside of stonemasonry traditions. As he has said, "I like to get into the history of a use of a material and play with that, and also do something that is not a part of that history, so you see the material anew."

Neither of Puryear's proposals for Tufts were ultimately realized, but the models serve as an archival record of the artist's ideas about public work at that moment in time. In addition, the proposed forms and materials have appeared in some of Puryear's subsequent works. *Connecting* (2018), for example, is reminiscent of *Stone Bow*'s arcing form and rounded granite bases.

PLATE 4. *Stone Bow*, 1985
Graphite, 17⅞ × 27½ in.
(45.4 × 69.85 cm)

PLATE 5. *Maquette for "Stone Bow"* (unrealized), 1980s
Painted wood, 9 × 36 × 18 in.
(22.9 × 91.4 × 45.7 cm)

OPPOSITE: PL. 5

PL. 4

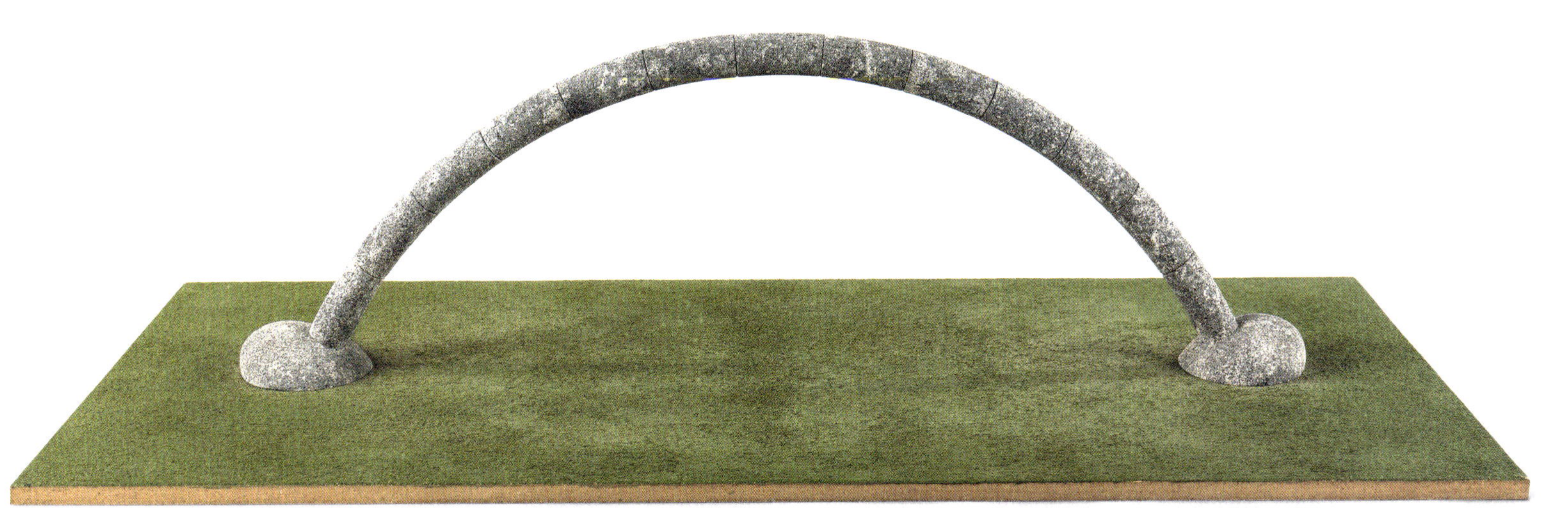

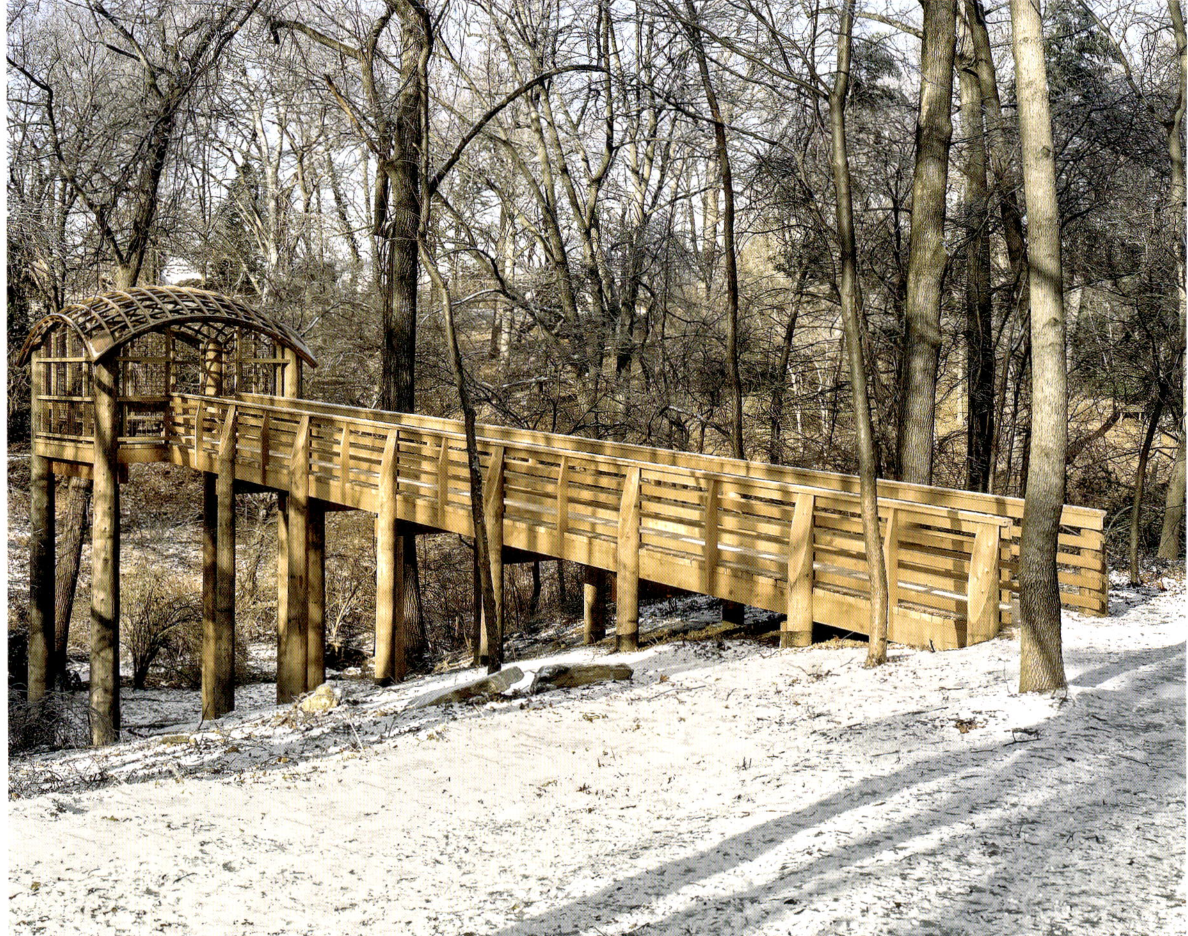

PL. 6

Pavilion in the Trees was commissioned by the Fairmount Park Art Association (now the Association for Public Art) in Philadelphia as part of its series Form and Function, which invited artists to create site-specific commissions for the park between 1980 and 1993. The work was constructed using three kinds of wood: debarked western red cedar, white oak, and redwood. The gridded canopy was built with the assistance of Bob Taylor, a woodworker who specialized in custom millwork.

Puryear has said, "I would never insist that the *Pavilion in the Trees* be called sculpture. I would say that it is a public amenity designed by a sculptor, which tried to invest a public facility with a bit more poetry than it otherwise might have." The spindly latticework of the process model conveys the airy, open sense of the final work, which rises high into a group of trees, evoking the feeling of being in a treehouse.

PLATE 6. *Pavilion in the Trees*, 1993–94
Red cedar, white oak, redwood, and chain-link fencing, pavilion: 11 × 16 × 16 ft. (335.3 × 487.7 × 487.7 cm); walkway: 60 in. (152.4 cm) wide × 60 ft. (1,828.8 cm) long; overall height: 35 ft. (1,066.8 cm)
Commissioned by the Fairmount Park Art Association, Philadelphia

PLATE 7. *Maquette for "Pavilion in the Trees,"* 1981
Wood, 16 × 38¾ × 10⅞ in. (40.6 × 98.4 × 27.6 cm)

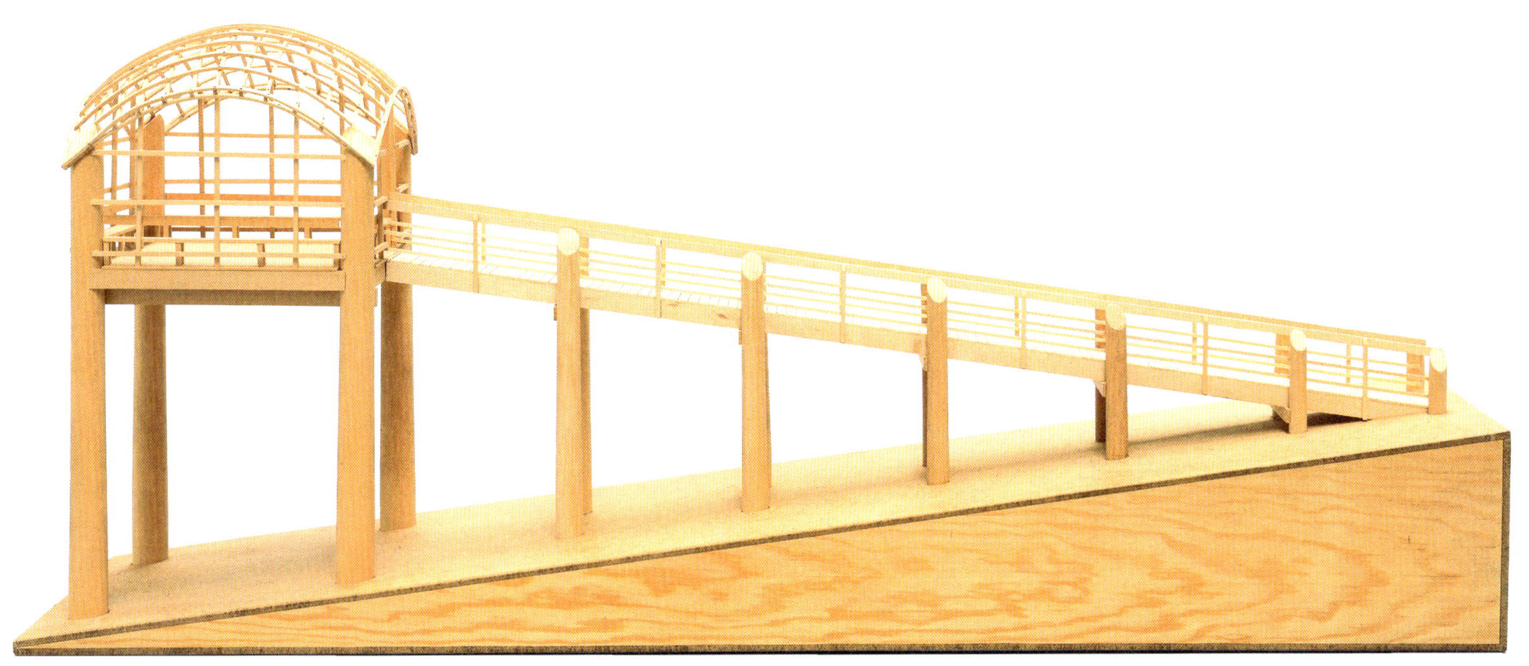

PL. 7

PLATE 8. *Pavilion in the Trees*, 1993–94
Red cedar, white oak, redwood, and chain-link fencing, pavilion: 11 × 16 × 16 ft. (335.3 × 487.7 × 487.7 cm); walkway: 60 in. (152.4 cm) wide × 60 ft. (1,828.8 cm) long; overall height: 35 ft. (1,066.8 cm)
Commissioned by the Fairmount Park Art Association, Philadelphia

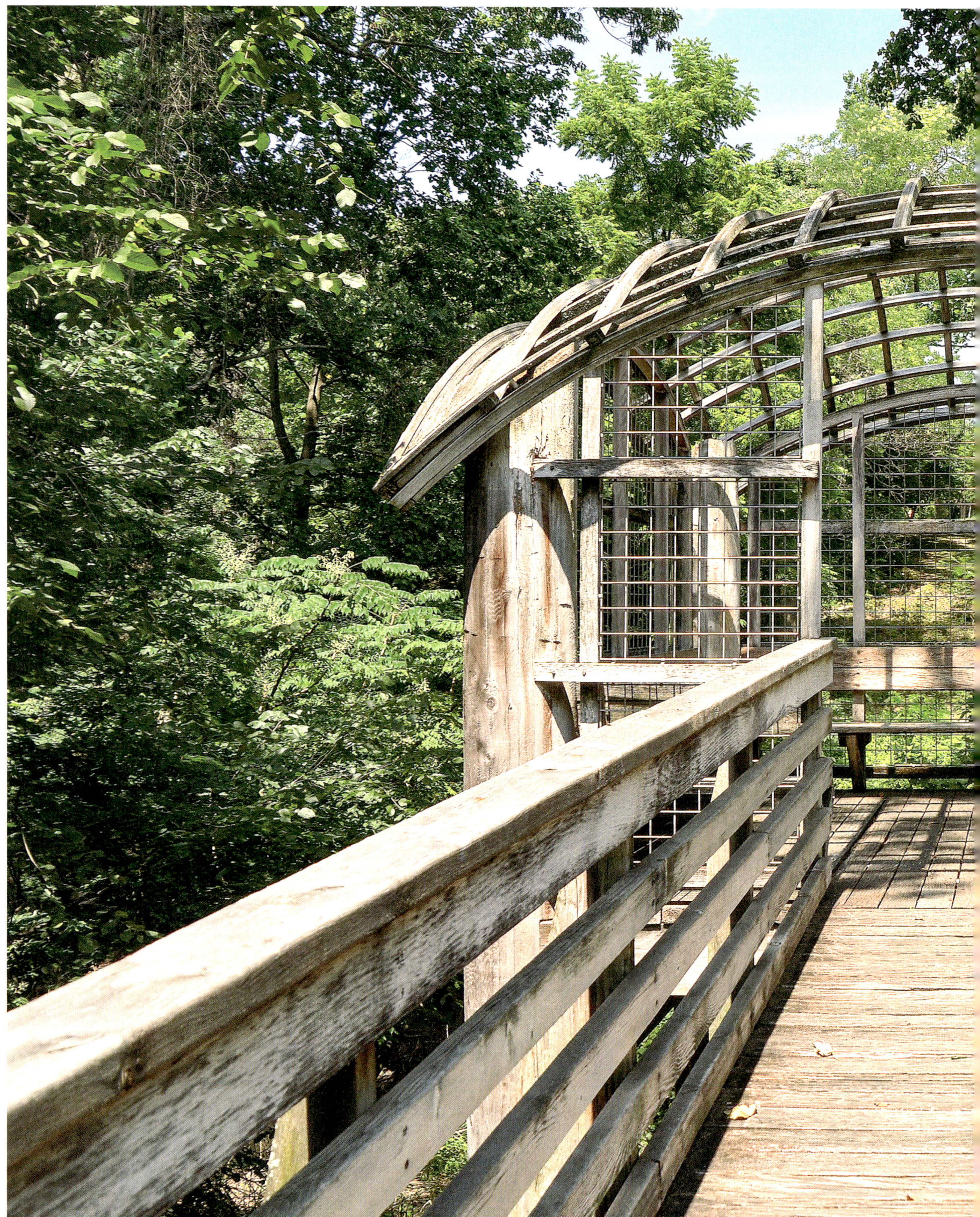

PL. 8

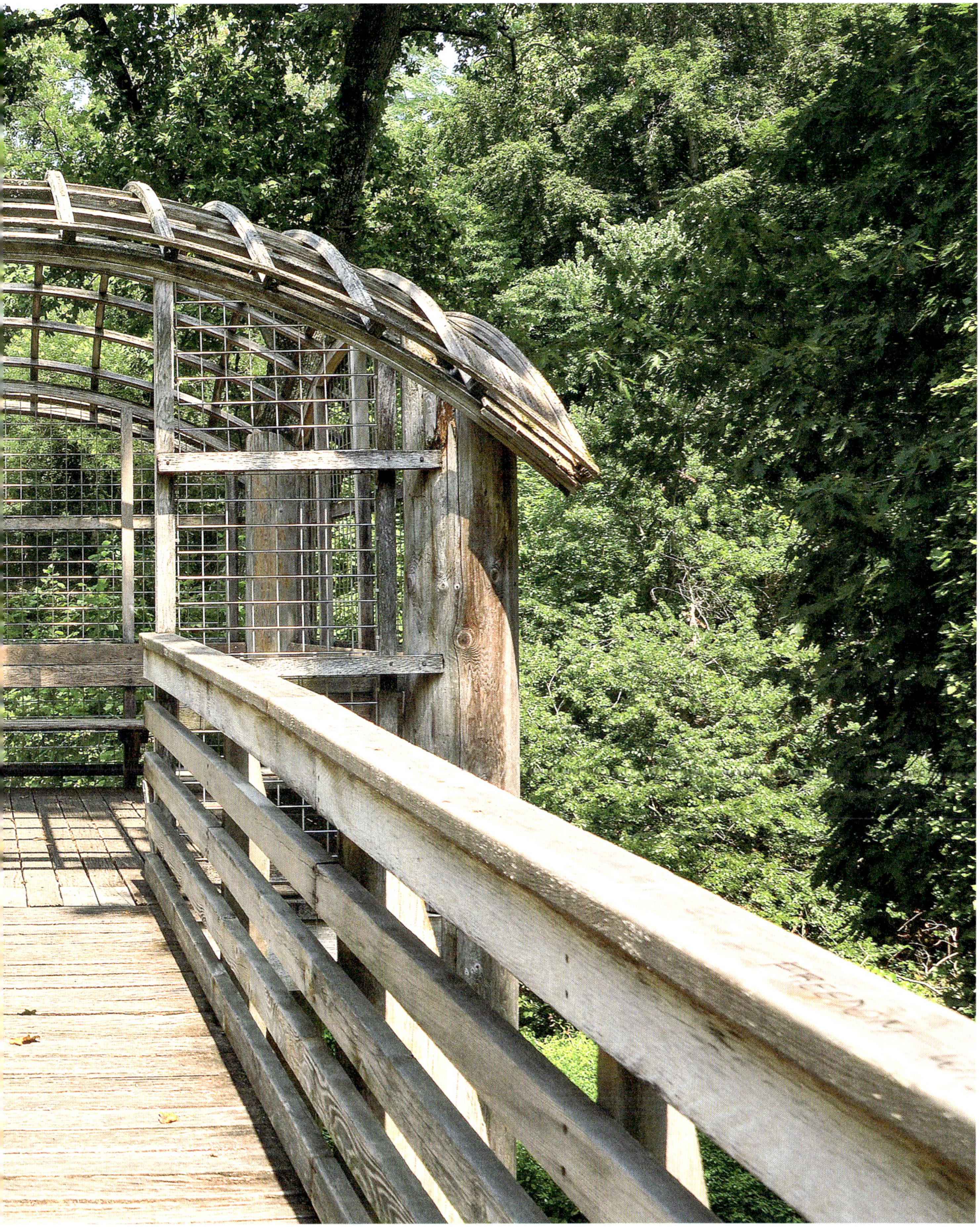

Commissioned for the sesquicentennial of Gettysburg College, in Pennsylvania, *Sentinel* is Puryear's first work in masonry. Puryear chose to work with fieldstone after viewing many local structures made of this material. In so doing, he paired a traditional, regional process with an abstract, contemporary sculpture—a notable approach in a town that is home to many bronze monuments to the Civil War. Describing this process, Puryear has recalled that he used "the fieldstone and mortar that had been used in barns and houses in that area of Pennsylvania by the German settlers for centuries—but to use those materials to make something that's very clearly mine."

To make *Sentinel*, Puryear crafted a latticed wooden mold at his Chicago studio and transported it to the site. There, he worked with a recent graduate from Gettysburg's art program, Nick Micros, to lay fieldstone into the mold. Fieldstone was plentiful on campus, making it possible for Puryear to source materials from areas of the college that were under construction. After the sculpture was completed, the hollow center was filled with cement. The maquette, however, is created from wood that Puryear carved by hand and painted to resemble stones and mortar.

PLATE 9. *Maquette for "Sentinel,"* c. 1981
Painted wood, 10¾ × 8¼ × 3½ in. (27.3 × 21 × 8.9 cm)

PLATE 10. *Sentinel*, 1982
Mortared fieldstone,
10 ft. 6 in. × 8 ft. 6 in. × 42 in.
(320 × 259.1 × 106.7 cm)
Commissioned by Gettysburg College, Pennsylvania

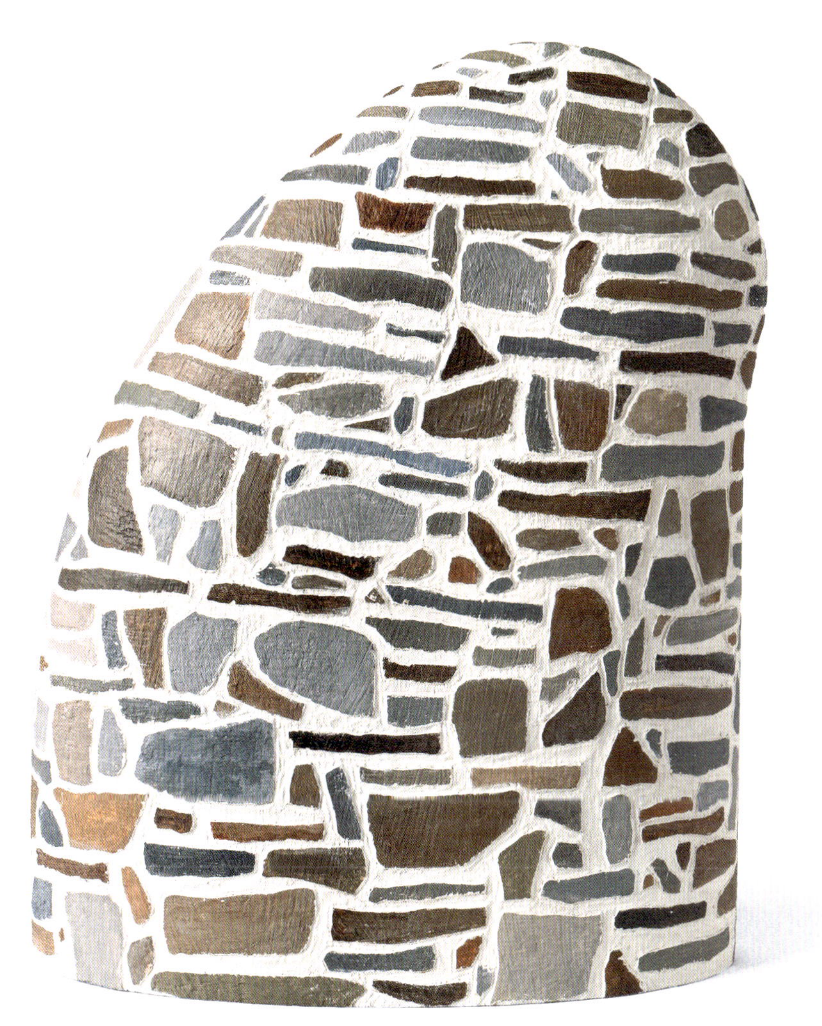

PL. 9

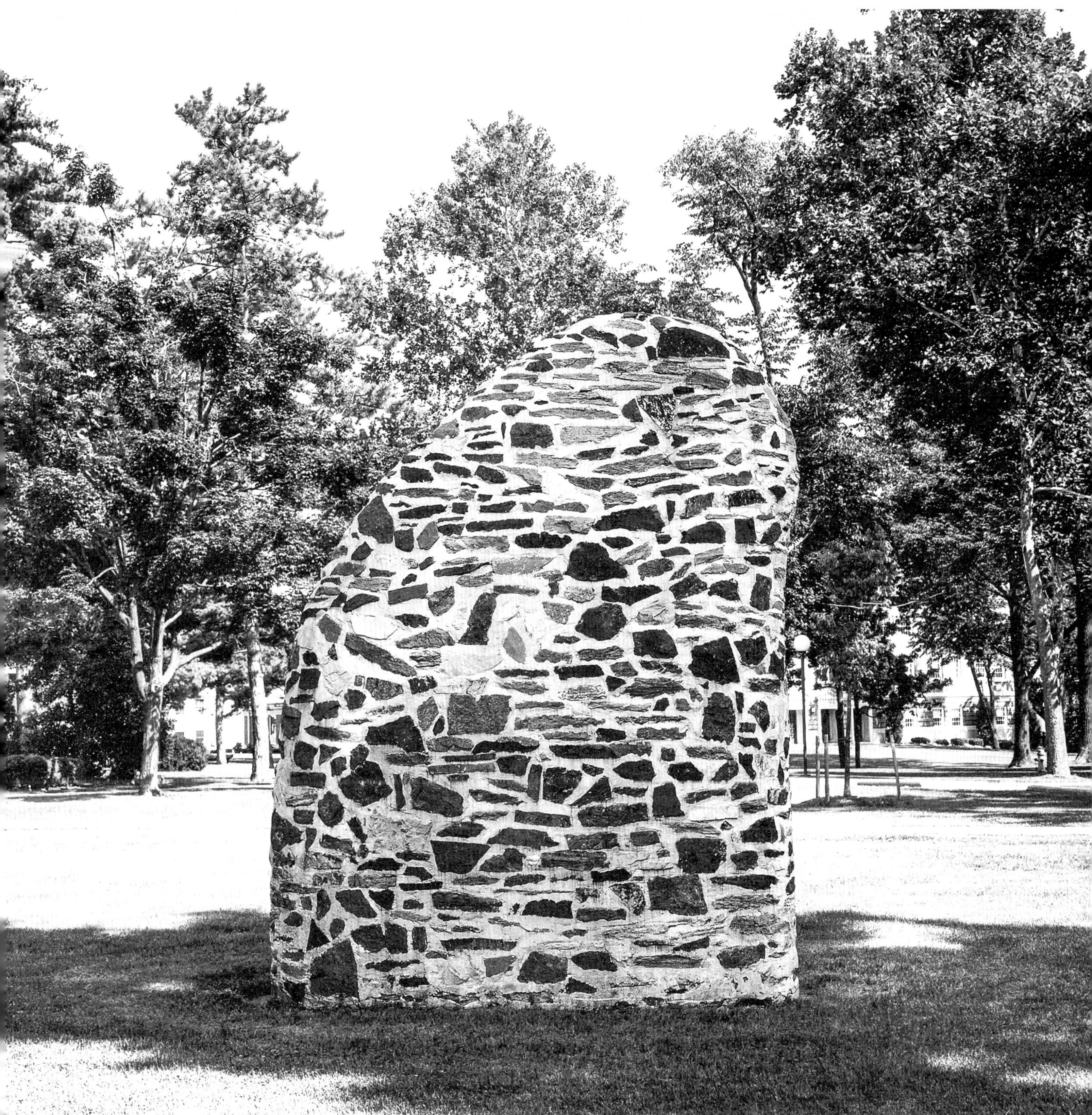

PL. 10

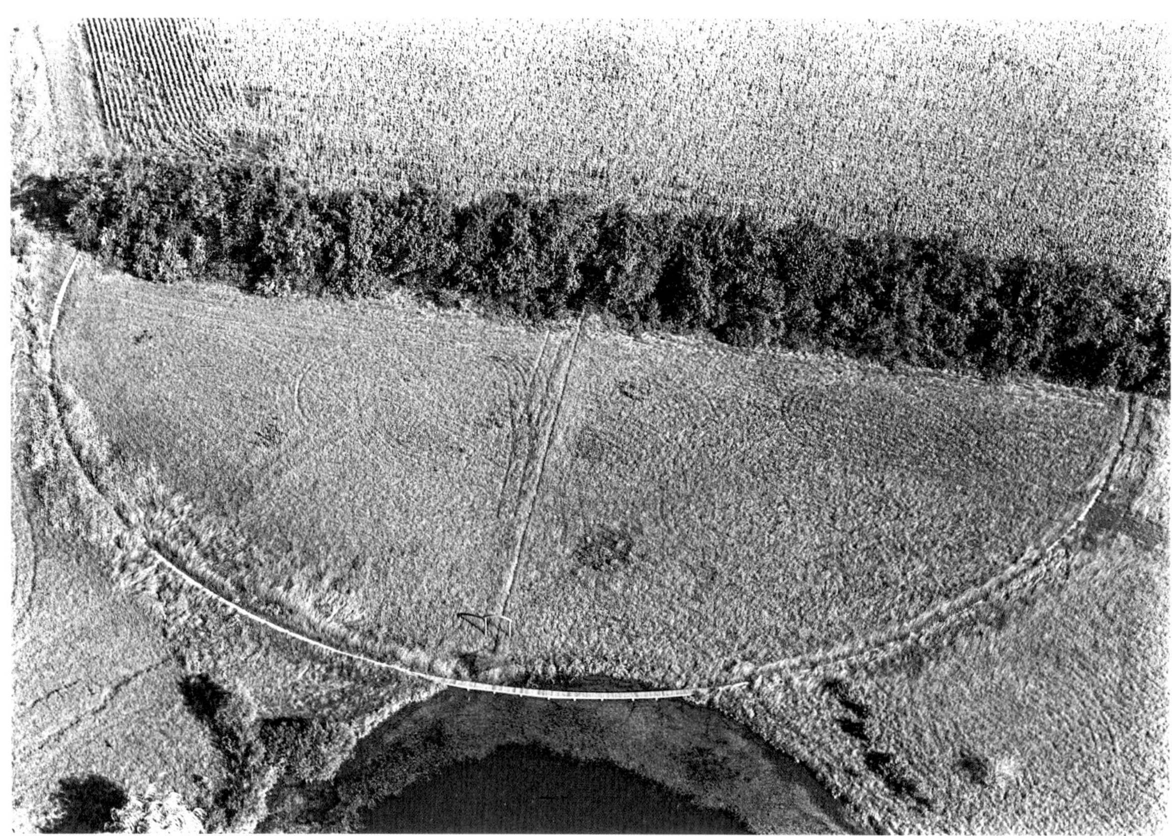

PL. 11

The scale of Puryear's *Bodark Arc*, permanently installed at Nathan Manilow Sculpture Park on the grounds of Governors State University in University Park, Illinois, is vast: a visitor gains an understanding of the work's entirety only by walking through it. (It can also be viewed in full from an airplane or an aerial photograph.) The titular "arc" is a half-circular path in a meadow. The central point of this arc's radius holds a small bronze seat that Puryear created, based on the style of a type of chair used in West Africa. The chair becomes the fixed center point around which the semicircular path revolves. This arched path continues even where the landscape does not: Puryear added a wooden bridge for an area where the circle extends over the edge of an existing pond.

The title refers to a hedgerow of Osage orange trees, native to the lands of the Osage Nation, in the Midwestern United States, grown near the work's site. The Osage people used the tree's hard wood to make bows. When early settlers began to plant these trees, the French term *bois d'arc*, which means "bow wood," was corrupted, becoming "bodark." The arcing shape of Puryear's land art is also reminiscent of the form of an archer's bow, pierced by an arrow straight through the middle.

PLATE 11. *Bodark Arc*, 1982
Earth, wood, Osage orange trees, asphalt, stones, and cast bronze, 196 ft. (5,974.1 cm) radius
Commissioned by Governors State University, installed at Nathan Manilow Sculpture Park, University Park, Illinois

PLATE 12. *Bodark Arc*, 1982
Graphite on ivory wove paper, 6 × 9 in. (15.2 × 22.9 cm)

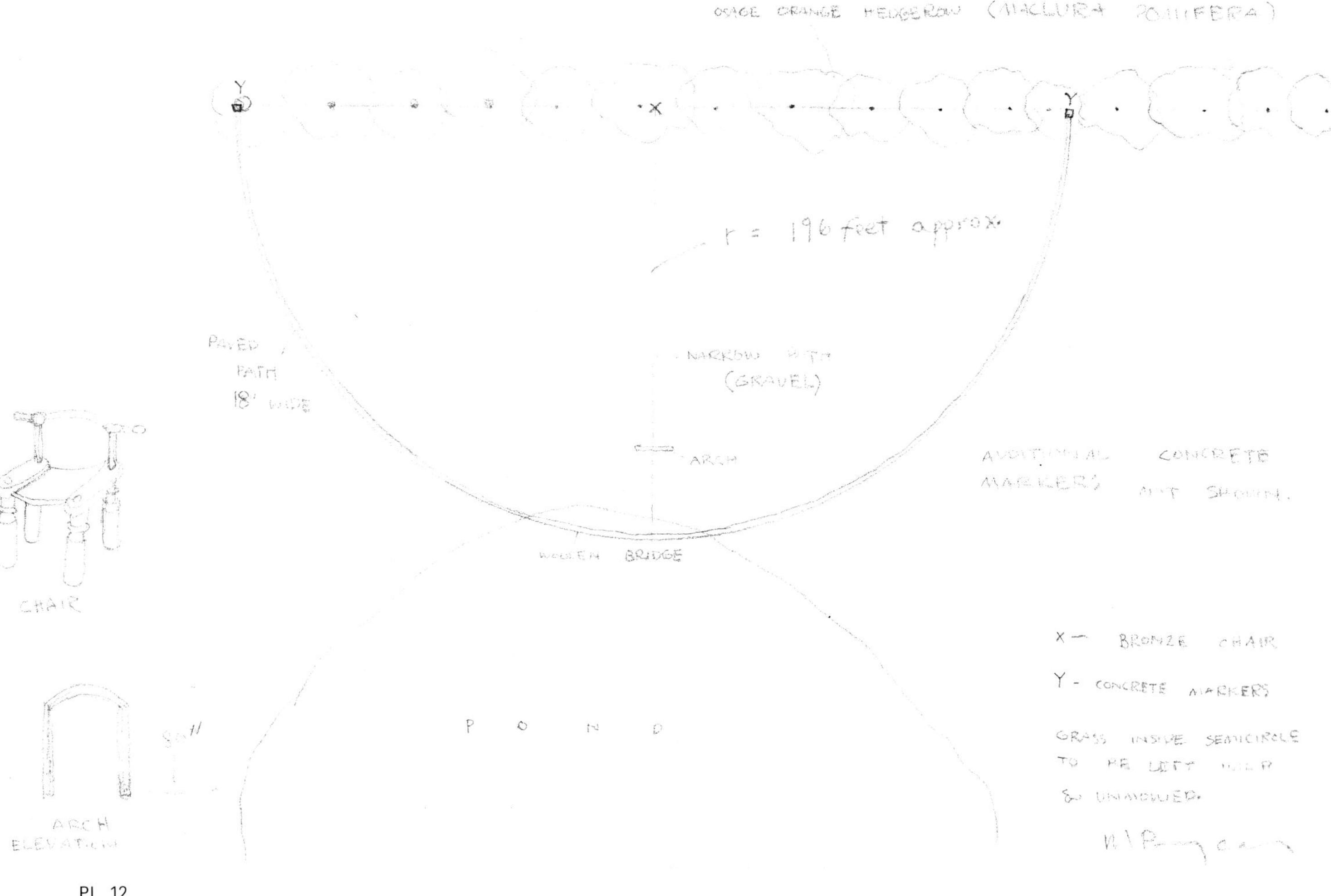

OSAGE ORANGE HEDGEROW (MACLURA POMIFERA)
Y
X
Y
r = 196 feet approx.
PAVED PATH 18' WIDE
NARROW PATH (GRAVEL)
ARCH
ADDITIONAL CONCRETE MARKERS NOT SHOWN.
WOODEN BRIDGE
CHAIR
P O N D
ARCH ELEVATION
X — BRONZE CHAIR
Y - CONCRETE MARKERS
GRASS INSIDE SEMICIRCLE TO BE LEFT WILD & UNMOWED.

PL. 12

The twin fourteen-foot granite columns of *Gog & Magog (Ampersand)*, which transition from rectangular to conical forms, one an inversion of the other, stand as sentinels at the entrance to the Walker Art Center's Minneapolis Sculpture Garden. When making maquettes for the work prior to its fabrication in stone, Puryear roughly cut the wood he was working with and then tooled the rest so it would be smooth. Wanting to replicate the dual textures of the wooden models in the final work, Puryear retained the natural "bark" of the granite—the naturally broken face of the stone as it came out of the quarry—on some parts, and smoothed the remainder of the sculptures' surfaces with a lathe.

In naming the work, Puryear was thinking less of religious connotations than of the sculptures of two mythical giants named Gog and Magog, also referred to as Gogmagog and Corineus, at Guildhall in London. Those figures, initially constructed from papier-mâché and then later remade out of carved wood, were used as part of festivals and public events beginning in the early 1400s.

Worried that certain audiences might take umbrage with the use of a biblical reference in the title, Martin Friedman, the Walker's director at the time the works were installed, asked Puryear if he would consider changing the title. In accordance with Friedman's request, Puryear dropped the names, leaving only "&" remaining. Years later, Puryear reverted to the original title, leaving "Ampersand" as a parenthetical nod to that moment in the sculpture's history.

PLATE 13. *Gog & Magog (Ampersand)*, 1987–88
Granite, east column: 13 ft. 7 in. × 36 in. × 36 in. (414 × 91.4 × 91.4 cm); west column: 13 ft. 11 in. × 36 in. × 36 in. (424.2 × 91.4 × 91.4 cm)
Walker Art Center, Minneapolis

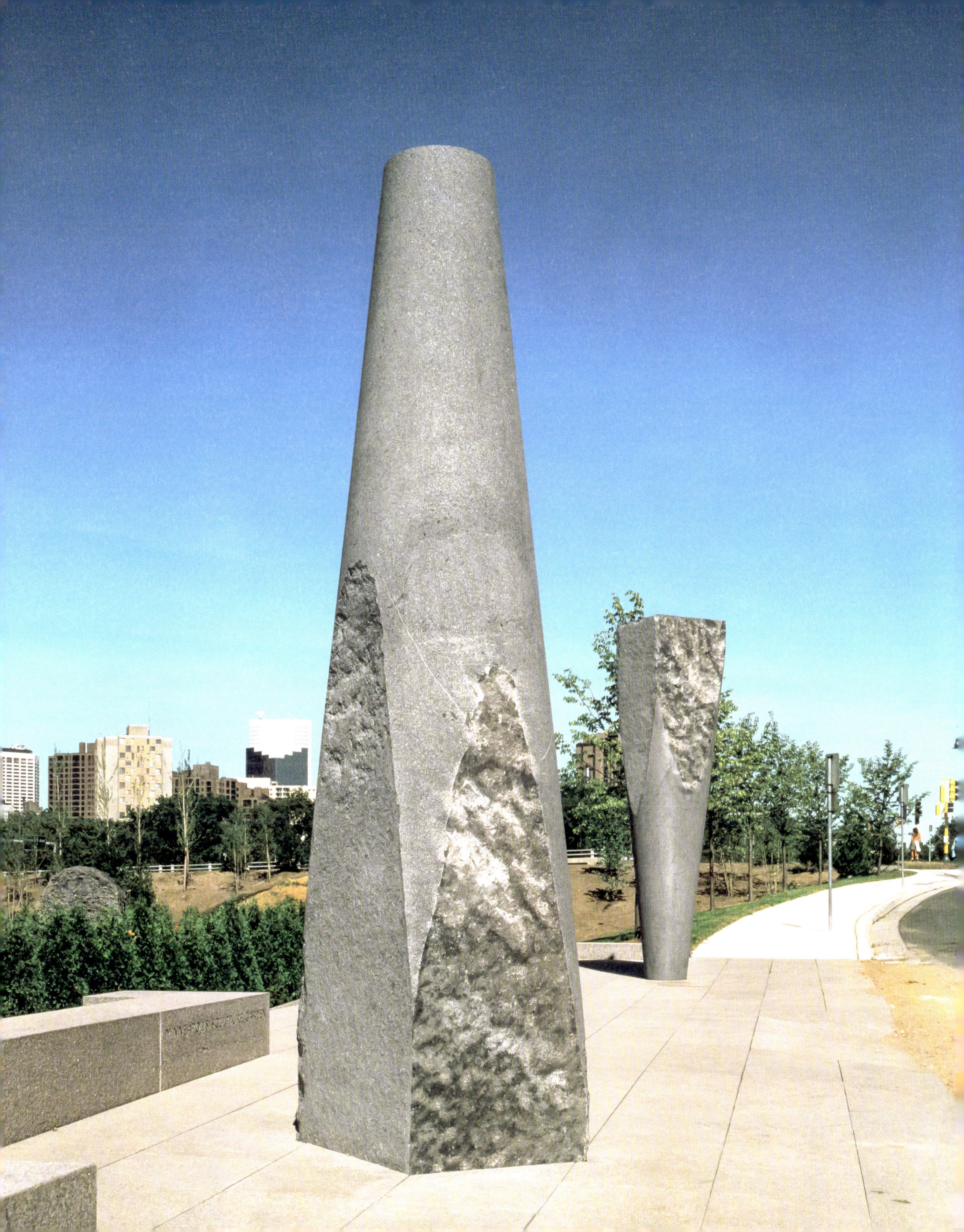

In his 1991 proposal for a sculpture commission for the United States Holocaust Memorial Museum in Washington, DC, Puryear wrote:

> *How can the Holocaust be addressed in sculptural terms?*
> *In the face of such an enormous human tragedy and the profound evil which produced it, beauty becomes mute.*
> *The way must be cleared for individual reflection.*
> *Dense interior space became the central element in my response.*
> *Literal palpable depth, and density. Literal evidence of destruction.*
> *Stillness, stasis.*
> *(Dignity, respect)*

Puryear's work was to have been a bronze sculpture, patinated black, cast from a charred cube of intersecting wooden timbers. The artist intended the work to serve as an artifact of a violent process to convey a sense of loss and desolation. While the project was ultimately not realized, for its installation at Storm King, Puryear charred this maquette to reflect the visual and emotional impact he intended for the sculpture.

PLATE 14. *Proposal for the Holocaust Memorial Museum* (unrealized), 1991, refabricated 2023
Charred wood (to have been cast in bronze and patinated black), 7 × 7 × 7 in. (17.8 × 17.8 × 17.8 cm)

PLATE 15. *Proposal for the Holocaust Memorial Museum* (unrealized), 1991
Graphite on ivory wove paper, 23 × 29 in. (58.4 × 73.7 cm)

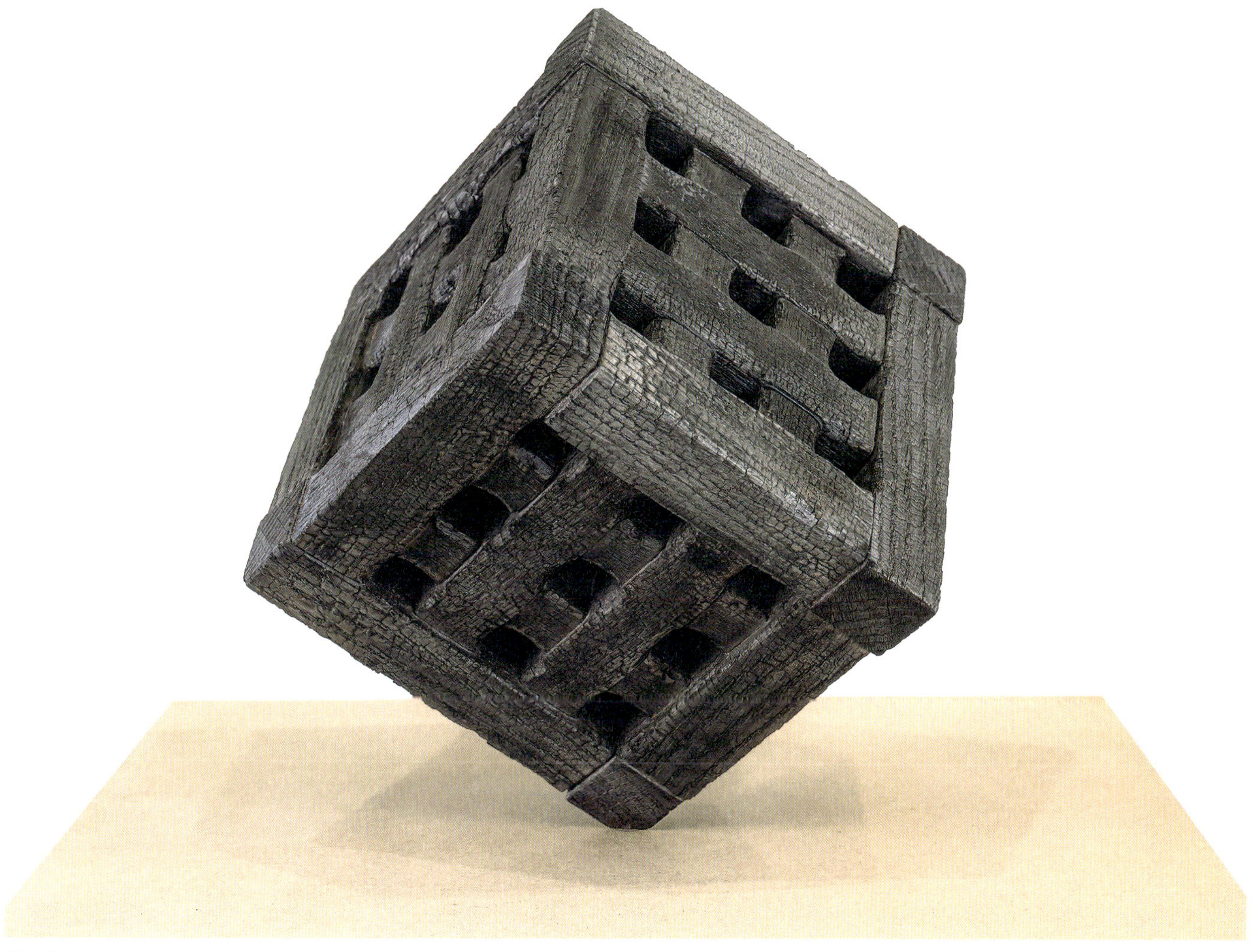

PL. 14

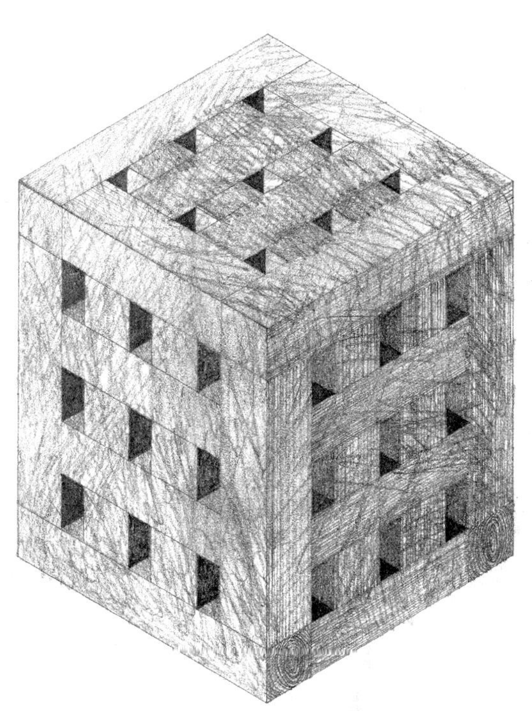

PL. 15

Puryear's *North Cove Pylons*, a site-specific installation at Battery Park City, in New York, function as beacons, to be seen from either land or water. For Puryear, it was important that the illumination of his sculptures come from within the work: both are lit internally, with the light projecting upward from below.

One pylon is made from tiered granite forms that seem to push downward like arrows; the base is swollen, as though collapsing under the weight of this movement and pressure. The other is open and airy, constructed from latticed stainless steel lantern forms, emanating upward from a perfectly cylindrical granite base. Together, they illustrate the dichotomous tension between downward momentum and ascent.

PLATE 16. *Maquettes for "North Cove Pylons,"* 1992
Wood, wire, and paint, north pylon: 25½ × 2 × 2 in. (64.8 × 5 × 5 cm); south pylon: 19½ × 2⅝ × 2⅝ in. (49.5 × 6.7 × 6.7 cm)

PLATES 17, 18. *North Cove Pylons*, 1995
Granite and stainless steel, north pylon: 72 ft. 3 in. × 68 in. (2,202.2 × 172.7 cm); south pylon: 56 ft. 8 in. × 7 ft. × 7 ft. (1,727.2 × 213.4 × 213.4 cm)
Commissioned by Battery Park City Authority, New York

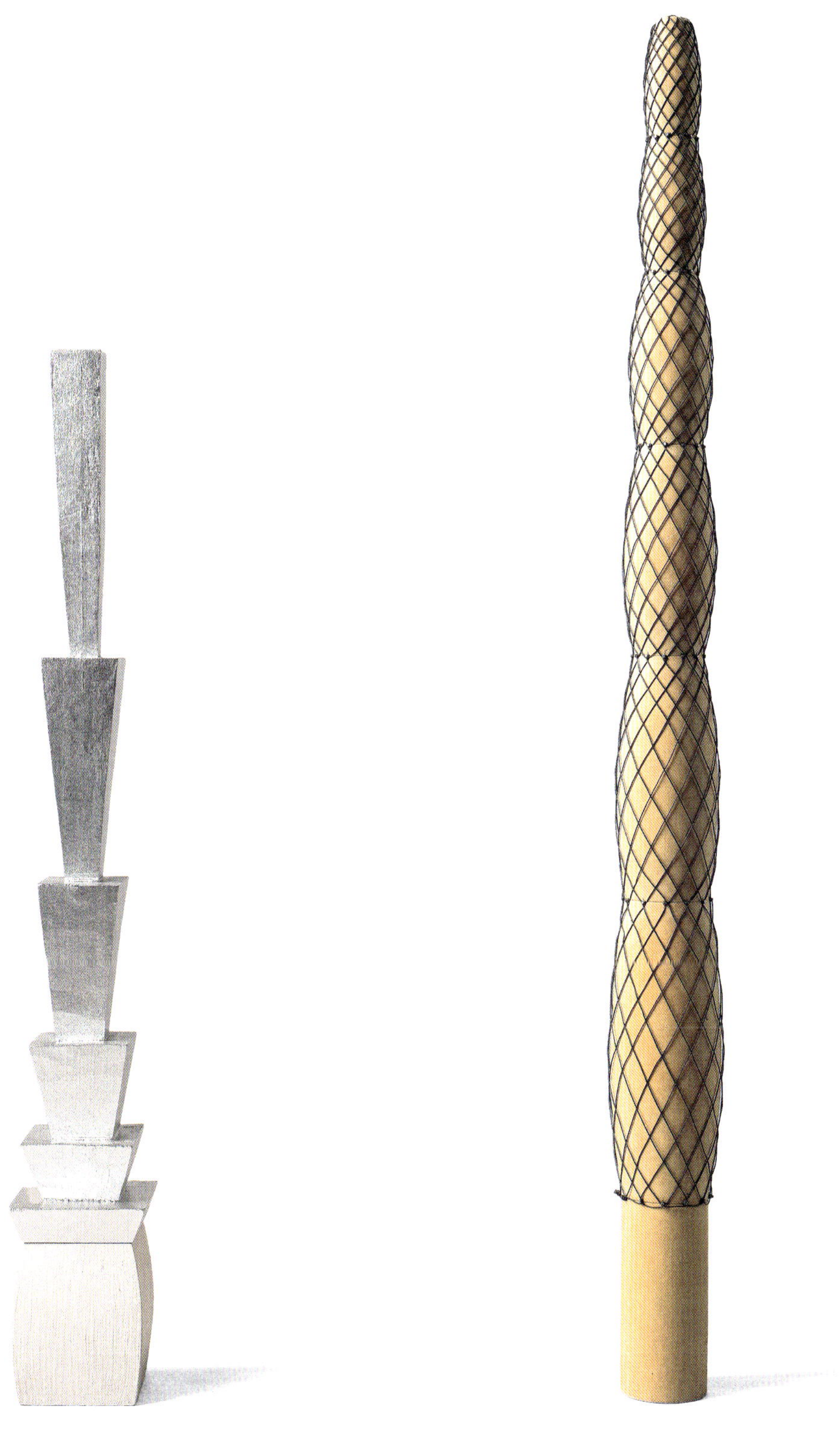

PL. 16

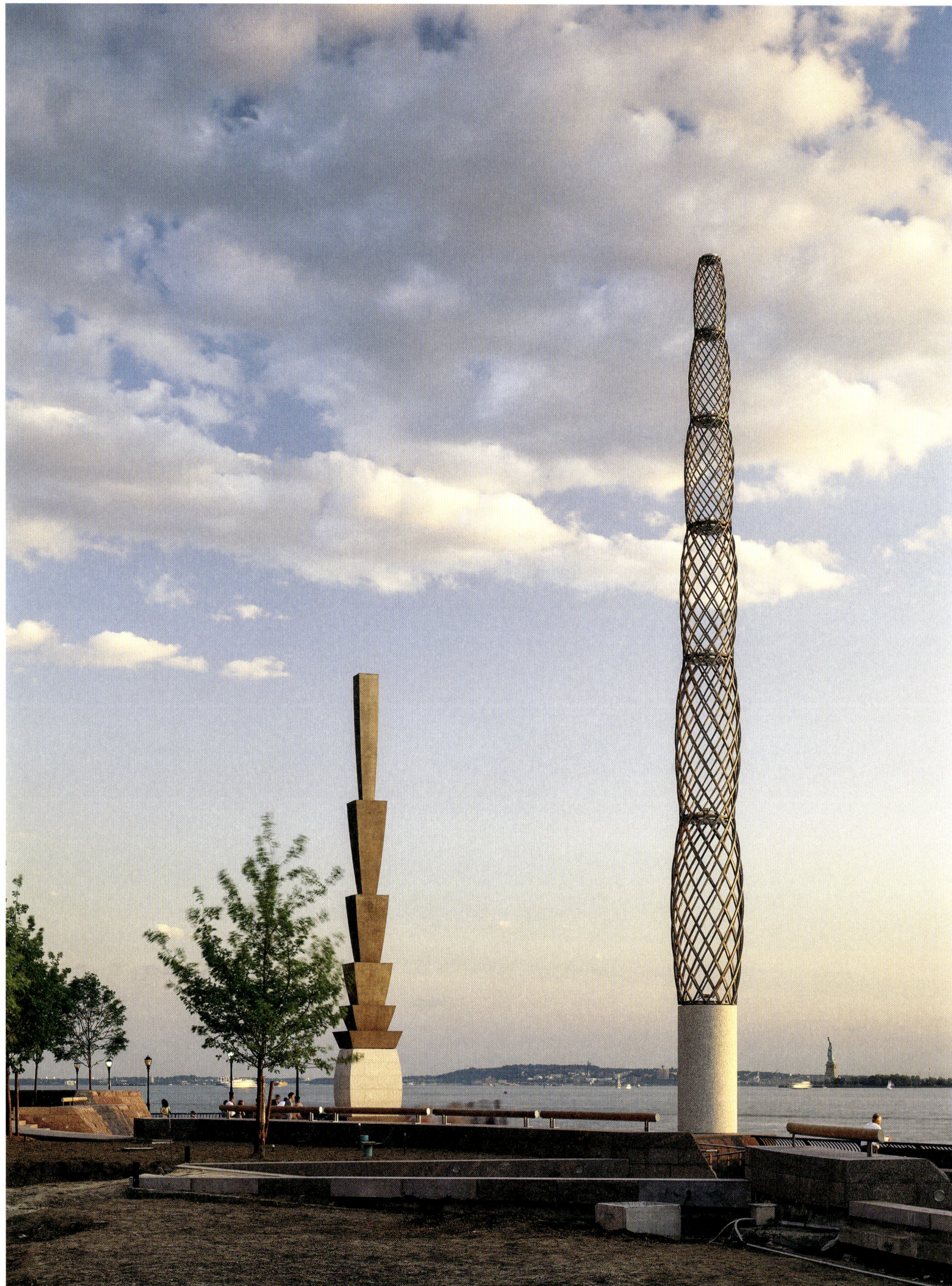

PL. 17

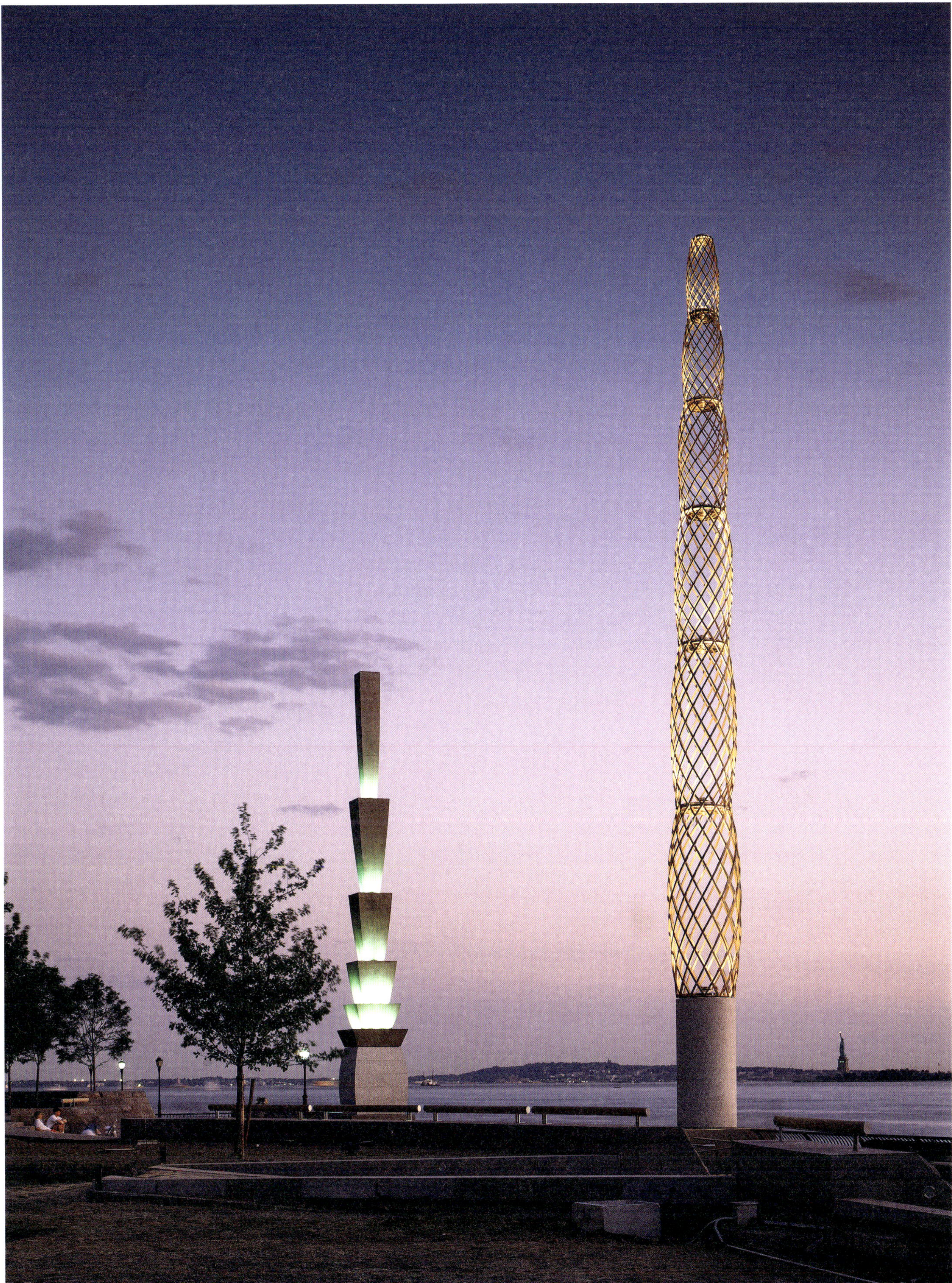

PL. 18

Puryear's 1997 commissioned work for the University of Washington's Seattle campus, *Everything That Rises*, was constructed from hammered bronze plates rather than cast bronze, which is more typical for the material. Instead of outsourcing this sculpture to a foundry, Puryear worked with a Kentucky company that created stills for liquor out of hammered metal and built up the work from parts. He emulated these stills because of his desire to create a sculpture that seemed to be holding a liquid: a bulbous double form that is just slightly larger on top than on bottom, as though a solution is rising in a pipette.

Puryear has acknowledged the title's reference to the Flannery O'Connor 1961 short story "Everything That Rises Must Converge," choosing, however, to omit the conclusion of the phrase. The artist has commented, "I like to give my work titles that are provocative and open up possible ways for people to look at the work and think about the work rather than close it down." For Puryear, the possibility of his works evoking associations beyond their physical forms has been a compelling factor in the decision to title them or leave them untitled.

PLATE 19. *Maquette for "Everything That Rises,"* 1993
Wood, 20⅛ × 21½ × 9⅜ in.
(51.1 × 54.6 × 23.8 cm)

PLATE 20. *Everything That Rises*, 1997
Formed plate bronze,
18 ft. 7 in. (566.4 cm) tall
Commissioned by the University of Washington, Seattle

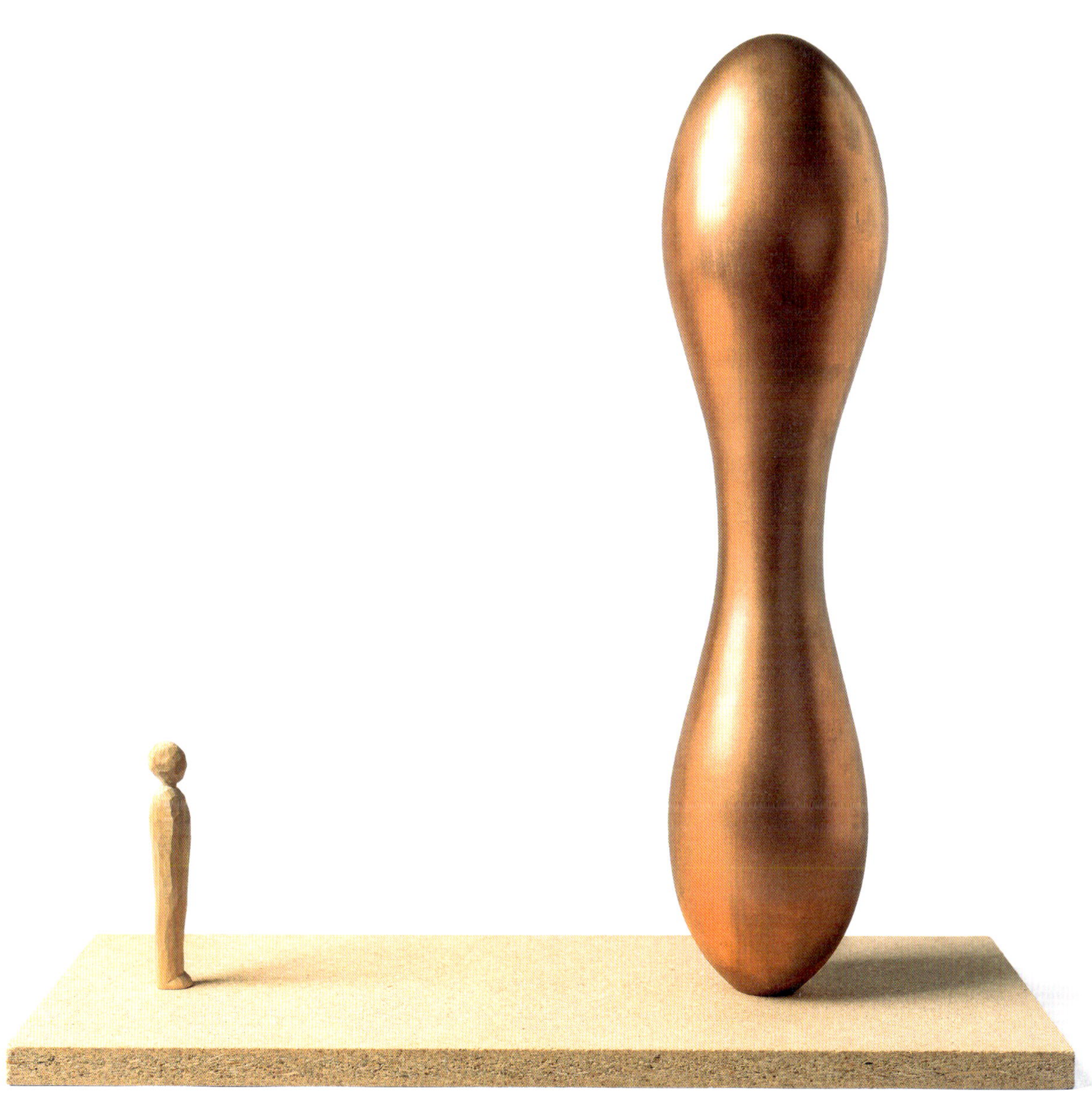

PL. 19

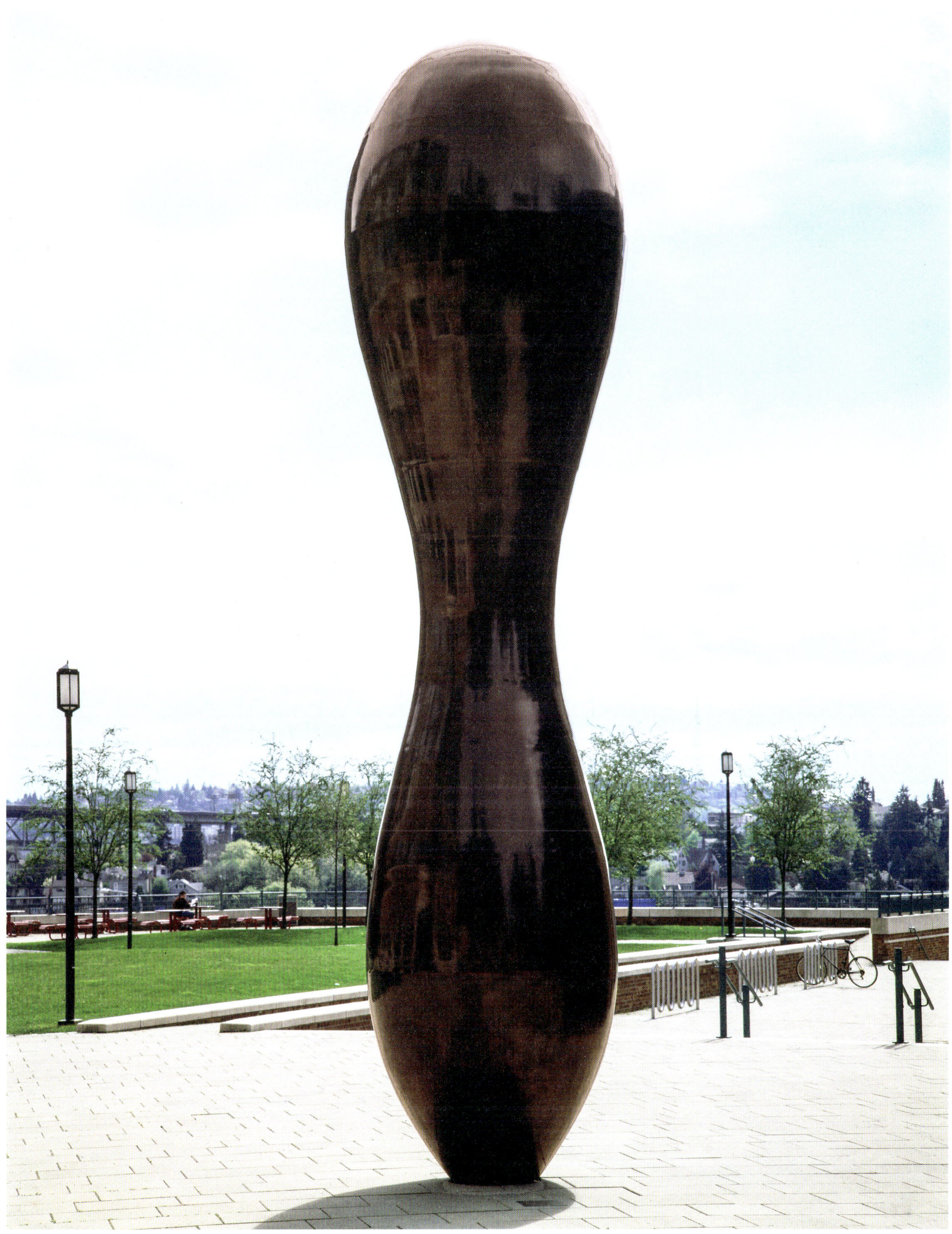

PL. 20

In the early 1990s Puryear was commissioned to build a site-specific work for Oliver Ranch, an estate and sculpture park in Sonoma County, California. Partnering with a local stonemason, Puryear constructed a sculpture that also serves as an architectural folly: an eighteen-foot wall with window- and door-like openings abutted by a bulging appendage. In its form, outlined in profile in a conté crayon drawing from about 1993, the sculpture for Oliver Ranch is a predecessor to Puryear's work for Storm King; unlike *Lookout*, however, the interior of the work at Oliver Ranch is accessible only by peering through the openings in the arched cedar grille that the artist constructed to cover the entrance. Puryear's drawings emphasize the importance of the apertures created by the interlocking wooden beams, which he rendered as solid black diamonds.

PLATE 21. *Untitled, Oliver Ranch*, c. 1993
Black conte crayon on Strathmore white wove paper, 23 × 29 in. (58.4 × 73.7 cm)

PLATE 22. *Untitled, Oliver Ranch*, c. 1993
Graphite and pen on paper, 12 × 23 in. (30.5 × 58.4 cm)

PLATES 23, 24. *Untitled (Oliver Ranch)*, 1994–95
Mortared fieldstone and red cedar, 18 × 17 × 24 ft. (548.6 × 518.2 × 731.5 cm)
Commissioned by Oliver Ranch Foundation, Geyserville, California

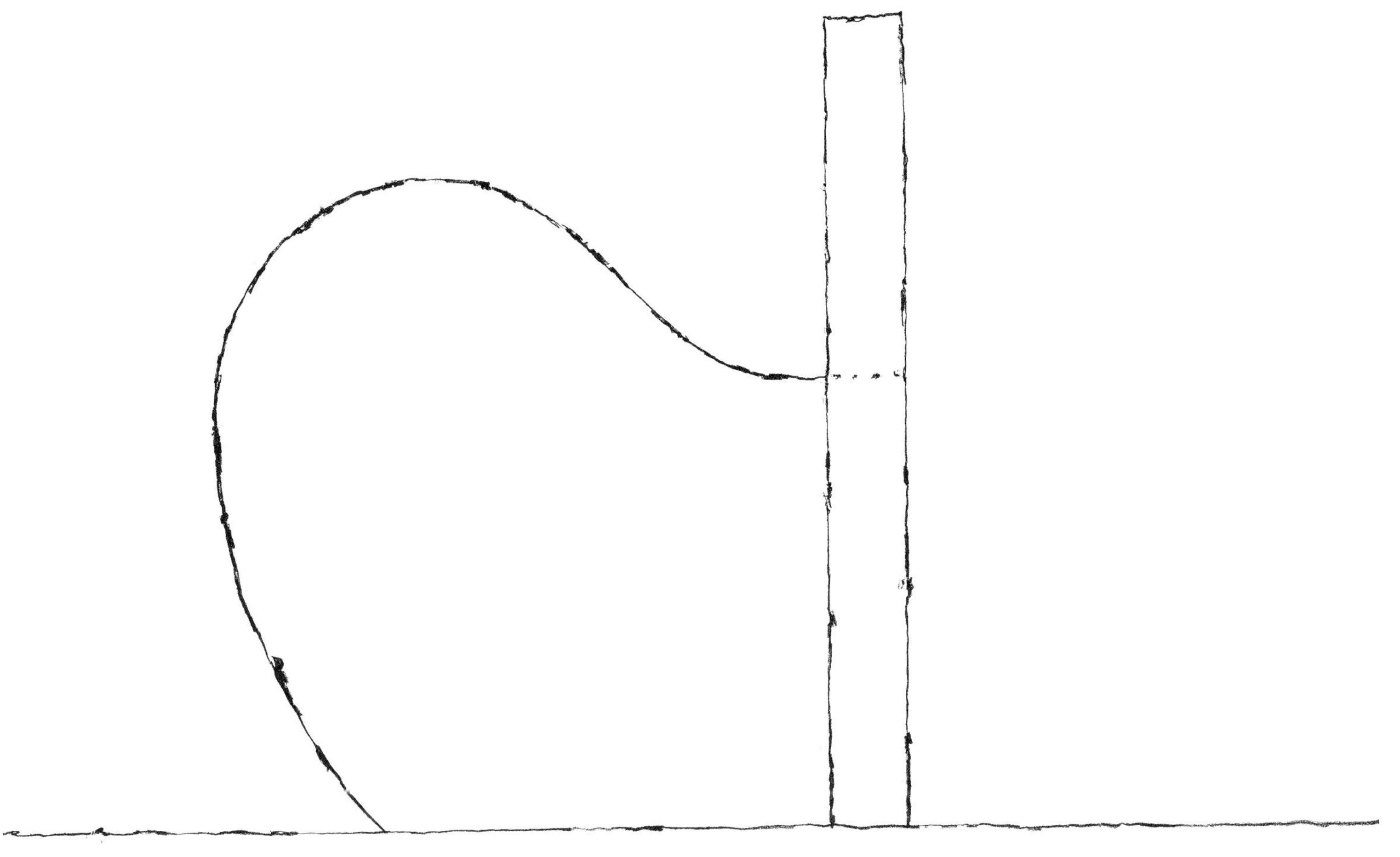

PL. 21

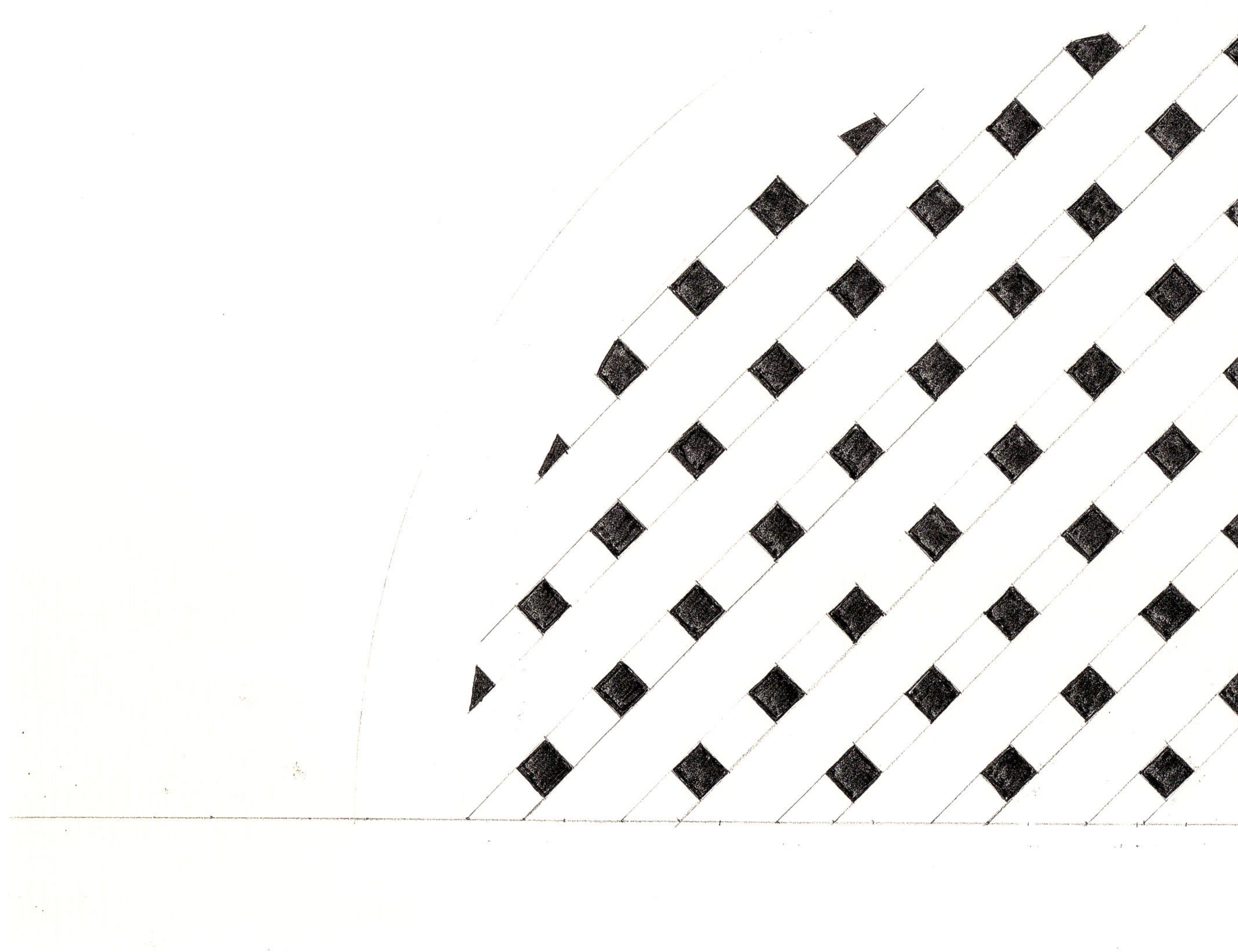

PL. 22

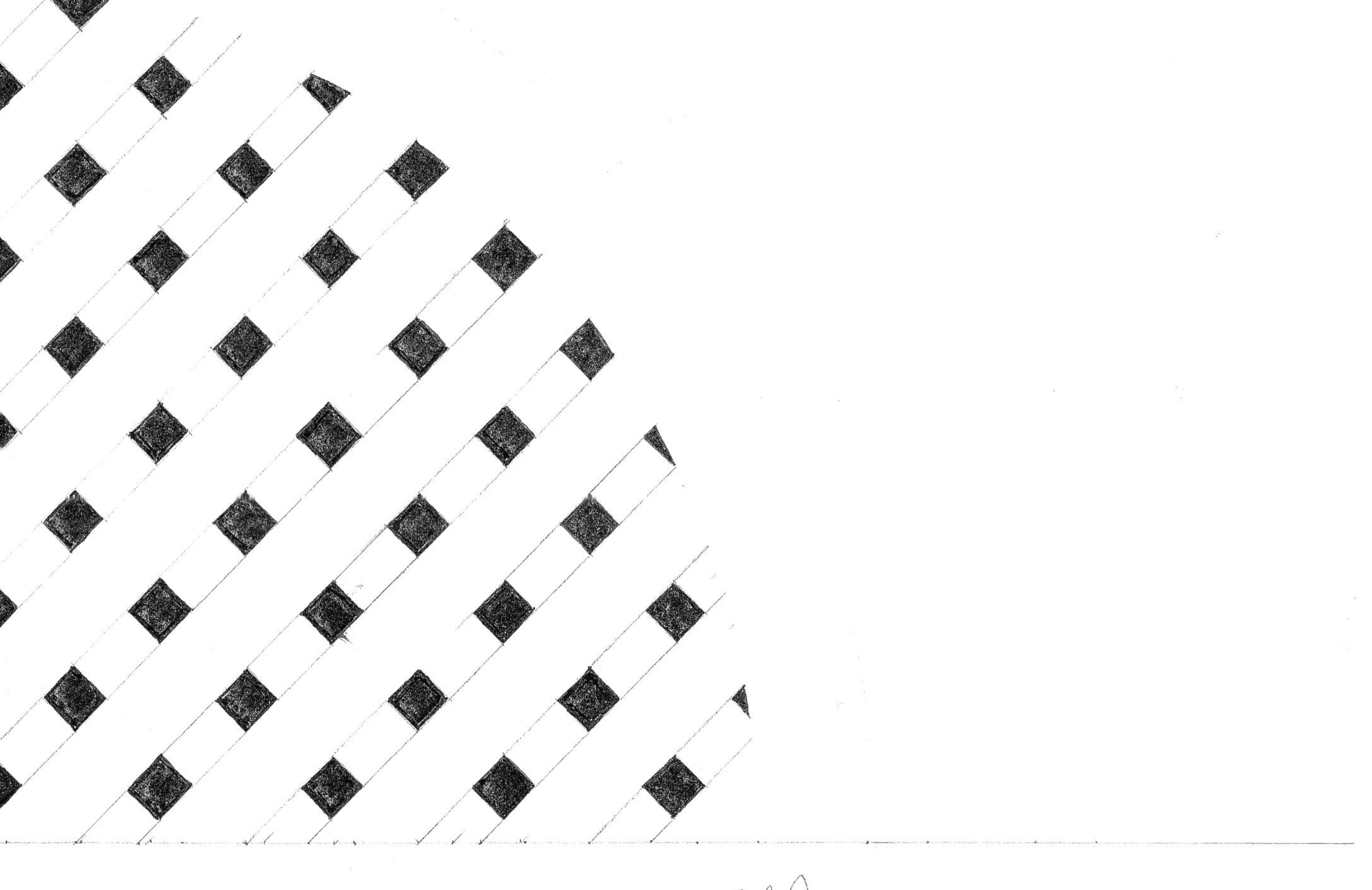

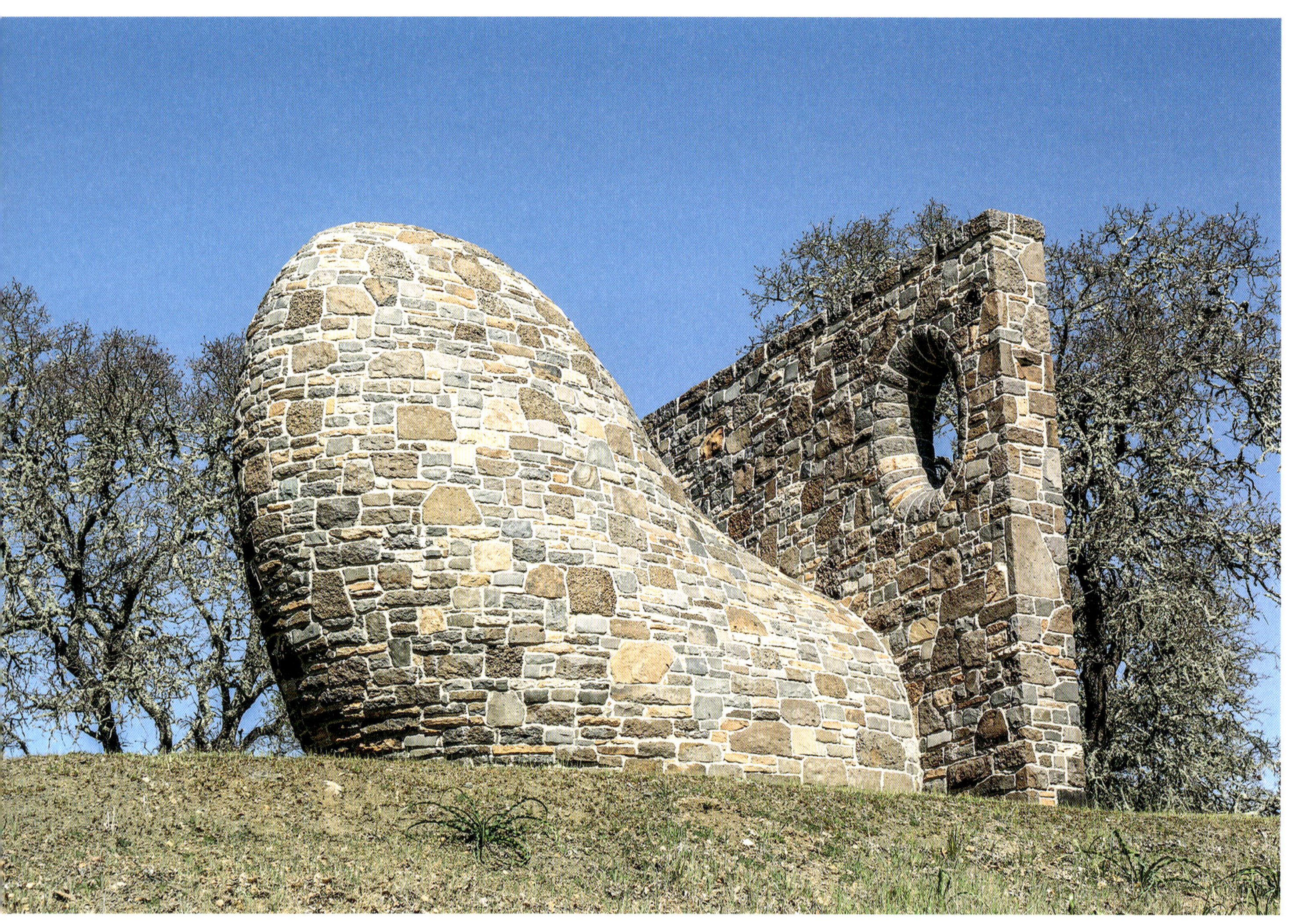

PL. 23

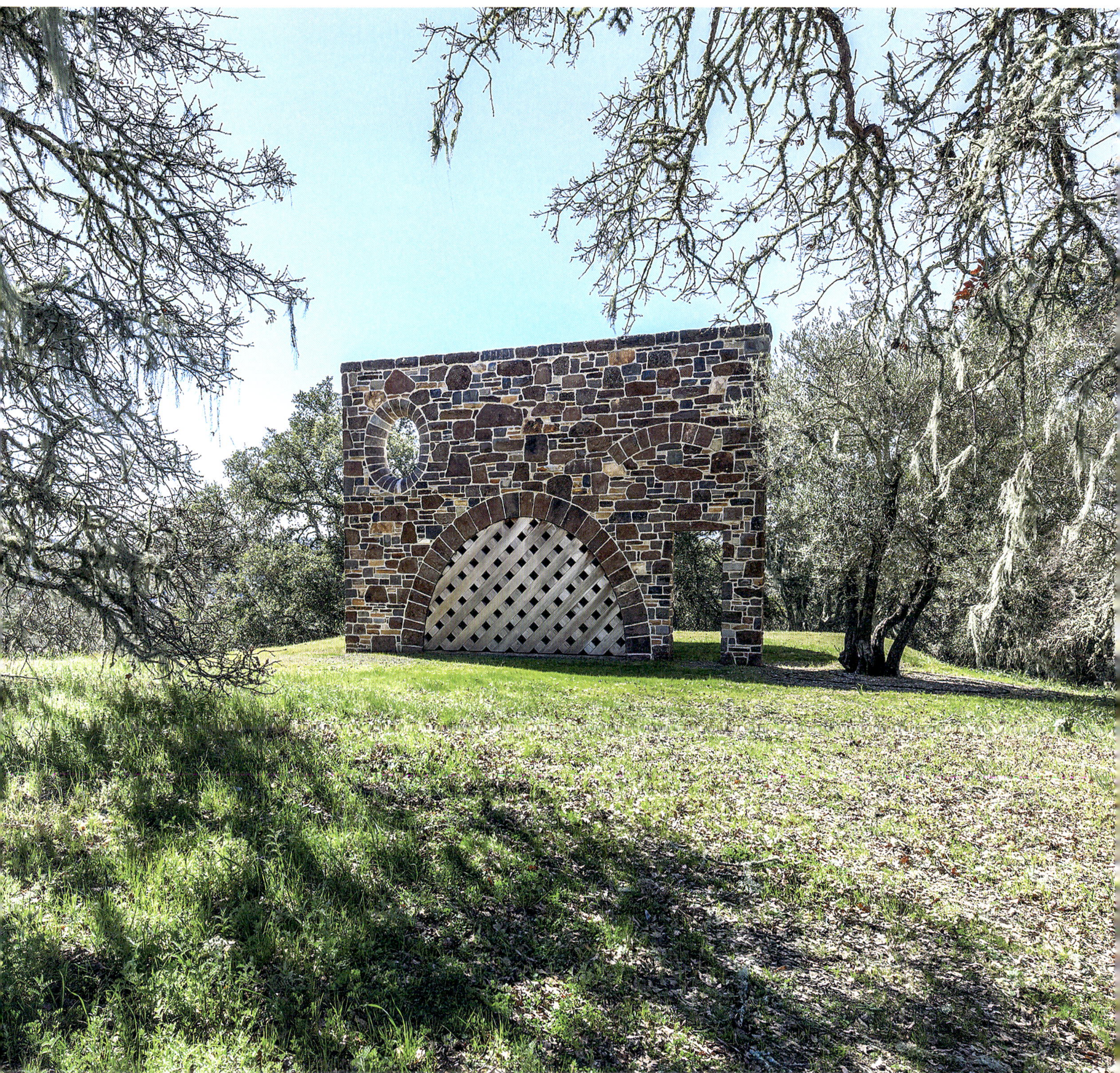

PL. 24

The form of *Bearing Witness* was inspired by abstracted imagery of the human head and neck. It was created in collaboration with Merrifield-Roberts, which specializes in the design and fabrication of sailboats that had previously worked on Claes Oldenburg and Coosje van Bruggen's *Spoonbridge and Cherry* (1988) for the Walker Art Center's sculpture garden. Puryear chose the company for its capacity to create domed concavities in sheet metal. *Bearing Witness* is crafted from hammer-formed and welded bronze, rather than cast. The artist has expressed that he is "more interested in the additive process of making forms, rather than modeling them and then having them translated in metal and cast."

The maquette for *Bearing Witness* was created with blocks of pine. To guide the fabrication of the final work, Puryear disassembled the maquette block by block, tracing these blocks and recording their dimensions. About this process Puryear has said, "Making wooden constructions is about assembly. Trying to think of a shape a priori and figuring out how to then construct that shape and put it together requires a certain kind of logic that happens when you are making a piece additively as opposed to subtractively."

PLATE 25. *Maquette for "Bearing Witness,"* 1994
Pine, 59¾ × 15 × 19½ in.
(151.8 × 38.1 × 49.5 cm)

PLATE 26. *Bearing Witness*, 1994–98
Bronze, 40 × 10 × 14 ft.
(1,219.2 × 304.8 × 426.7 cm)
Commissioned by the General Services Administration, Washington, DC

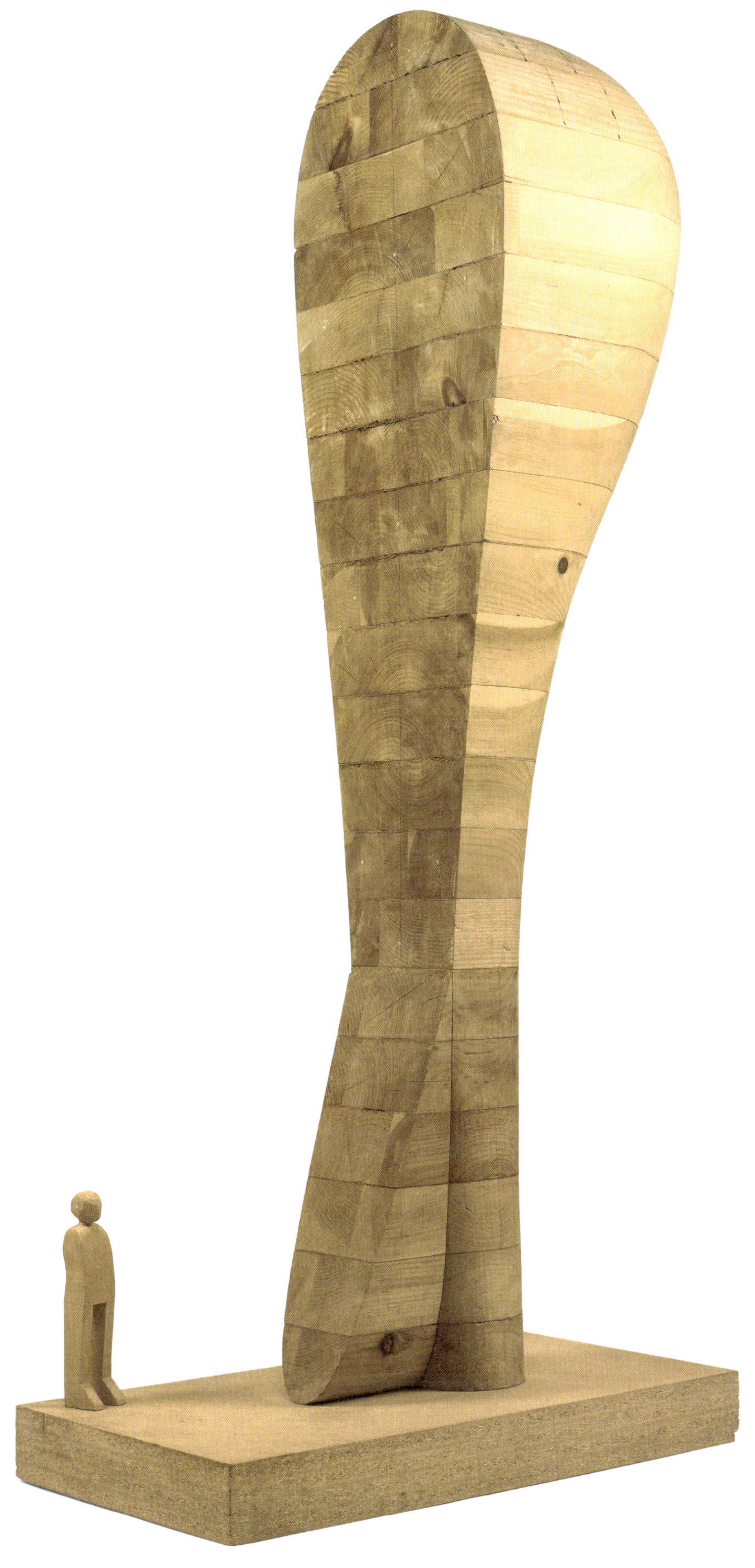

PL. 25

OPPOSITE: PL. 26

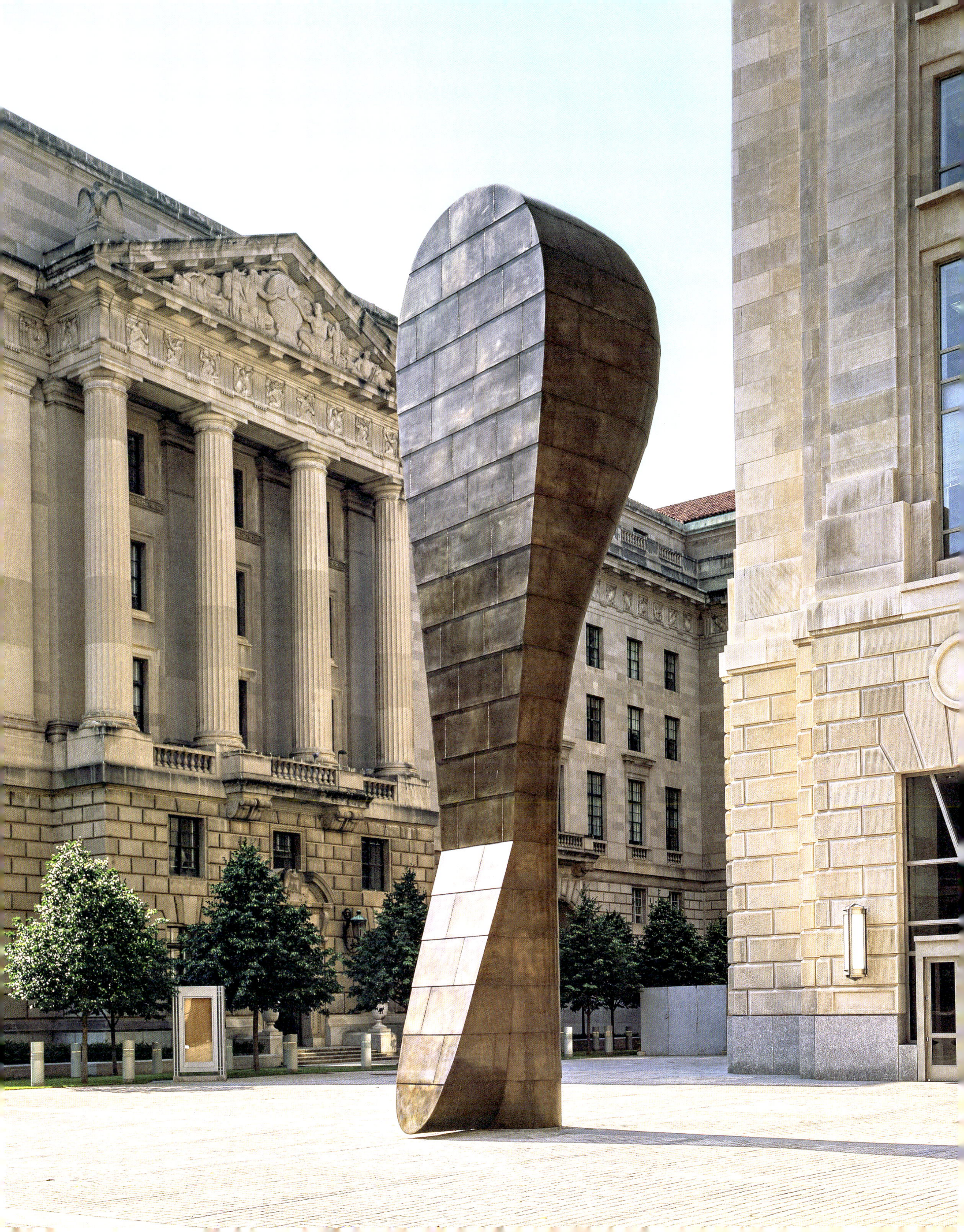

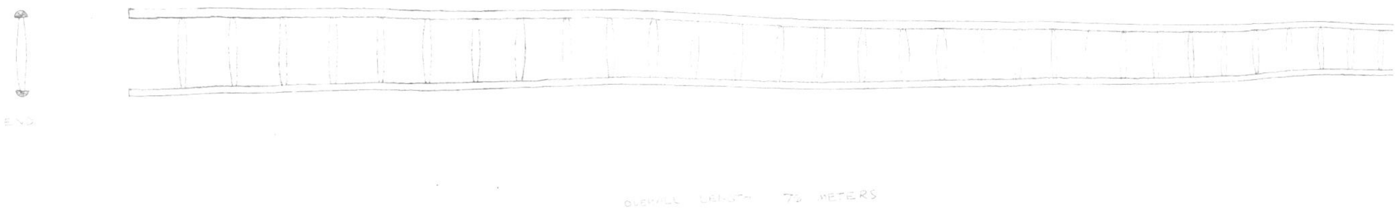

PL. 27

At the time he proposed a work for Tokyo International Forum, in 1995, Puryear was deeply interested in the concept of forced perspective. The sculpture he envisioned was a wooden ladder, two hundred fifty feet long, to be suspended diagonally in the atrium of the Forum, a massive meeting hall designed by Rafael Viñoly. With this proposal, Puryear wanted to explore the interplay between the physical tapering of the ladder and the illusion of the form diminishing in space as it receded into the distance.

The drawing Puryear used for his proposal measures over seven feet in length, and illustrates the narrowing of the ladder to an acute angle. Like Puryear's proposed sculpture, the length of the drawing necessitates a perspectival shift, forcing the viewer to move from side to side or step back to experience the work in its entirety.

A year later, Puryear realized a ladder sculpture incorporating forced perspective, on a comparatively modest scale: his 1996 work *Ladder for Booker T. Washington* is thirty-six feet tall and suspended vertically.

PLATE 27. *Tokyo International Forum Proposal*, 1995
Graphite on tracing paper,
15⅛ in. × 7 ft. 9½ in.
(38.4 × 237.5 cm)

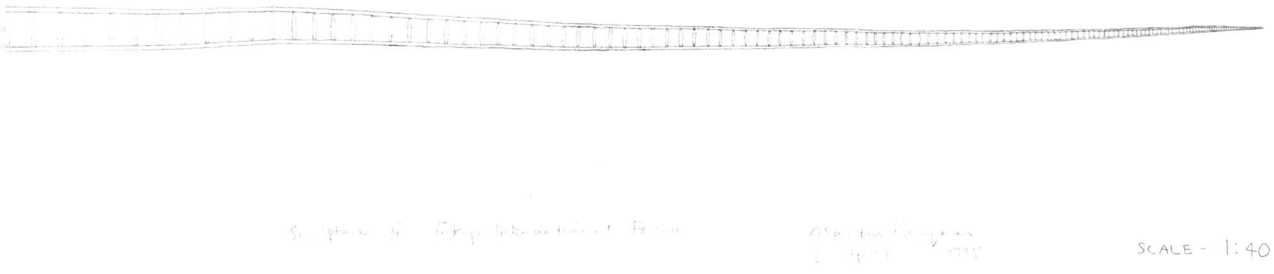

Sculpture for Tokyo International Forum

Martin Puryear
[illegible]

SCALE - 1:40

Following his time in the Peace Corps in Sierra Leone, from 1964 to 1966, Puryear traveled to Stockholm to study printmaking at the Royal Swedish Academy of Fine Arts. Outside of his classes, he honed his woodworking skills and gained an appreciation for Danish furniture-making for its ability to merge traditional craft with modernist production.

When Puryear returned to Sweden to create a commission for the Wanås Foundation, he drew on a traditional vernacular building material, thatch, which had been used widely for roofing across Scandinavia. At the outset, several craftspeople whom the artist approached for the project thought the shape of the work, an abstraction based on the form of a seated Buddha, was too complicated to achieve in the artist's chosen medium, but he ultimately found an expert thatcher who was willing to collaborate. However, Puryear has asserted, "I did not do it to test the material, I did it to realize the form."

Like many of Puryear's other process models, the maquette for *Meditation in a Beech Wood* is functional in addition to being a preparatory study: the artist sliced the model with a band saw in order to determine cross sections, reassembled it, and created two subsequent models to show the form of the wooden armature that provided structural support to the thatching.

PLATE 28. *Meditation in a Beech Wood*, 1996
Water reed thatched over timber frame, 14 ft. 7 in. × 16 ft. 5 in. × 11 ft. 2 in. (444.5 × 500.4 × 340.4 cm)
Commissioned by Wanås Foundation, Knislinge, Sweden

PLATE 29. *Maquette for "Meditation in a Beech Wood,"* c. 1995
Wood, 8 × 12 × 9 in. (20.3 × 30.5 × 22.9 cm)

PLATE 30. *Maquette for "Meditation in a Beech Wood,"* c. 1995
Wood, 9⅛ × 10⅝ × 6¾ in. (23.2 × 27 × 17.1 cm)

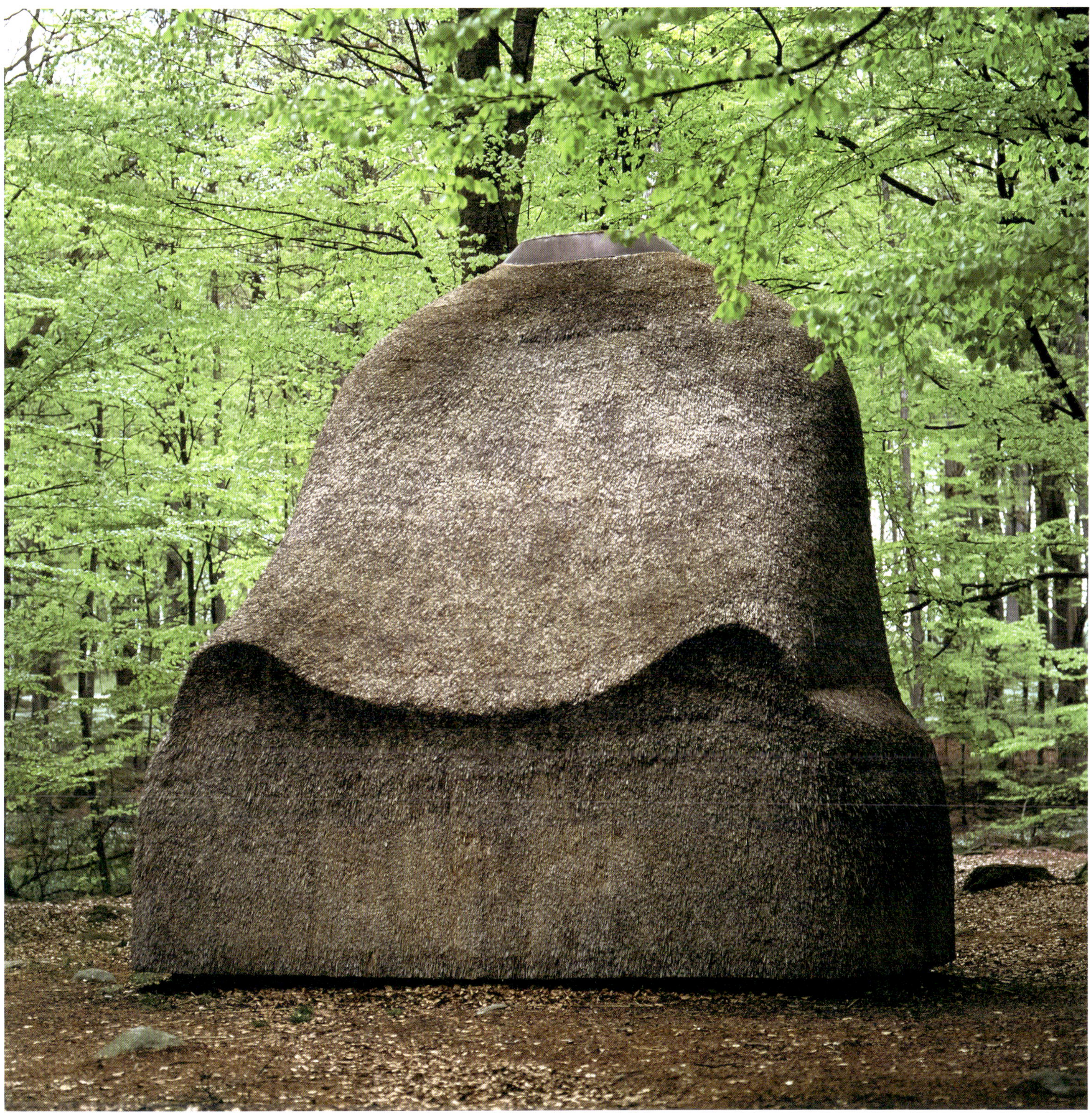

PL. 28

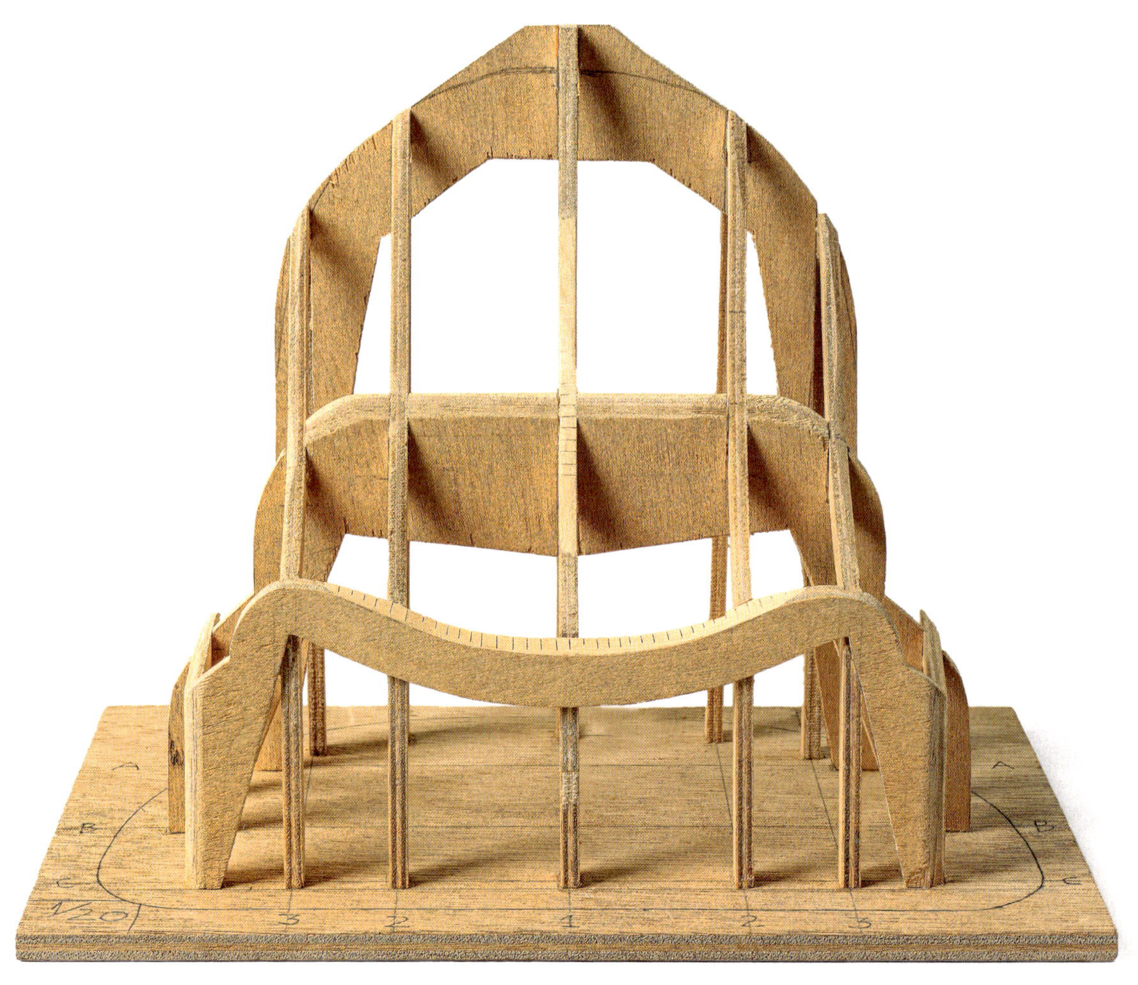

PL. 29

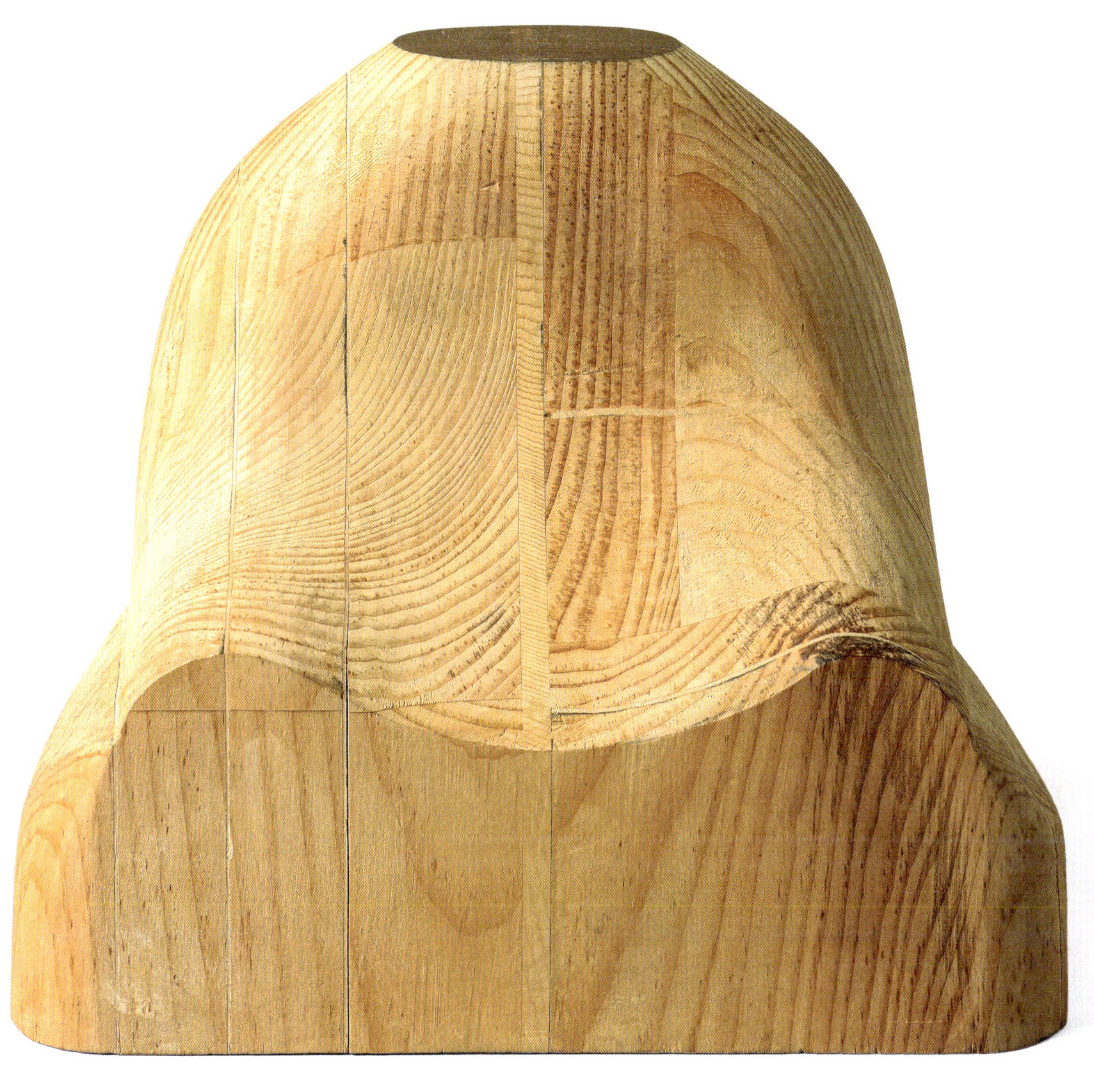

PL. 30

That Profile was commissioned for the opening of the new campus of the J. Paul Getty Museum in Los Angeles. It is installed in an expansive area and seen upon one's entry to the campus. The work's open gridded structure appears as a flat plane from one vantage point but is rounded from another. The viewer's experience of the work is as much about the contours of the metal shape as it is about the spaces framed between them—the geometric slices of sky and surrounding landscape.

Puryear chose the scale of the maquette of *That Profile* to be functional: he needed to be able to pack the model in his suitcase to show the design to his collaborators at the Getty and the fabricators of the work.

PLATE 31. *Drawing for "That Profile,"* c. 1997
Graphite on vellum,
29 × 23 in. (73.7 × 58.4 cm)

PLATE 32. *Maquette for "That Profile,"* 1997
Steel wire and wood,
23 × 48 × 38 in.
(58.4 × 121.9 × 96.5 cm)

PLATE 33. *That Profile*, 1999
Stainless steel and bronze,
45 ft. × 30 ft. × 11 ft. 4 in.
(1,371.6 × 914.4 × 345.44 cm)
Commissioned by The J. Paul Getty Trust, Los Angeles

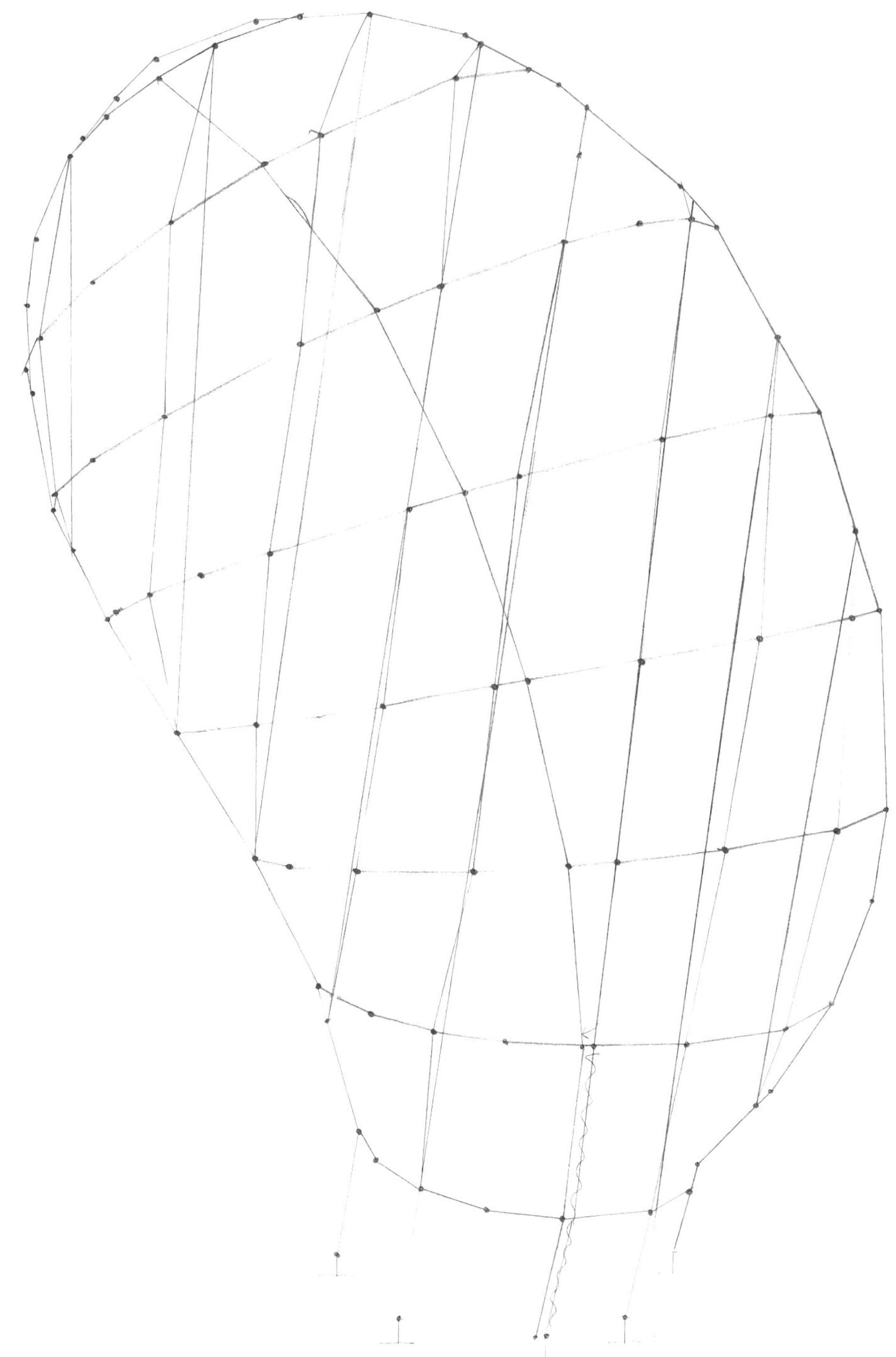

PL. 31

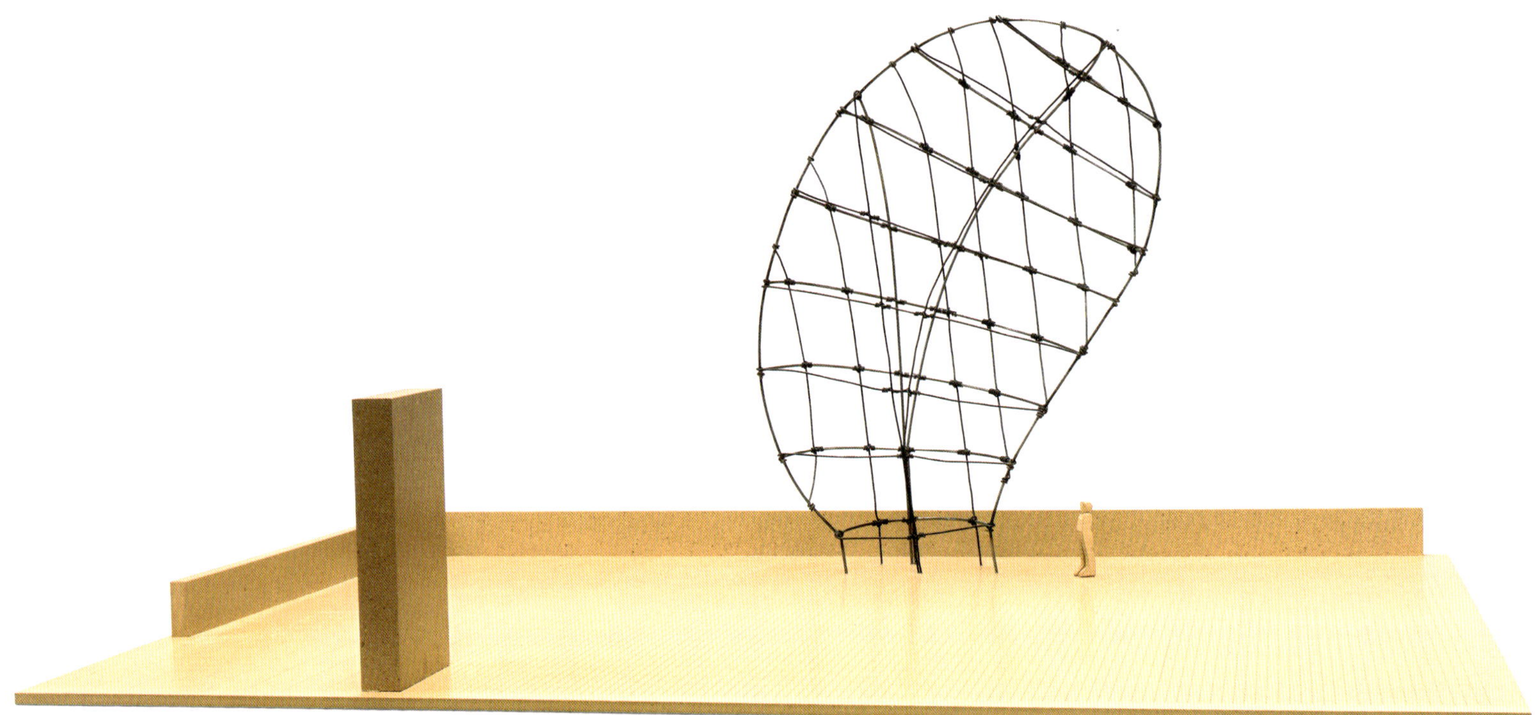

PL. 32

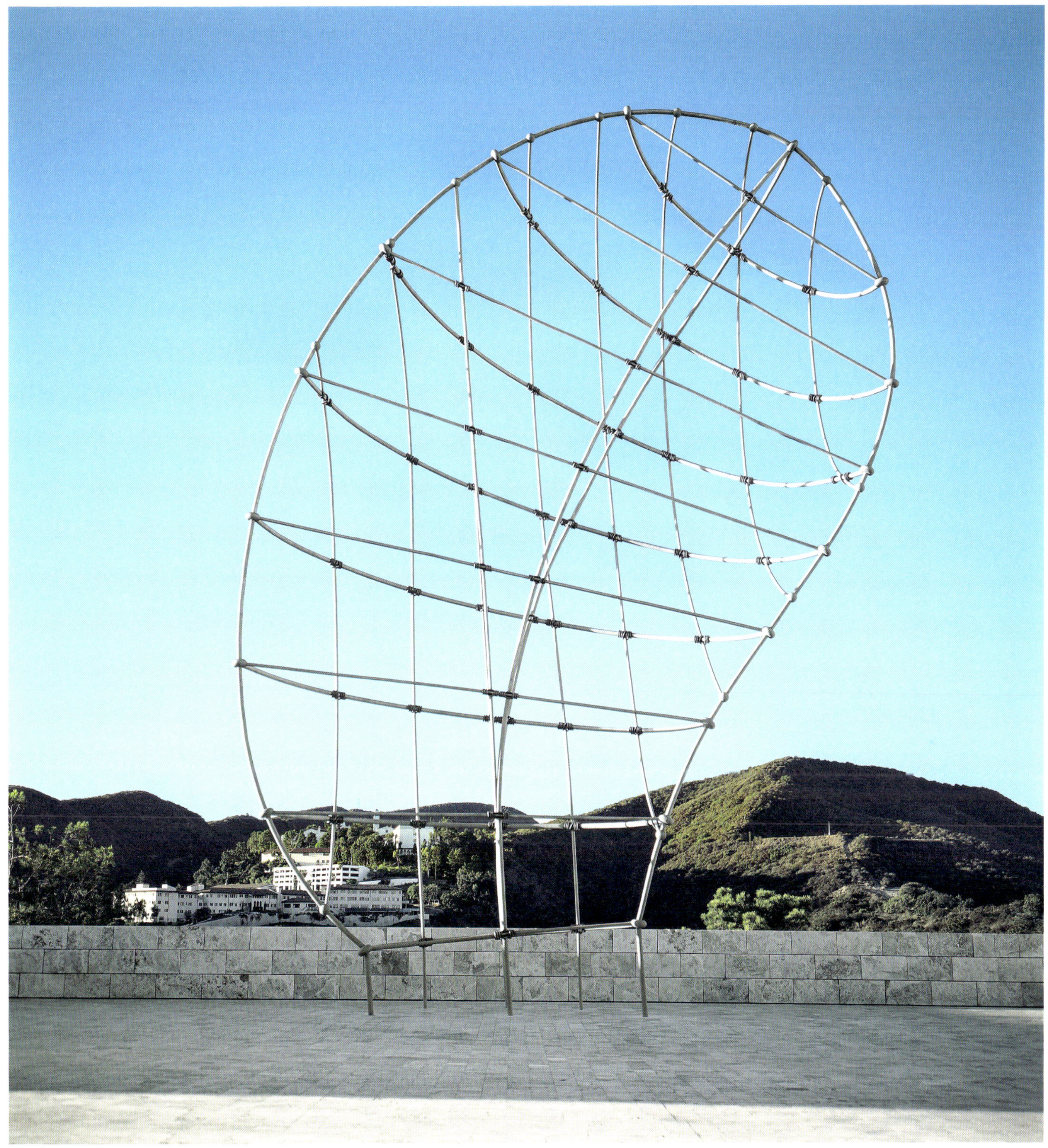

PL. 33

This Mortal Coil, commissioned for the Festival d'Automne à Paris, was on view for only two months at the Chapelle Saint-Louis de la Salpêtrière. The base of the work was constructed from heavy American red cedar timbers arranged as an inverted, conical spiral staircase. The construction became lighter as it spiraled upward, terminating in a muslin staircase supported on a fragile frame, appearing to defy gravity. The work's installation was complicated by the chapel's historic architecture, which Puryear was not permitted to alter in any way; instead, the sculpture had to rest on the church's existing structures.

Puryear originally approached the expert tradespeople of the French building guild, Les Compagnons du Devoir, about the fabrication of the work, but they balked at the idea of constructing something temporary after having trained in archival building practices meant to last for centuries. Puryear ultimately worked with theater set builders to realize the project using plywood and an aluminum ellipse that rested on the cornices of the upper reaches of the church. The spiraling sculpture was supported entirely with taut cables that French alpinists helped the artist to install.

PLATE 34. *This Mortal Coil*, 1998
Graphite on thin paper
14 × 11 in. (35.6 × 27.9 cm)

PLATE 35. *This Mortal Coil*, c. 1998
Graphite on paper, 37 × 21⅜ in. (94 × 54.3 cm)

PLATE 36. *This Mortal Coil*, 1999
Red cedar, stainless steel cable, aluminum, and muslin, 85 ft. 3⅝ in. × 39 ft. 4½ in. × 52 ft. 5⅞ in. (2,600 × 1,200.2 × 1,599.9 cm)
Commissioned for the Festival d'Automne à Paris, temporary installation at Chapelle Saint-Louis de la Salpêtrière, Paris

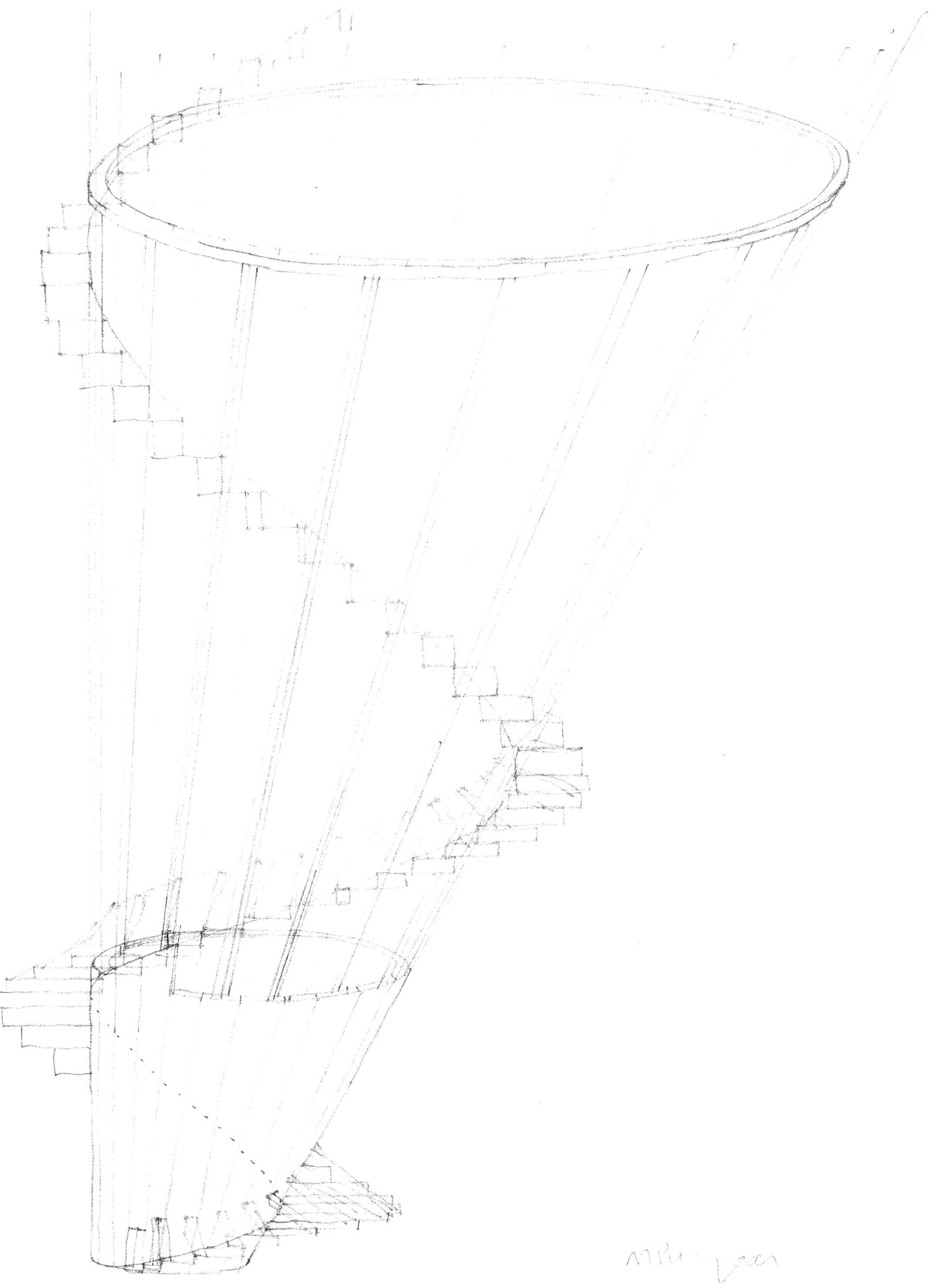

PL. 34

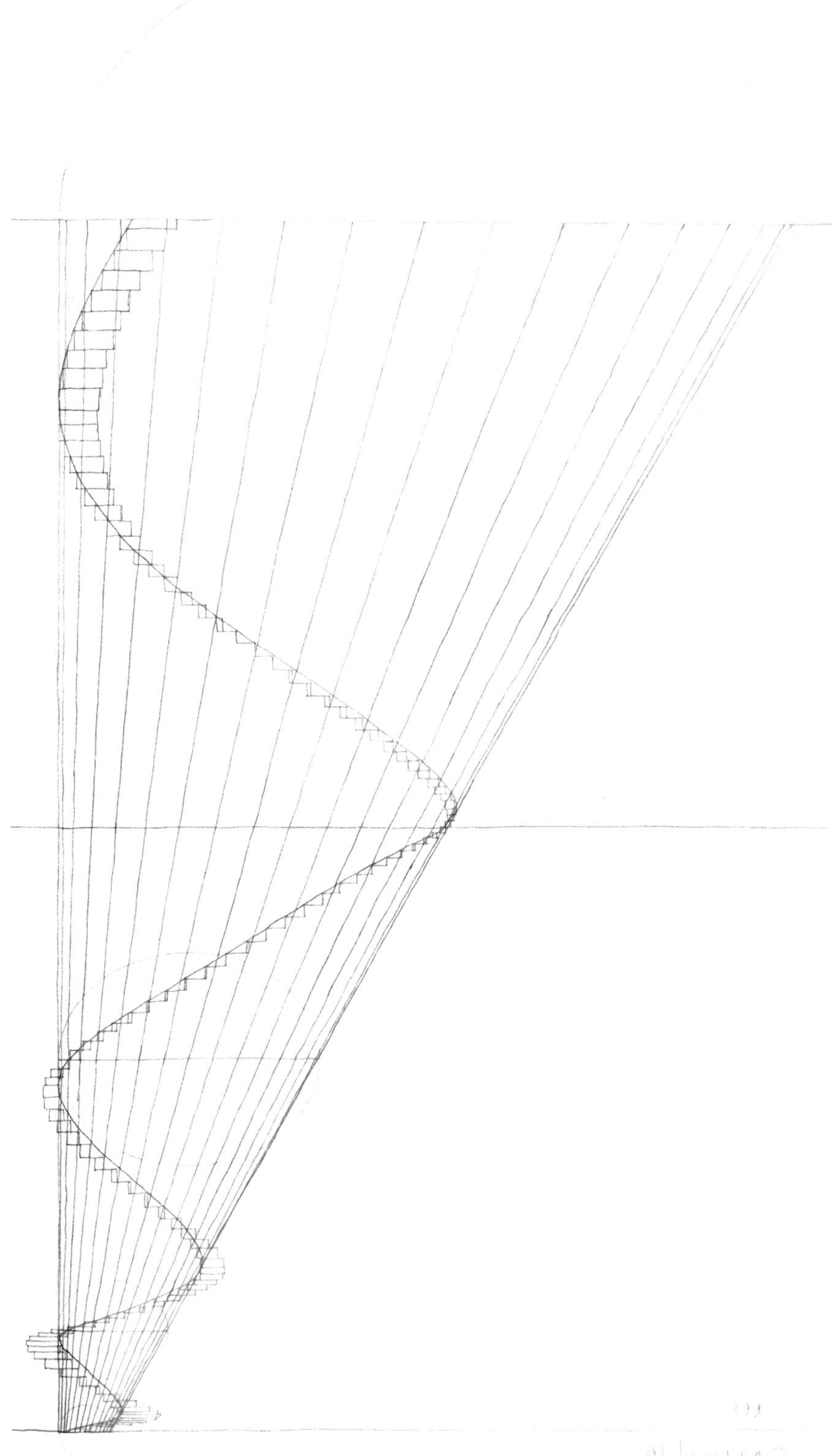

PL. 35

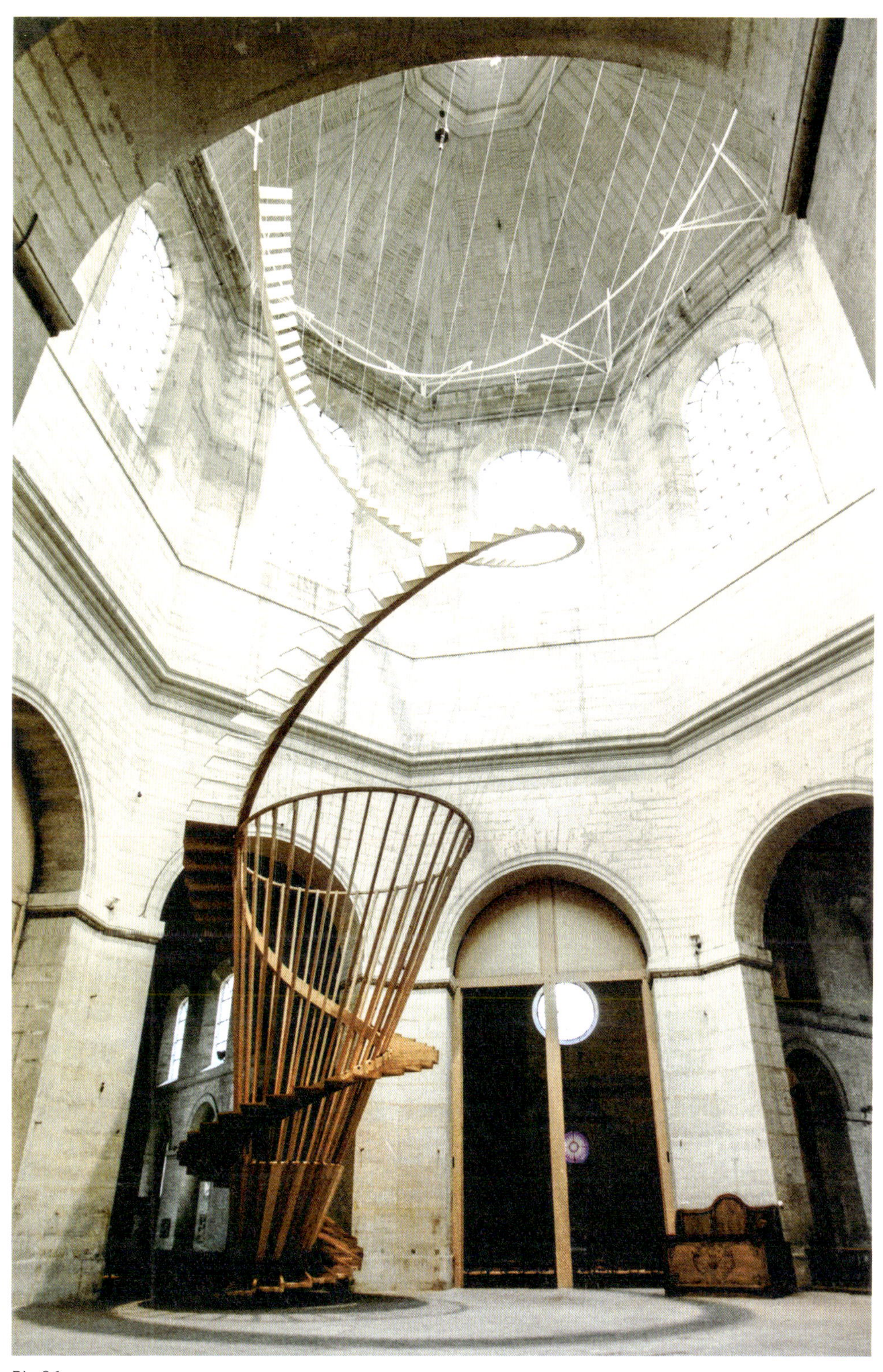

PL. 36

Guardian Stone, Puryear's first large-scale work made entirely out of granite, was constructed from multiple pieces of stone that were carved by hand to achieve the gentle curves of the form that the artist envisioned: the shape of a head and neck in abstraction. This process model served a functional role in the work's fabrication. The one-tenth scale painted wood maquette was cut into eighteen pieces, which were then traced and enlarged to ten times their original size to serve as templates for the industrial stone carvers with whom Puryear collaborated.

PLATE 37. *Maquette for "Guardian Stone,"* 2002
Painted wood, 22 × 17½ × 14 in. (55.9 × 44.5 × 35.6 cm)

PLATE 38. *Guardian Stone,* 2001–03
Granite, 18 ft. × 10 ft. × 12 ft. 3 in. (548.6 × 304.8 × 373.4 cm)
Commissioned by TV Asahi, Tokyo

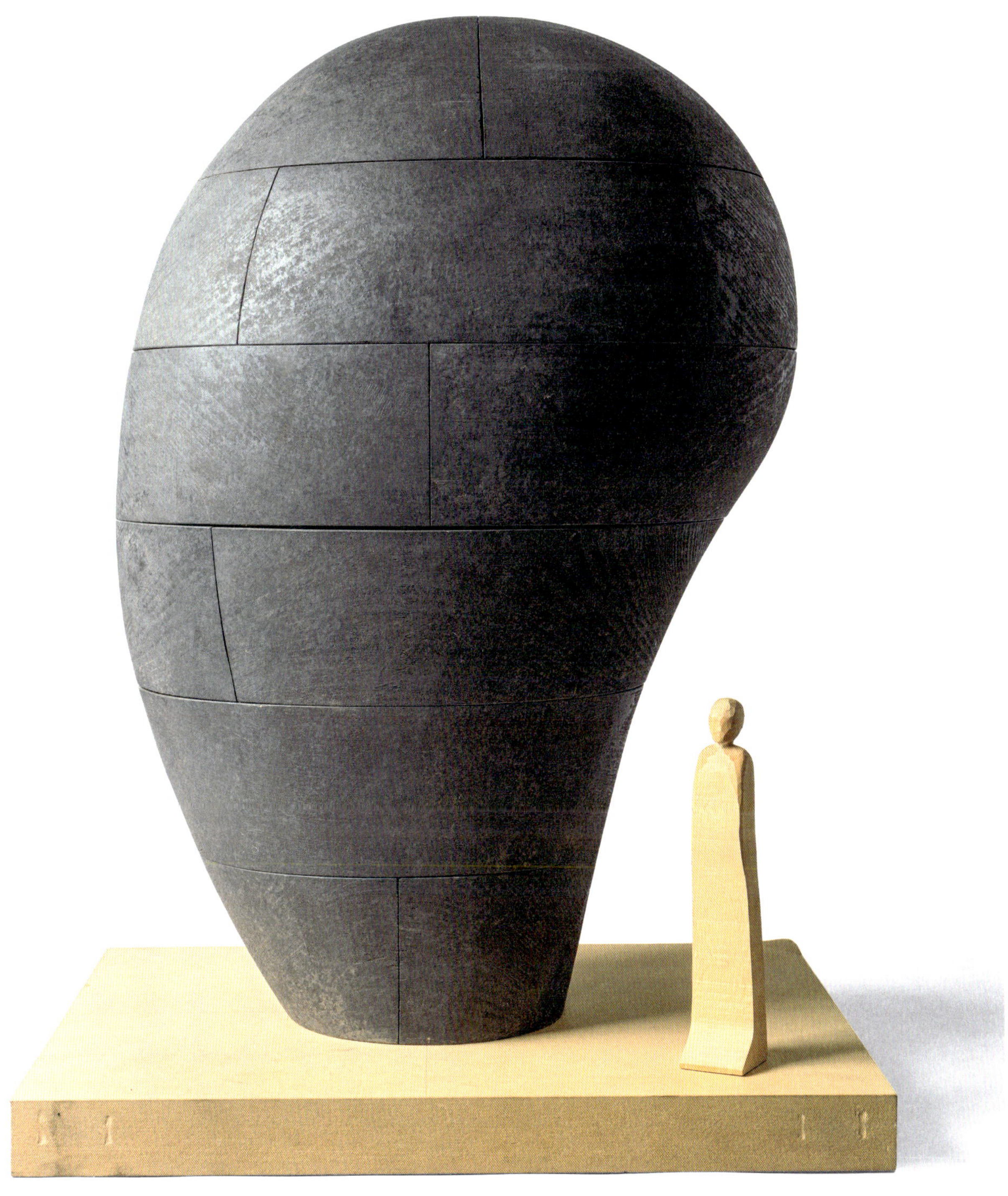

PL. 37

OPPOSITE: PL. 38

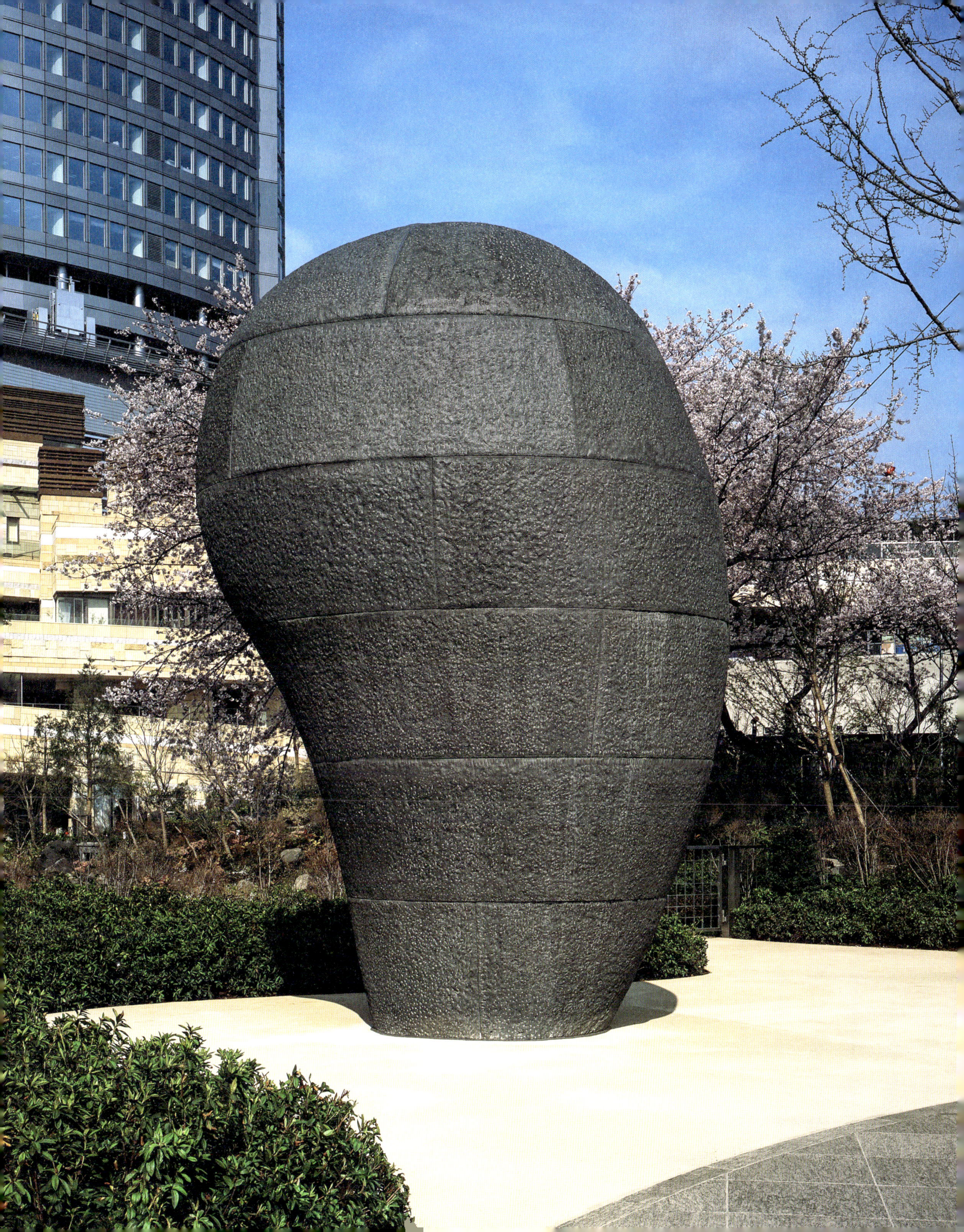

Carved from oriented strand board, a building material that Puryear often works with for model-making, and then cast in iron, *Shackled* retains some of the surface texture of the original. The work demonstrates how Puryear typically explores different forms over time in a variety of materials and at different sizes before realizing them at a monumental scale. In the year after making *Shackled*, Puryear completed drawings for *Big Bling* and *Creature from Iddefjord*, both of which bear formal similarities to this sculpture, and which would later become large-scale site-specific public works.

PLATE 39. *Shackled*, 2013
Iron, $27\frac{1}{2} \times 30\frac{5}{8} \times 8\frac{3}{8}$ in.
(69.8 × 77.8 × 21.3 cm)

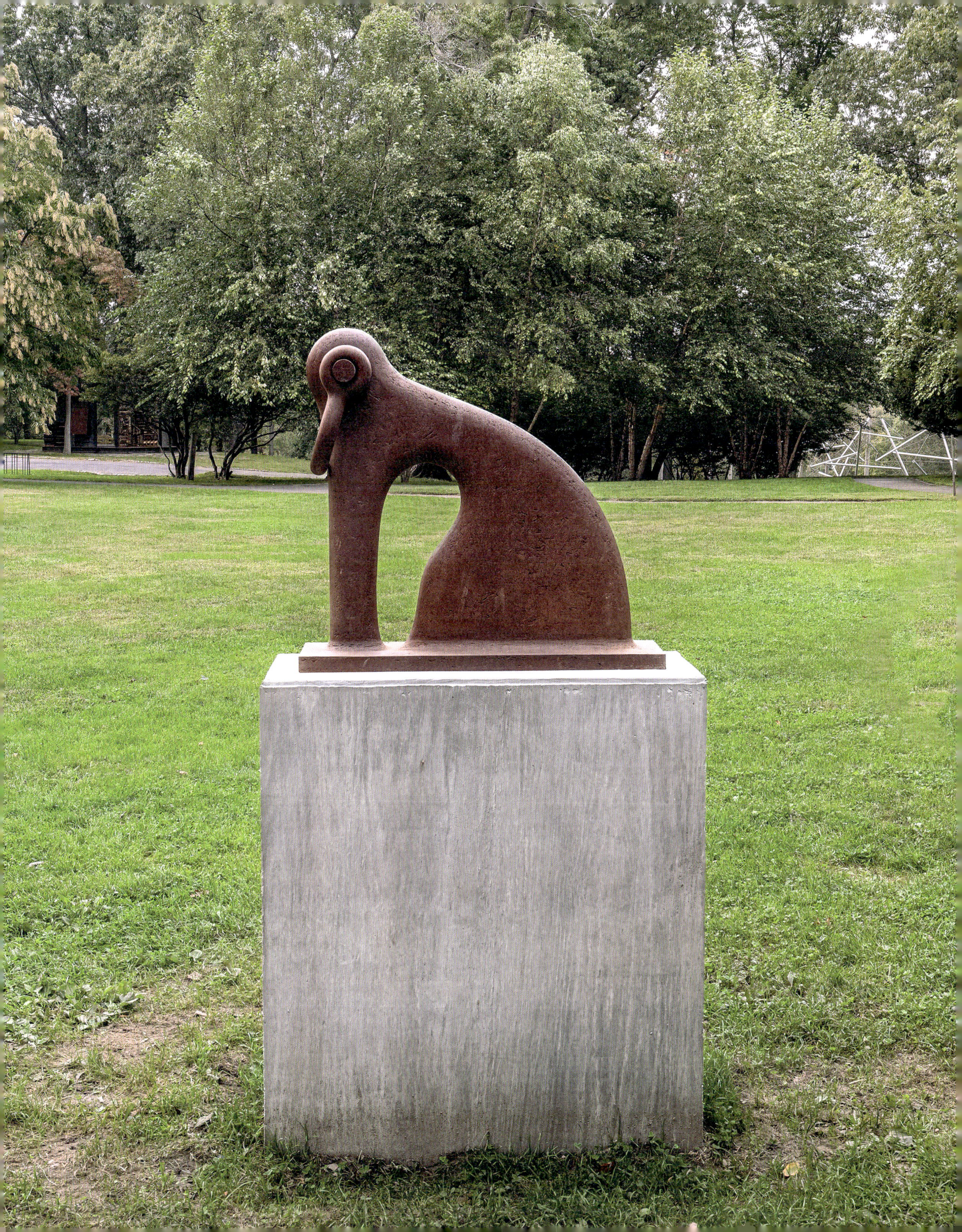

Before Puryear's forty-foot-tall sculpture *Big Bling* was constructed in conventional building materials by industrial fabricators, engineers, and model makers, the artist rendered the work, with its complexity of intricate intersecting grids, as a handmade wooden model. Commissioned for a temporary installation by the Madison Square Park Conservancy, Puryear intended the work to be in dialogue with New York City, saying, "I see you New York. I see how you grow and compartmentalize and stratify. I see how you beckon and promise (and also how you exclude). And crowning it all like a beacon, I see your wealth, your gilded shackle, the golden ring (the bling), the prize, our pride, maybe even our success."

To create the gilded shackle, the carved wooden original from Puryear's model was enlarged, modeled in fiberglass-covered foam, and applied with twenty-four-karat gold leaf. For Puryear, the word "shackle" suggests multiple connotations, including its industrial use in ships, and its more sinister historical use as a tool of bondage and subjugation of enslaved people. *Big Bling* is reminiscent of the form of Puryear's cast iron work, *Shackled* (2013).

PLATE 40. *Big Bling*, 2014
Graphite on paper,
50 × 42 in. (127 × 106.7 cm)

PLATE 41. *Big Bling*, 2016
Pressure-treated laminated timbers, plywood, chain-link fencing, fiberglass, and gold leaf, 40 × 10 × 38 ft. (1,219.2 × 304.8 × 38 cm)
Commissioned by Madison Square Park Conservancy, New York

PLATE 42. *Maquette for "Big Bling,"* 2014
Birch plywood, maple, and 22kt gold leaf,
40½ × 9⅛ × 40 in.
(102.9 × 23.2 × 101.6 cm)

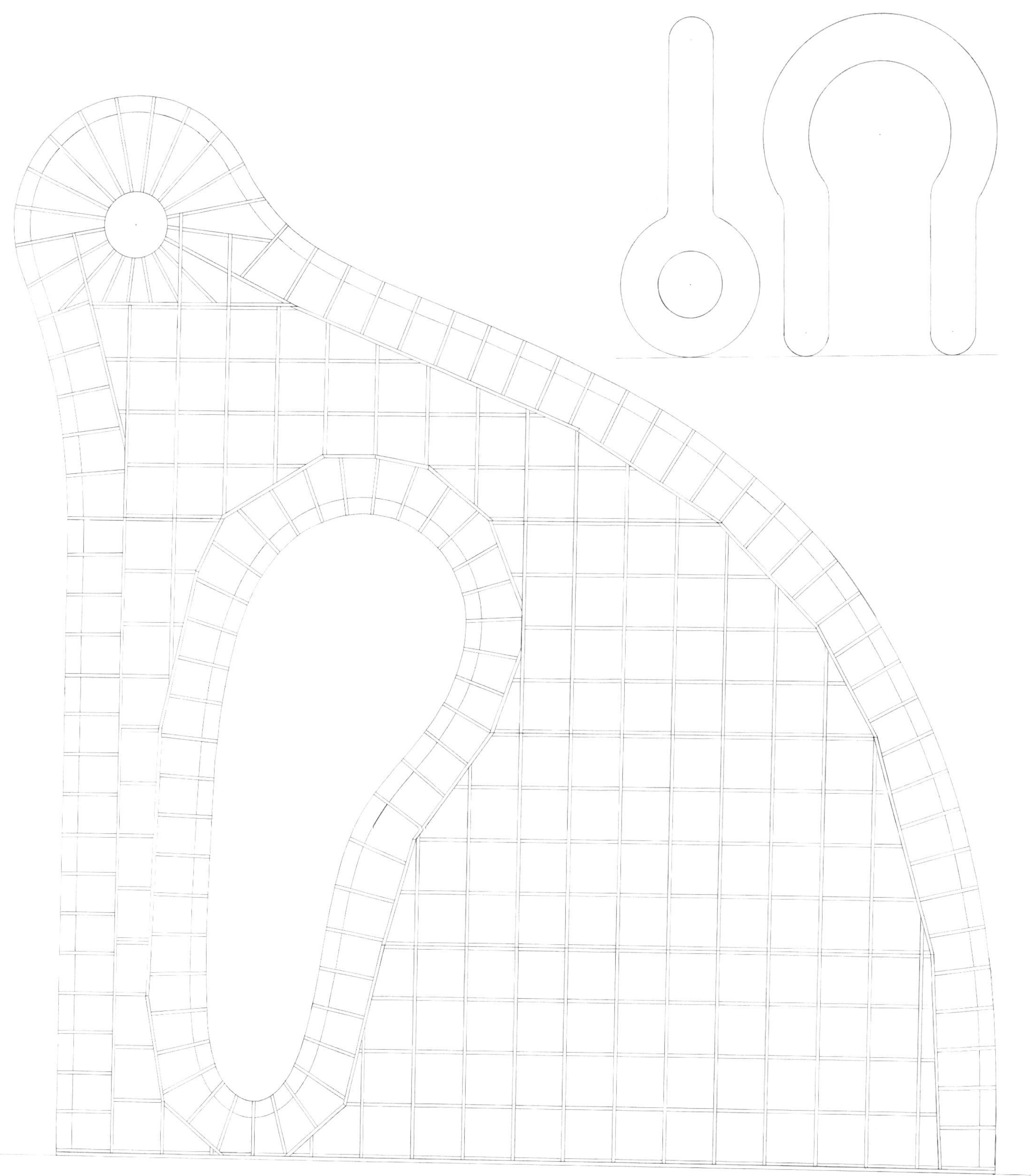

PL. 40

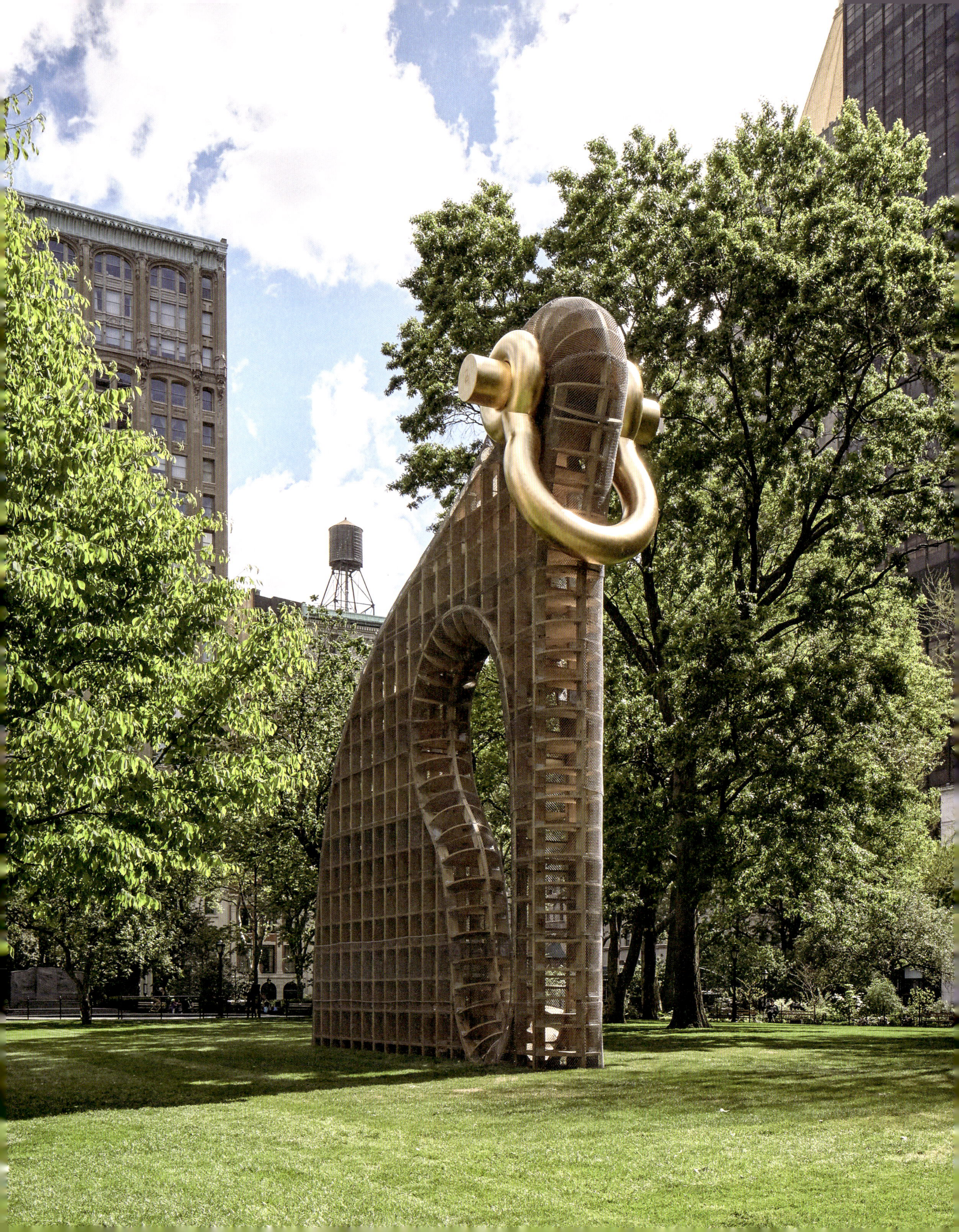

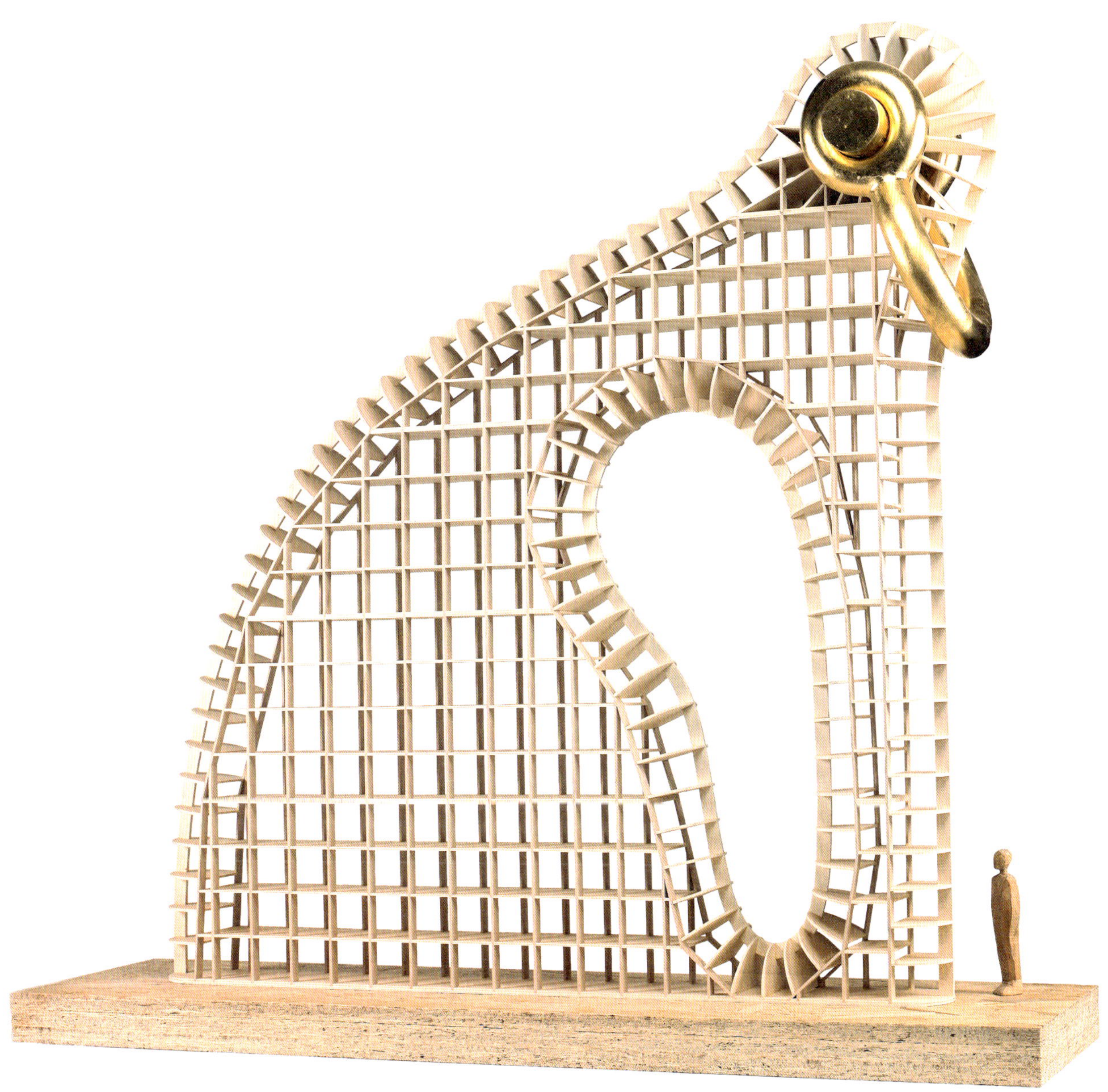

PL. 42

OPPOSITE: PL. 41

Puryear was commissioned to create *Slavery Memorial* by Brown University to mark and recognize the institution's long-unacknowledged profit from and engagement in the transatlantic trade of enslaved people. Puryear has likened the work—emerging from underground with links of broken chain—to "an unearthing of a buried truth." The artist chose to create the work in cast iron, rather than bronze, in order to use a material free from the high-minded associations and stature of traditional memorials, which he felt was inappropriate for this grim and shameful subject. With cast iron, Puryear also sought to make a connection between industry and slavery: "Slavery was, in fact, an industrial reality. It was a way this society created wealth. It was a way in which it measured wealth. To me, the memorial should reflect that. I hope that I have created an industrial artifact that is partially buried—mostly buried—but that will never, ever disappear from memory."

Puryear has expressed that the most important part of *Slavery Memorial* is the text inscribed into a plaque accompanying his sculpture. It reads:

> This memorial recognizes Brown University's connection to the trans-Atlantic slave trade and the work of Africans and African-Americans, enslaved and free, who helped build our university, Rhode Island, and the nation.
>
> In 2003 Brown President Ruth J. Simmons initiated a study of this aspect of the university's history. In the eighteenth century slavery permeated every aspect of social and economic life in Rhode Island. Rhode Islanders dominated the North American share of the African slave trade, launching over a thousand slaving voyages in the century before the abolition of the trade in 1808, and scores of illegal voyages thereafter.
>
> Brown University was a beneficiary of this trade.

PLATE 43. *Maquette for "Slavery Memorial," Brown University*, 2014
Ductile cast iron and stainless steel, 9 × 15½ × 16½ in.

PLATE 44. *Slavery Memorial, Brown University*, 2014
Ductile cast iron, stainless steel, and granite, sculptural element: 55 in. × 8 ft. × 8 ft. (139.7 × 243.8 × 243.8 cm); granite element: 43⅜ × 39½ × 30 in. (110.2 × 100.3 × 76.2 cm)
Commissioned by Brown University, Providence, Rhode Island

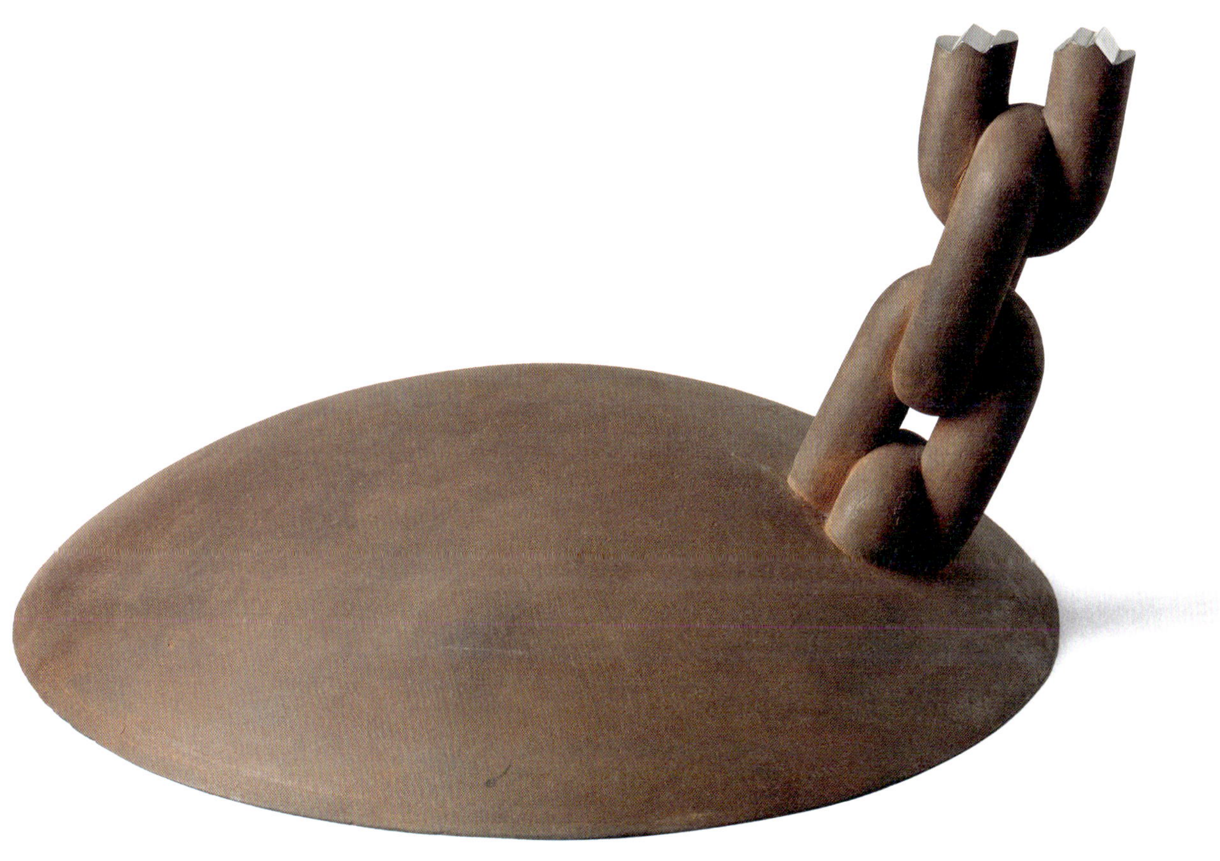

PL. 43

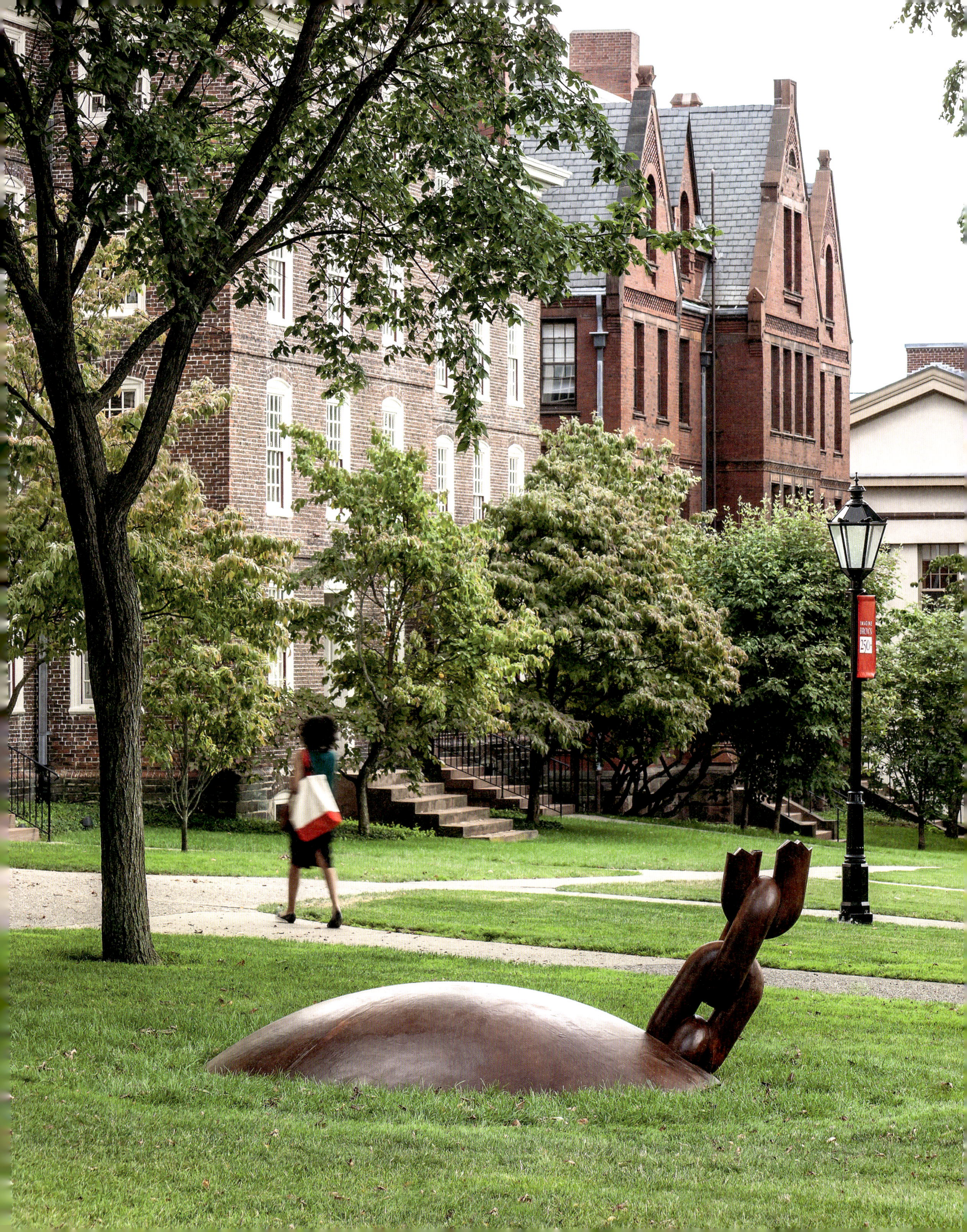
IMAGINE
BROWN
250+

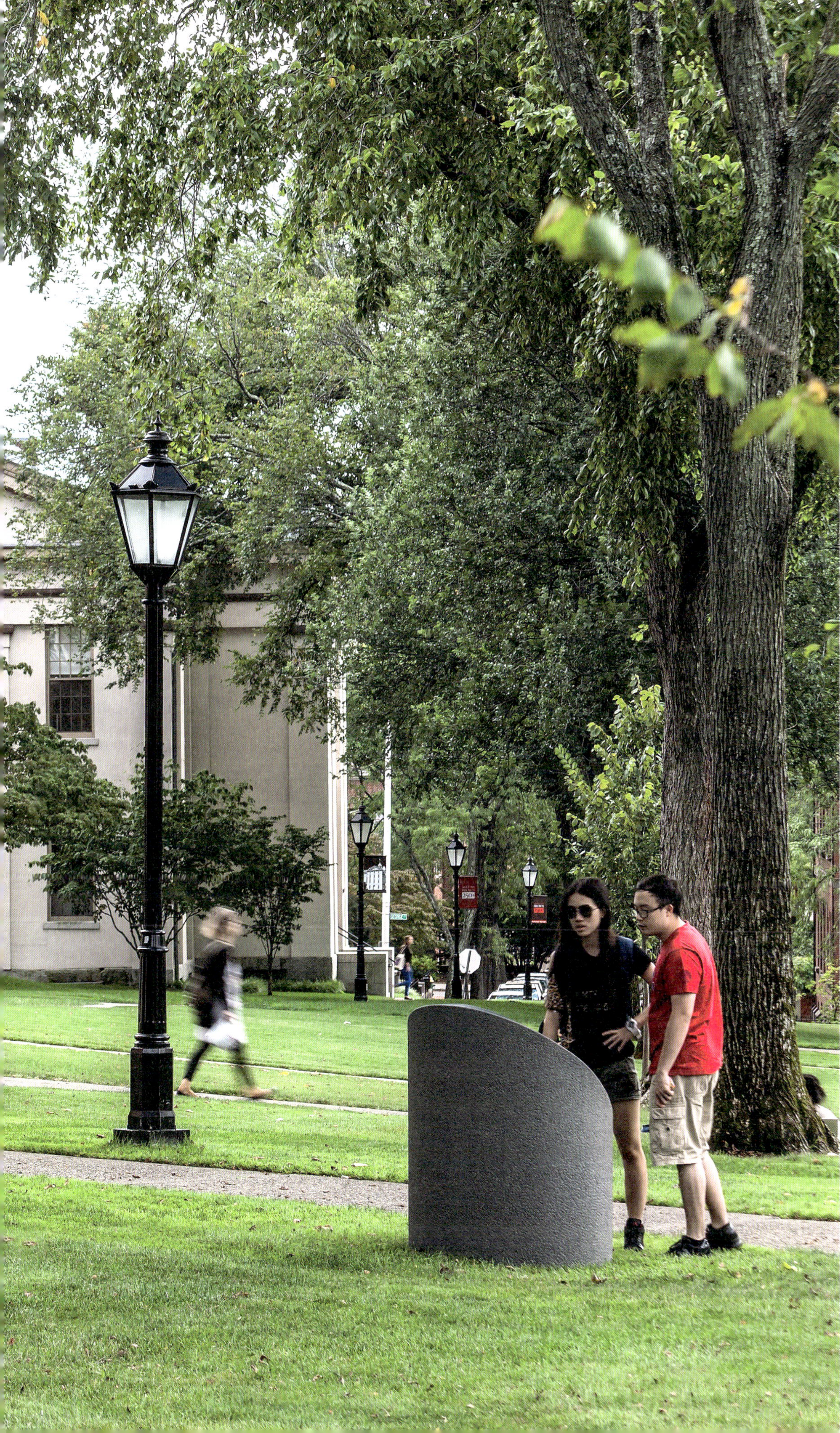

PL. 44

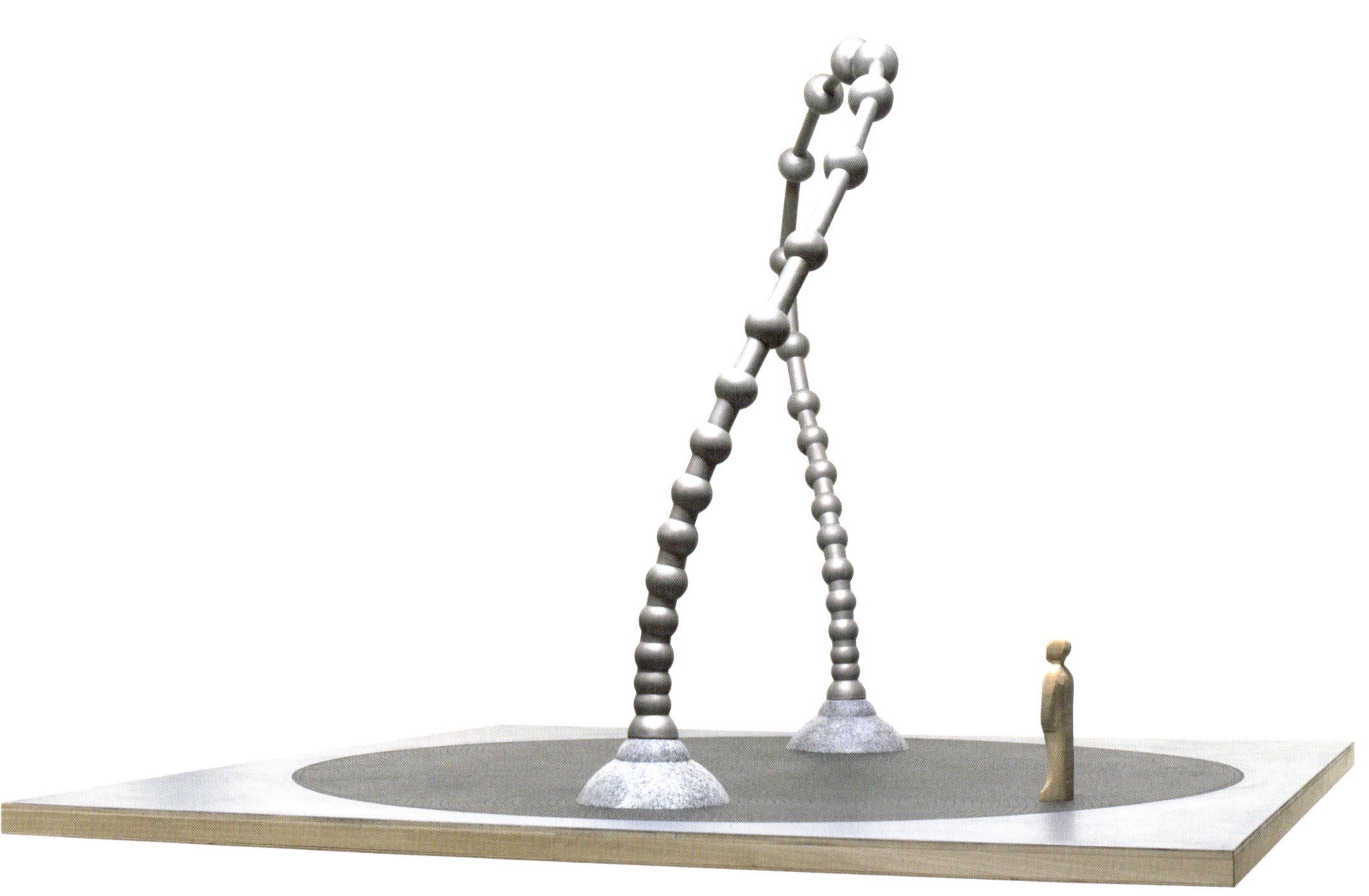

PL. 45

Puryear intended the top of this swooping steel arc sitting on curved granite bases, which reaches over thirty feet tall, to be visible from outside the ten-foot-high opaque walls of the United States Embassy in Beijing. For Puryear, *Connecting*'s form is reminiscent of a knotted string "meandering in space." The accompanying drawing shows Puryear's plans for the paving pattern—dark cobblestones arrayed in the configuration of the symbol for yin and yang—a detail visible only from within the embassy.

PLATES 45, 46. *Maquette for "Connecting,"* 2016
Stainless steel and painted wood, 50 × 68¼ × 68¼ in. (127 × 173.4 × 173.4 cm)

PLATES 47, 48. *Connecting*, 2018
Stainless steel with granite bases, 31 ft. (944.9 cm) tall
Commissioned by FAPE, installed at the U.S. Embassy, Beijing

PLATE 49. *Paving Pattern for "Connecting,"* c. 2016
Graphite on paper, 23 × 23 in. (58.4 × 58.4 cm)

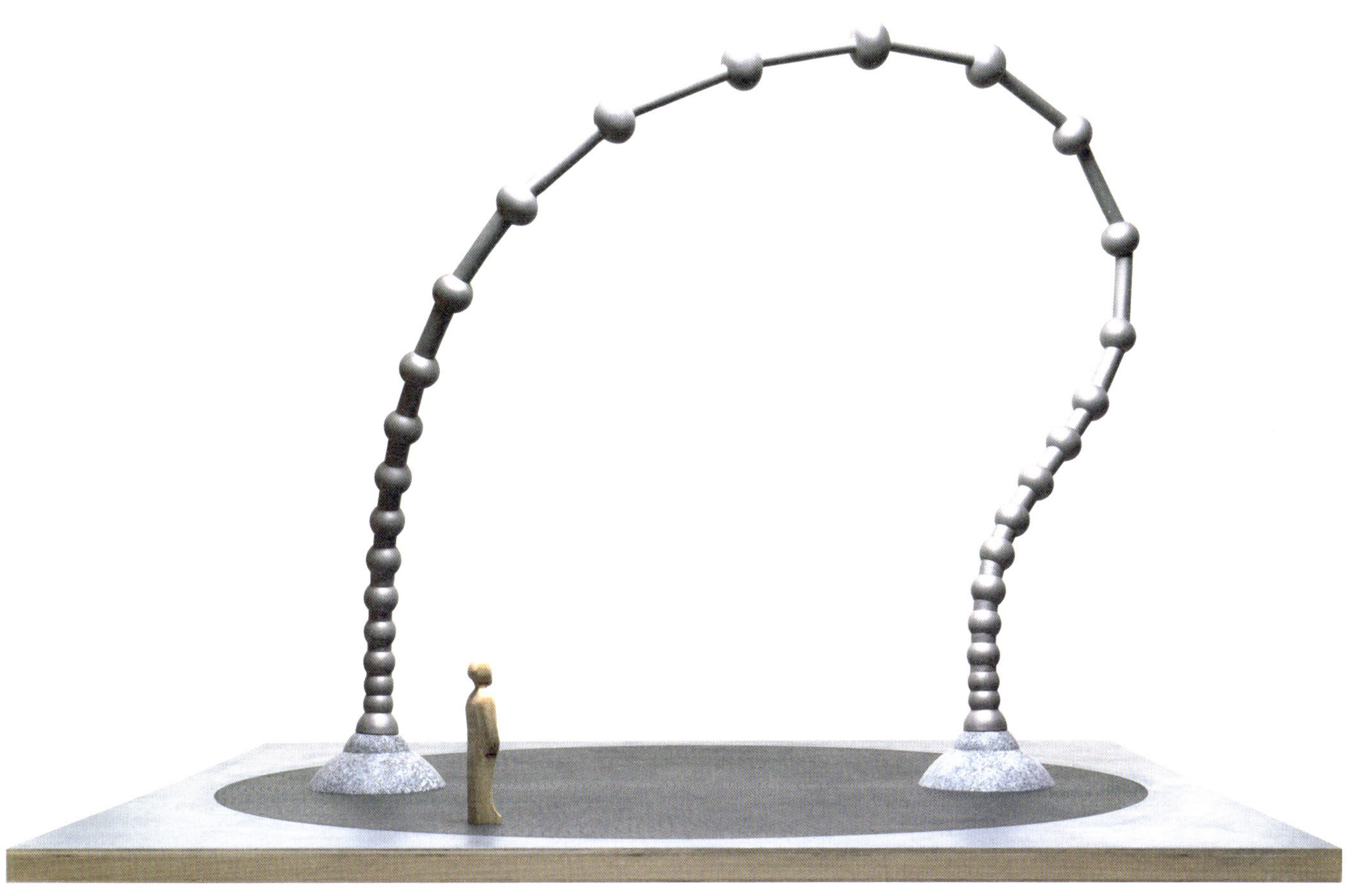

PL. 46

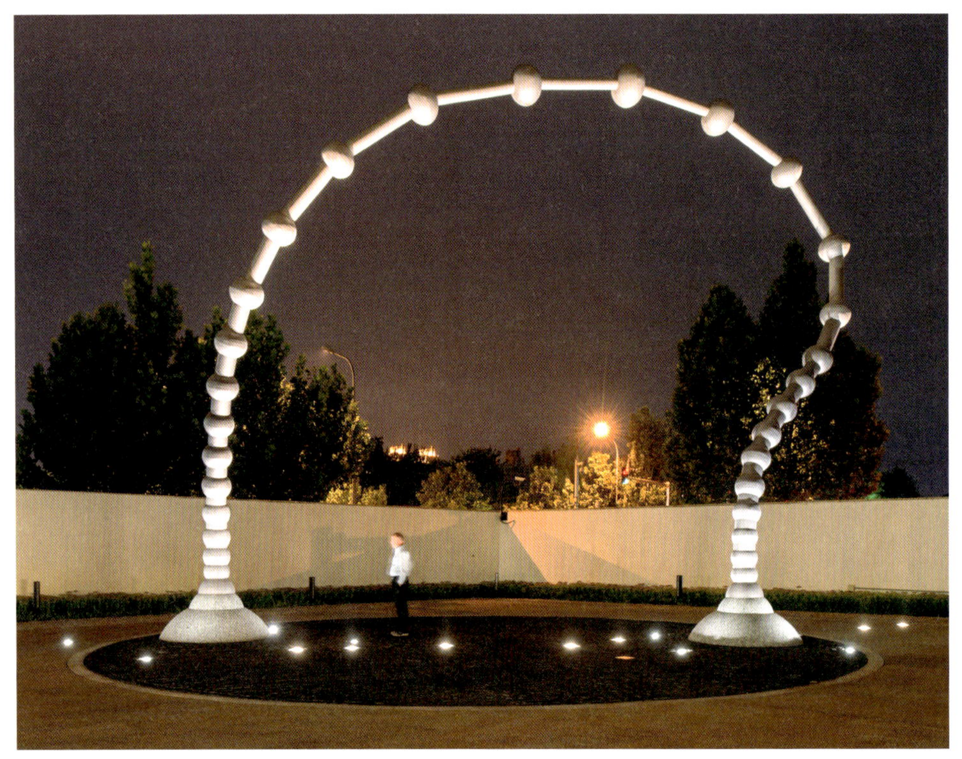

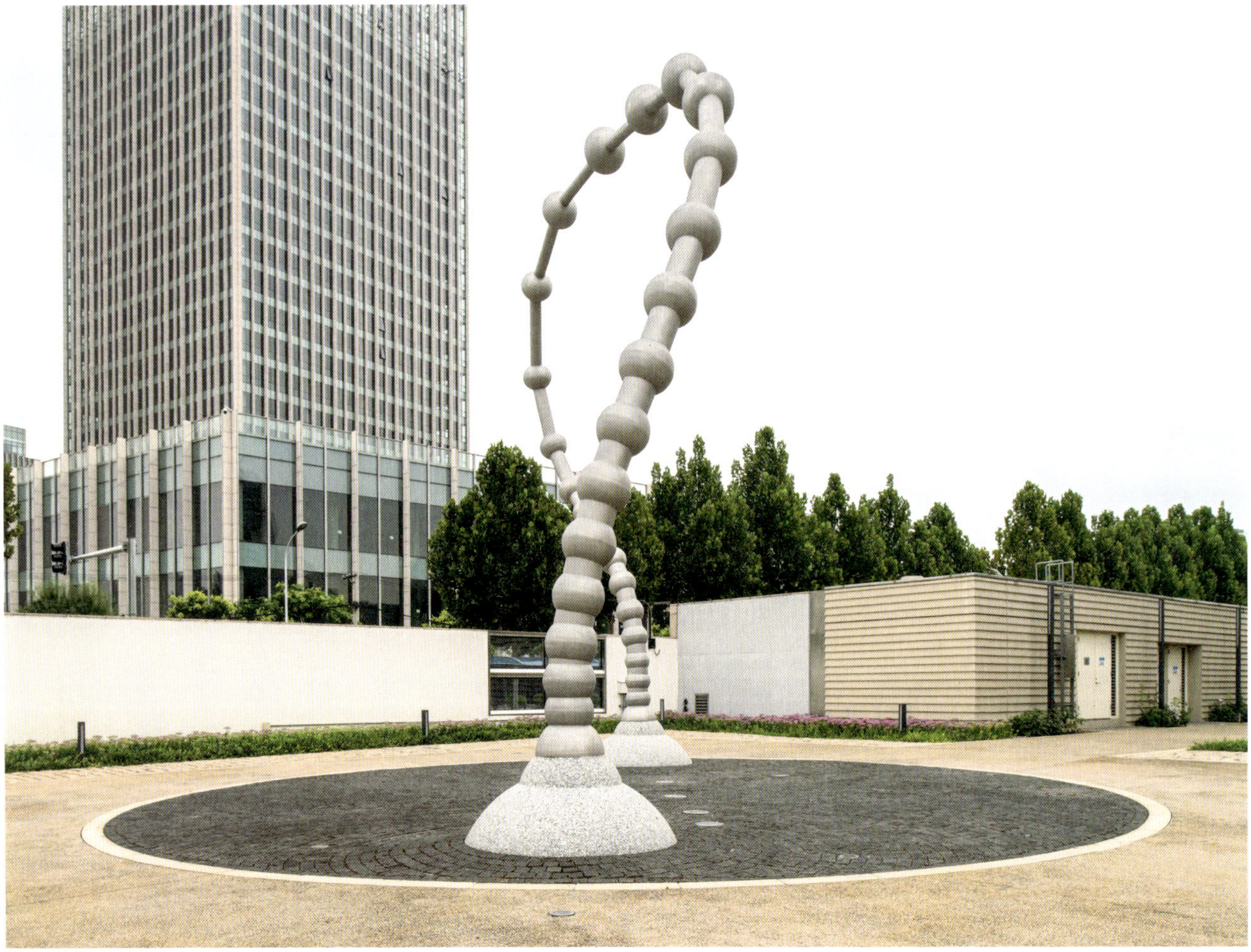

PLS. 47, 48

PL. 49

Puryear has described this model for an unrealized project as a "tube within a tube." The work was to be constructed using standard building parts, including the largest size of steel pipes available, measuring approximately two feet in diameter. Puryear envisioned that the component parts would be welded together and then galvanized.

The proposed site for the work was the corner of a sloping street in San Francisco. By situating the sculpture on an elevated plinth, Puryear intended for viewers to encounter work from below even when they walked up to it.

PLATE 50. *Proposal for Site in San Francisco* (unrealized), 2017
Wood, 27½ × 30⅝ × 8⅜ in.
(69.8 × 77.8 × 21.3 cm)

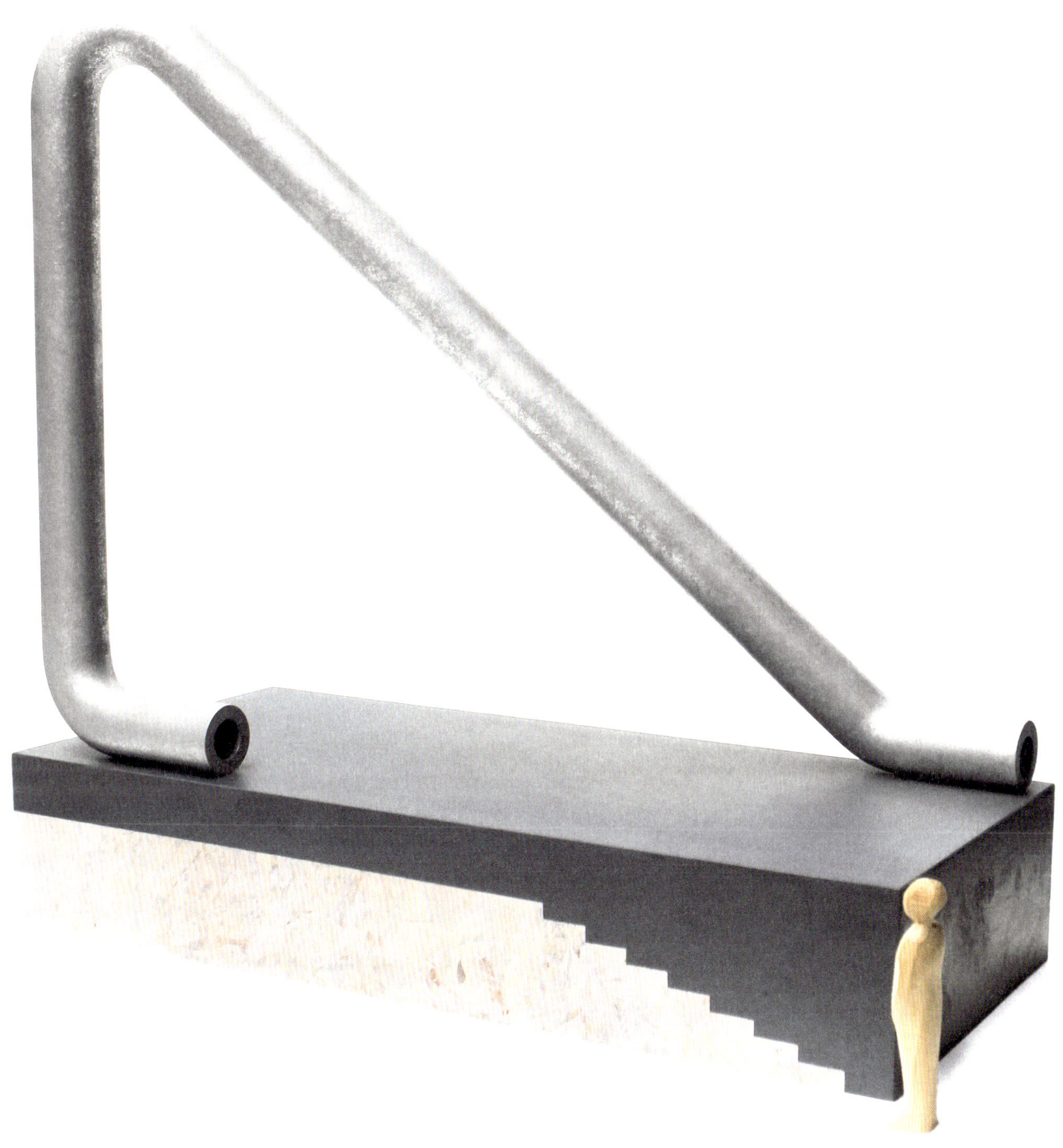

In 2019 Puryear represented the United States at the Venice Biennale. While it is one of the highest national honors that can be awarded to an artist, Puryear felt conflicted about taking on this role during a time of deep national division. He has written:

> I was profoundly disturbed by the level of weaponized resentment, fear, and ignorance that characterized the 2016 presidential election and the administration that followed. My anguish at seeing what was happening to the country found its way into my art.

The work that Puryear created for the forecourt outside the exhibition pavilion took the form of an enormous tracery screen that obscured the building's Federal-style facade behind a wooden sunburst with a reflective center (the "monstrance"). The screen was supported from behind by a dark, spiraling buttress (the "volute"), reminiscent of a malevolent dragon's tail.

Inside the pavilion Puryear exhibited sculptures that explored the ways in which notions of American exceptionalism and freedom are complicated by our fraught national history.

PLATE 51. *Maquette for "Swallowed Sun (Monstrance and Volute),"* 2018
Oriented strand board, pine, maple, paint, and laser-cut acrylic, 17½ × 33¾ × 16¼ in. (44.5 × 85.7 × 41.3 cm)

PLATES 52, 53. *Swallowed Sun (Monstrance and Volute)*, 2019
Southern yellow pine, steel, polyester, canvas, and rope, 22 ft. 8 in. × 44 ft. × 24 ft. 3 in. (690.9 × 1,341.1 × 739.1 cm)
Temporary installation at the U.S. Pavilion, 2019 Venice Biennale

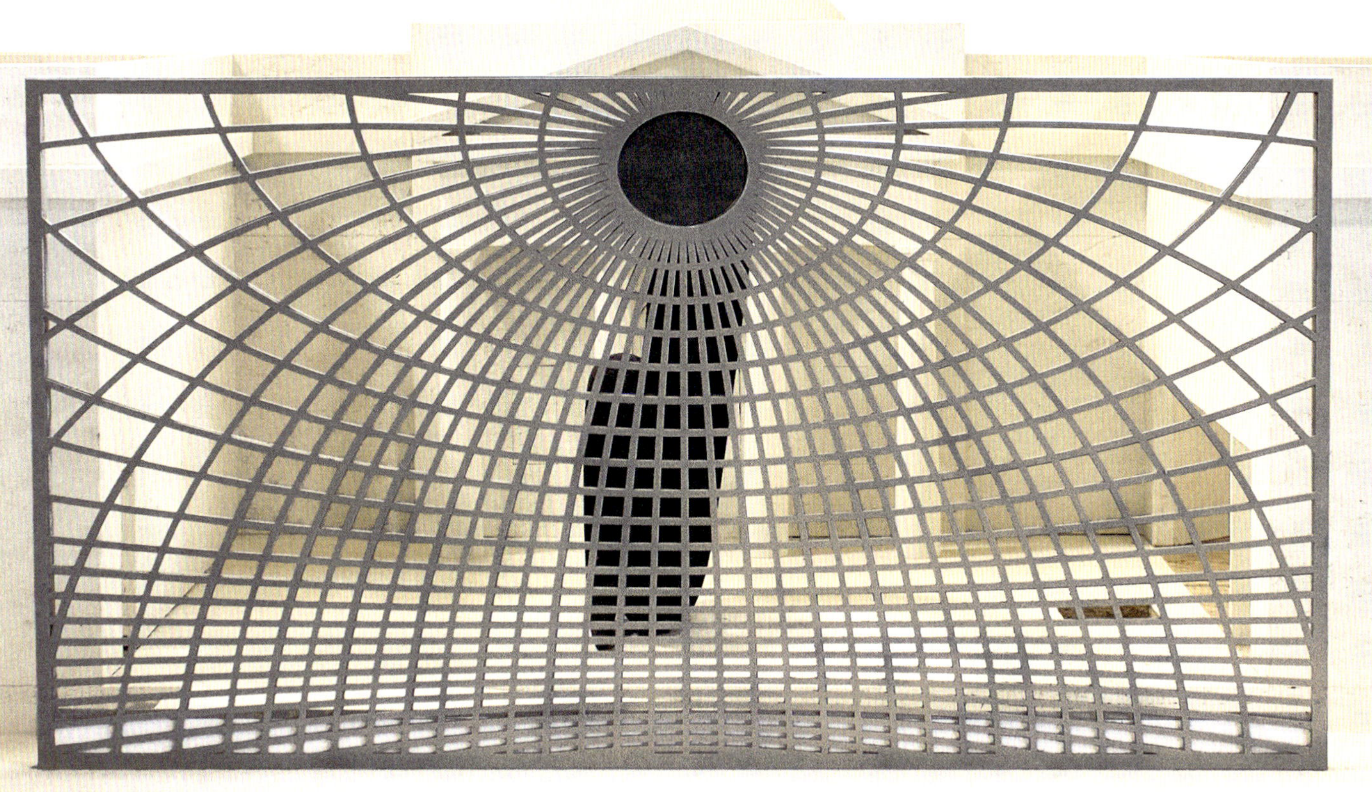

PL. 51

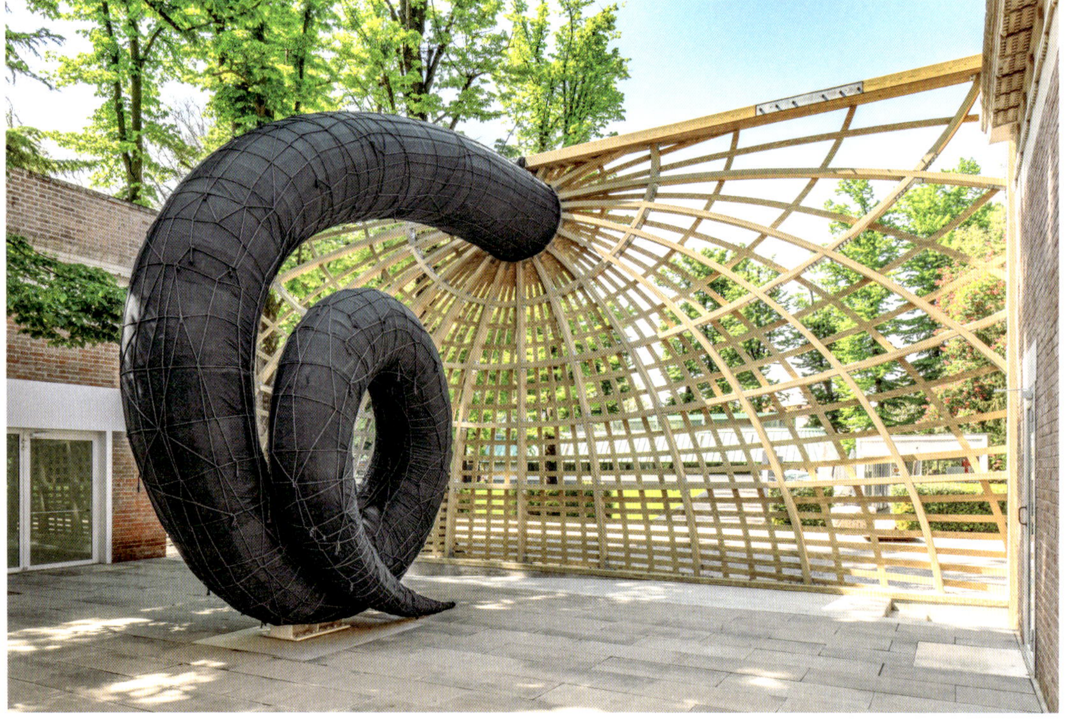

PL. 52

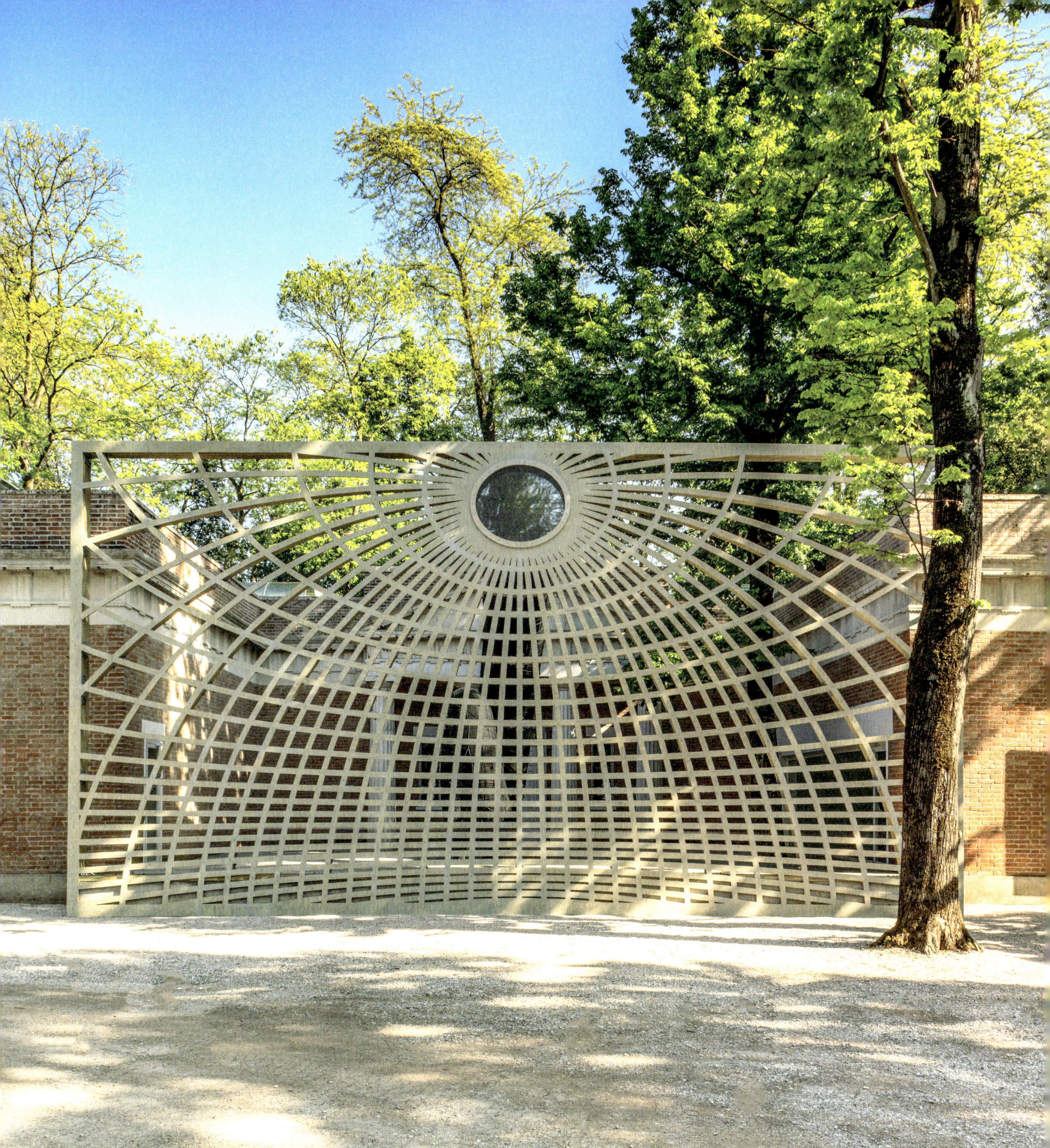

PL. 53

Creature from Iddefjord, installed outside Oslo's central Deichman Library and proximate to the Oslo Opera House, is named for a notable fjord in southern Norway, from which forty-two blocks of granite were quarried to construct it. On one side, the work appears as a flat plane; on the other, it is rounded and biomorphic. To walk through and around the sculpture is a process of discovery.

Although not visible from the maquette, the work has a different surface texture on each side: one is a smooth, carved surface, while the other maintains the rough natural surface of split granite from when it was quarried. Of the work's form, Puryear has said, "I think of it as a crouching creature, but also as a stone construction. One side is like architecture with a flat wall with a sharply cut opening, while the other side has a flowing, more organic shape." *Creature from Iddefjord* was created with a process of construction similar to that of Puryear's *Guardian Stone* (2001–03) in Tokyo, but here the smooth contours between pieces of granite were achieved with computer-guided cutting and finished by hand-chiseling.

PLATE 54. *Creature from Iddefjord*, c. 2014
Graphite on paper, 12½ × 19 in. (31.8 × 48.3 cm)

PLATES 55, 56. *Maquette for "Creature from Iddefjord,"* 2020
Poplar and paint, 29½ × 18 × 31½ in. (74.9 × 45.7 × 80 cm)

PLATES 57, 58. *Creature from Iddefjord*, 2020
Granite, 25 × 22 × 12 ft. (762 × 670.6 × 365.8 cm)
Commissioned by Sparebankstiftelsen, installed Deichman Library, Oslo

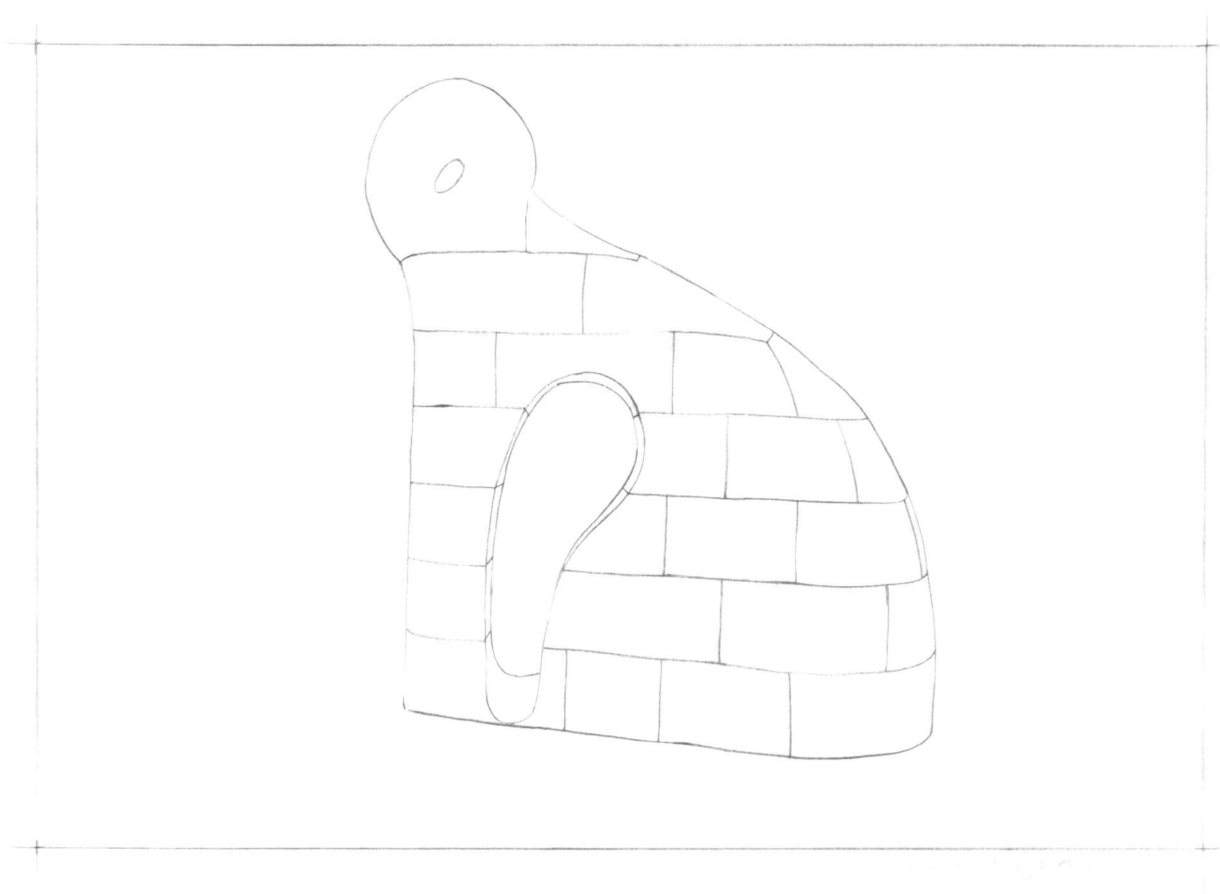

PL. 54

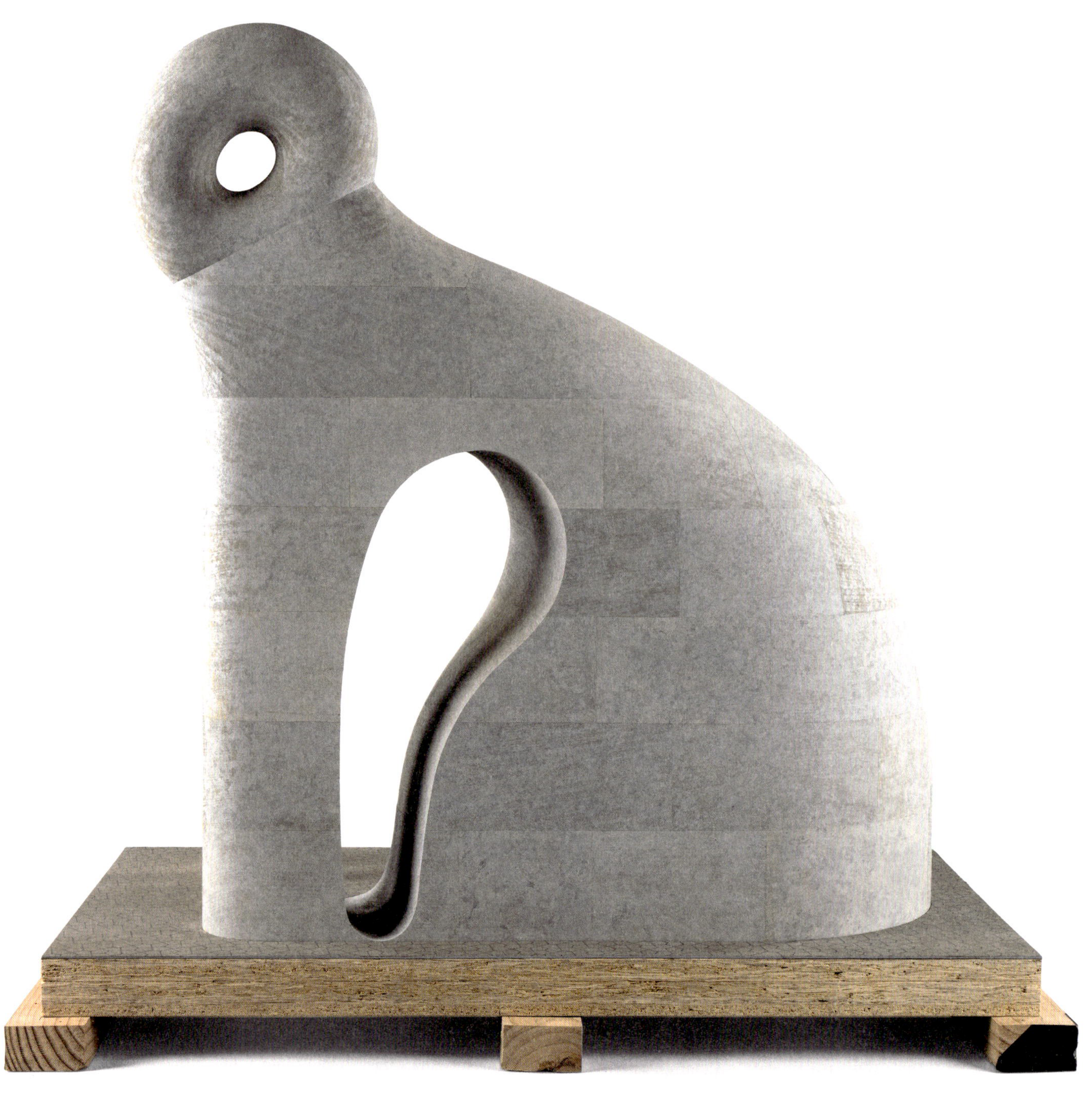

PL. 55

OPPOSITE: PL. 56

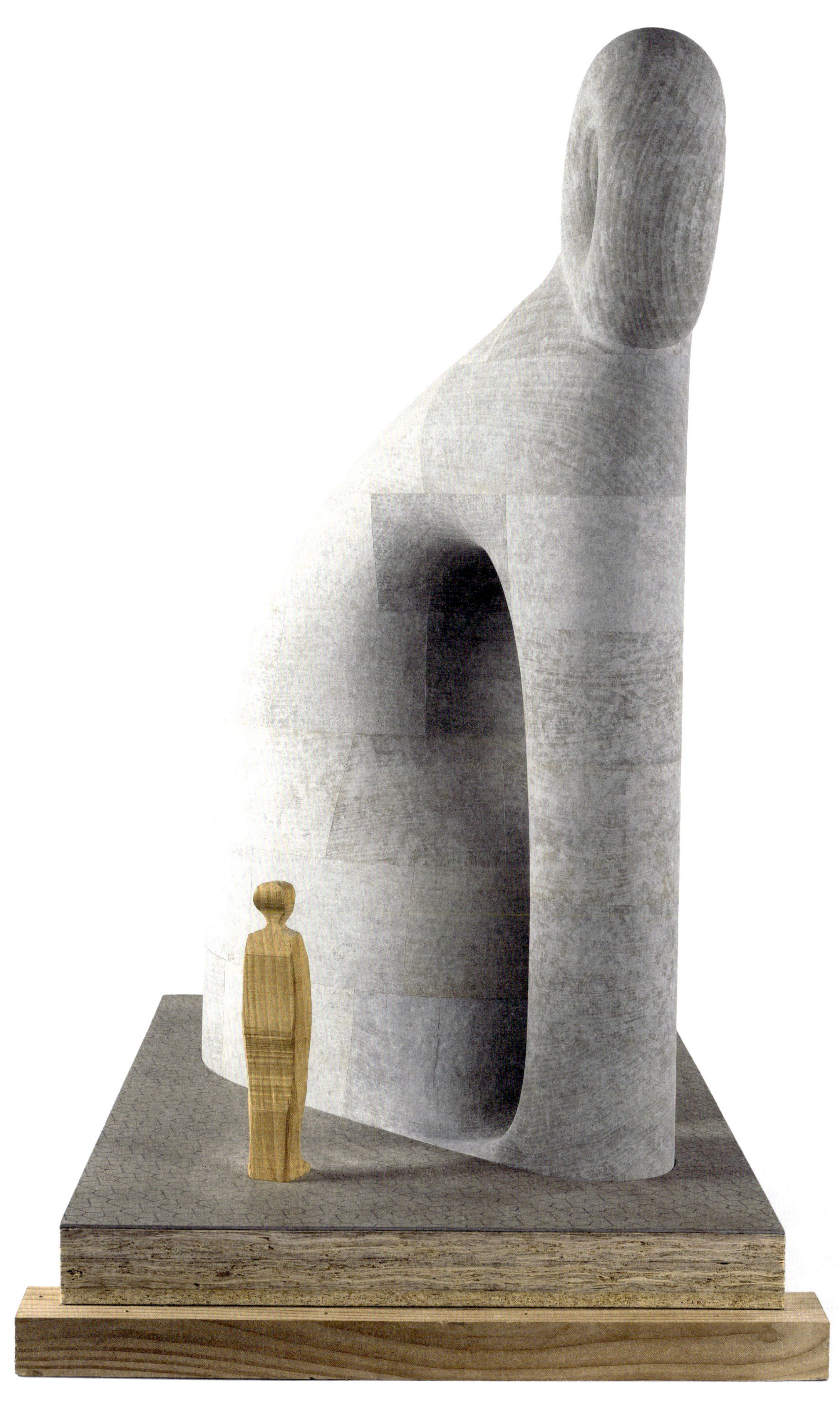

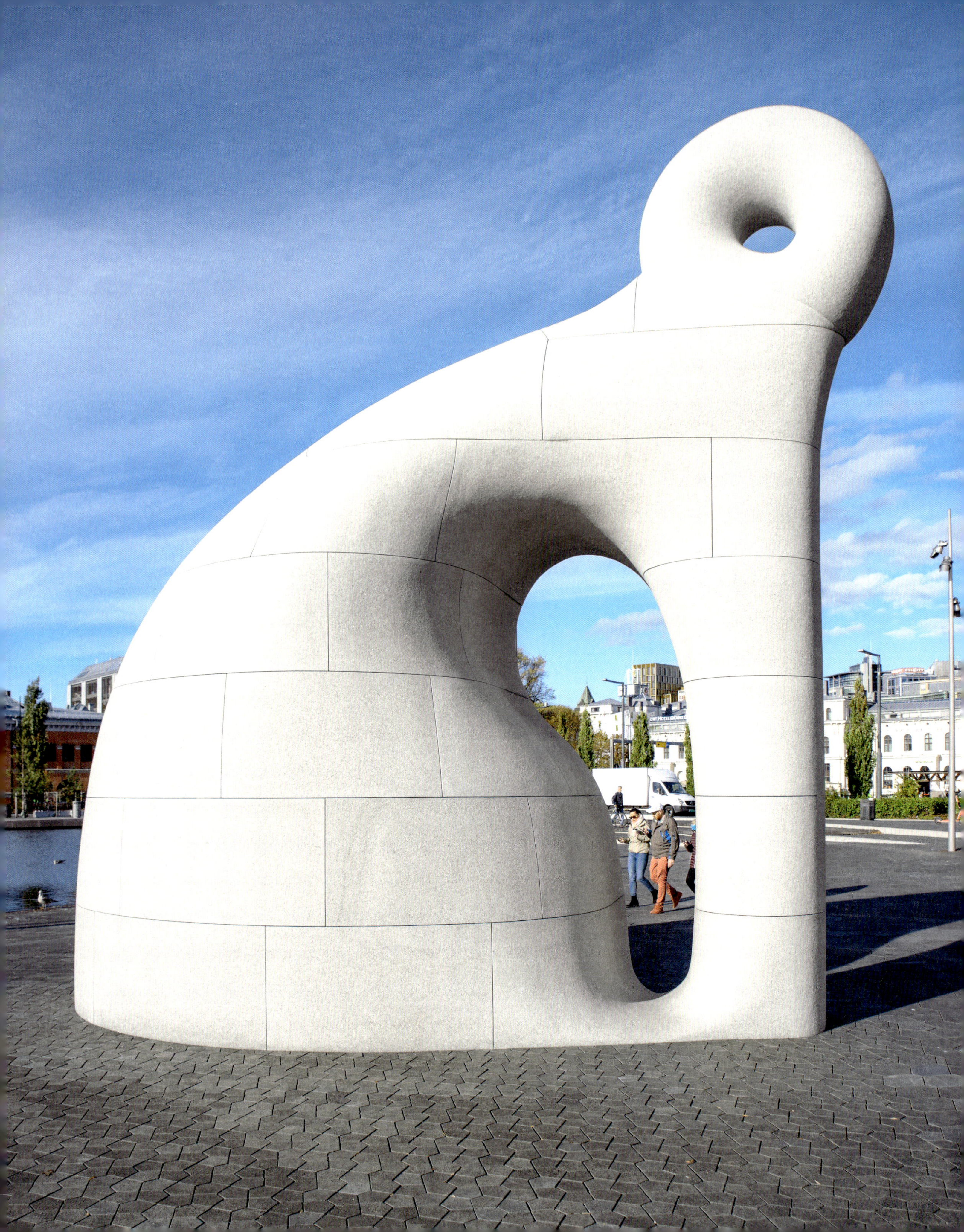

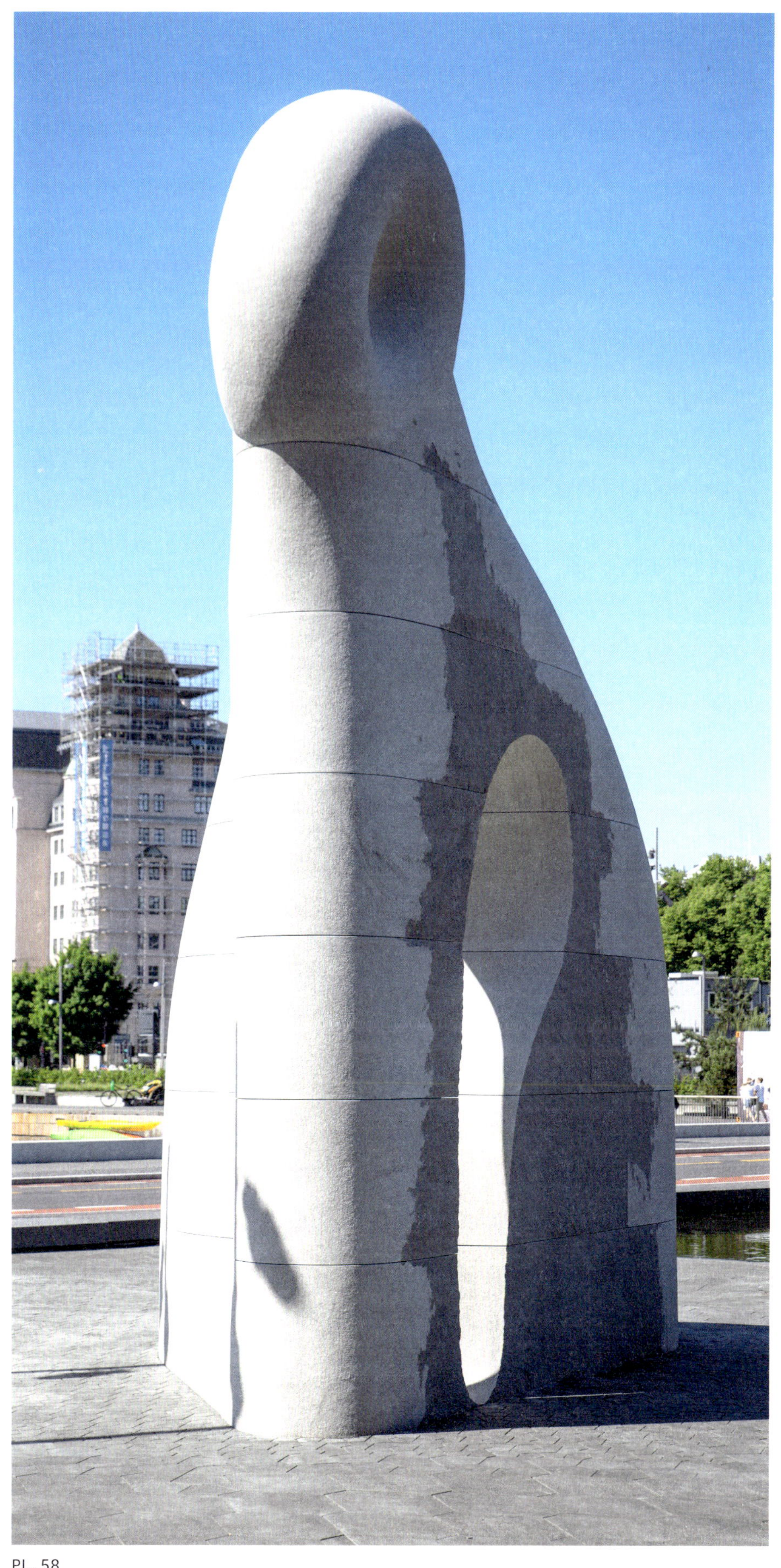

PL. 58

OPPOSITE: PL. 57

For his Storm King commission, Puryear worked through a series of models over the course of a decade, starting with an outline of the shape in pine, then moving toward high-density polyurethane and wood, painted to show the individual bricks and cobbles of the completed work.

The model-making continued even as construction on the full-size commission began, enabling the artist and his team of masons to consider different vaulting strategies, test the strength of bonds between brick and mortar, and determine the shape in which the bricks atop the masonry dome would come together. In addition to serving as study aids for the fabrication and completion of the work, the models provide a record of the process.

Two drawings from different stages in the design process demonstrate the refining of *Lookout*'s engineering from thirteen segments of brick to nine. Set at a series of gradually increasing angles, the segments allow the form to transition from a masonry arch into a dome. The team of masons began construction at the arch, laid over a wooden formwork, creating it as a line of bricks perpendicular to the ground. To end each section and begin anew, the team made angled cuts through bricks they had already laid, creating a new angle for the following segment of coursed brick. When the work reached the ninth segment, the bricks courses were laid horizontally, forming a dome.

PLATE 59. *First Wooden Model for Storm King Commission*, 2016
Wood, 9¾ × 9¾ × 9¾ in.
(24.8 × 24.8 × 24.8 cm)

PLATE 60. *Brick Sculpture for Storm King Art Center (Thirteen Segments)*, 2018
Graphite on paper,
23 × 29 in. (58.4 × 73.7 cm)

PLATE 61. *Maquette for "Lookout,"* 2018
Painted high-density urethane foam and painted wood, 19½ × 32 × 34 in.
(49.5 × 81.3 × 86.4 cm)

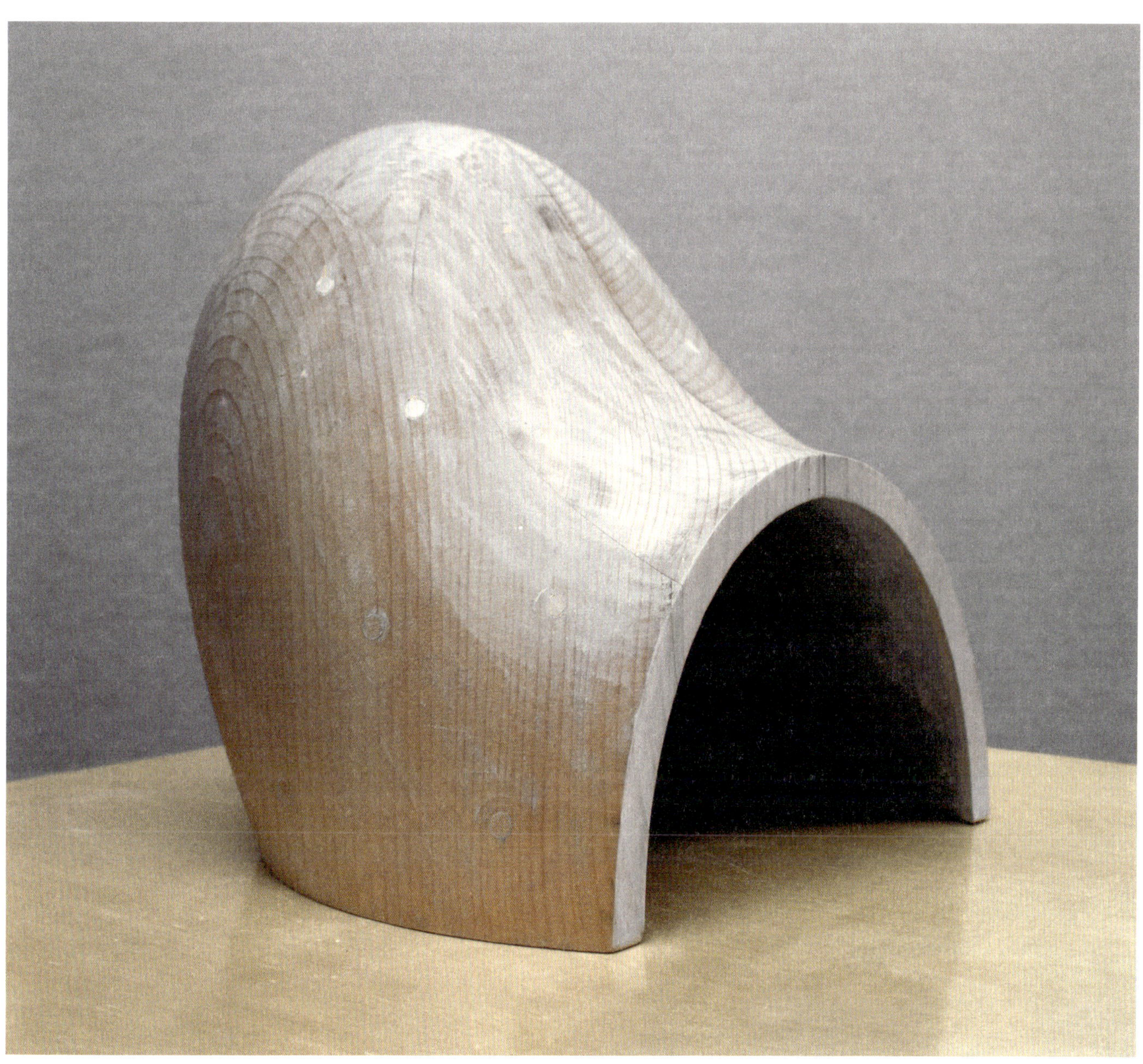

PL. 59

PL. 60

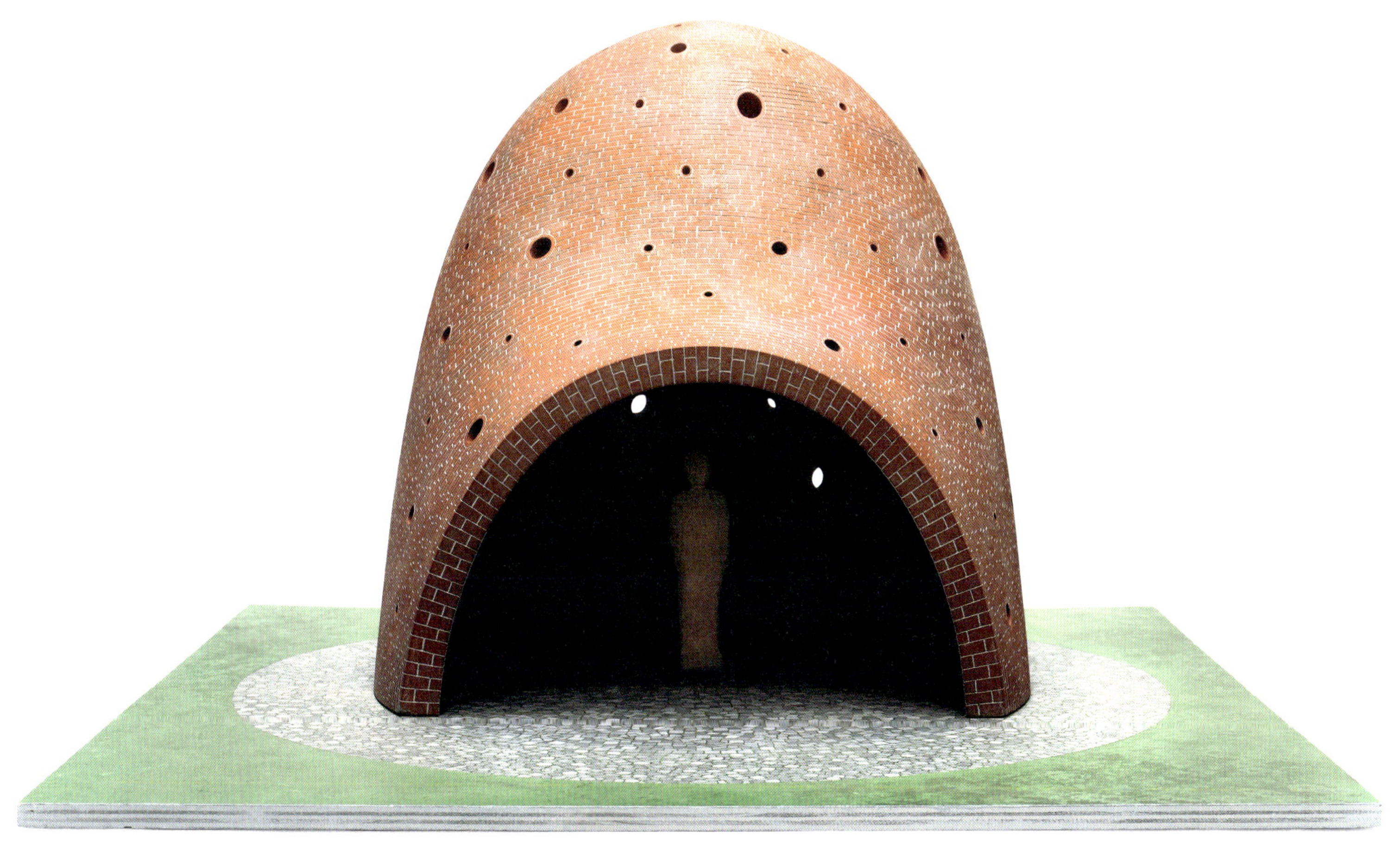

PL. 61

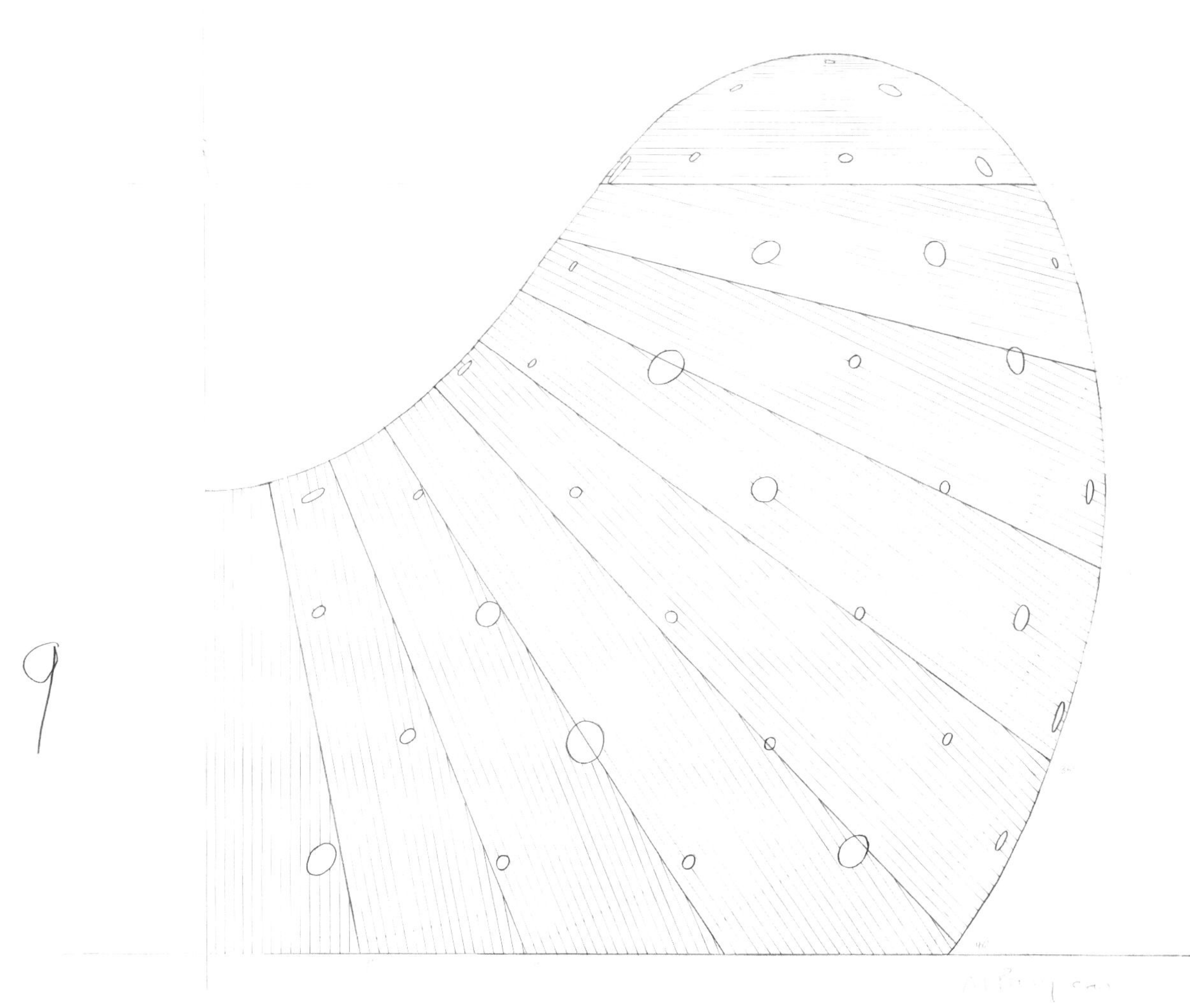

PL. 62

PLATE 62. *Brick Sculpture for Storm King Art Center (Nine Segments)*, 2021
Graphite on vellum,
23 × 29 in. (58.4 × 73.7 cm)

PLATE 63. *Final Nine-Segment Masonry Maquette for "Lookout,"* 2023
Painted high-density urethane foam and painted wood, 40 in. (101.6 cm) high

OPPOSITE: PL. 63

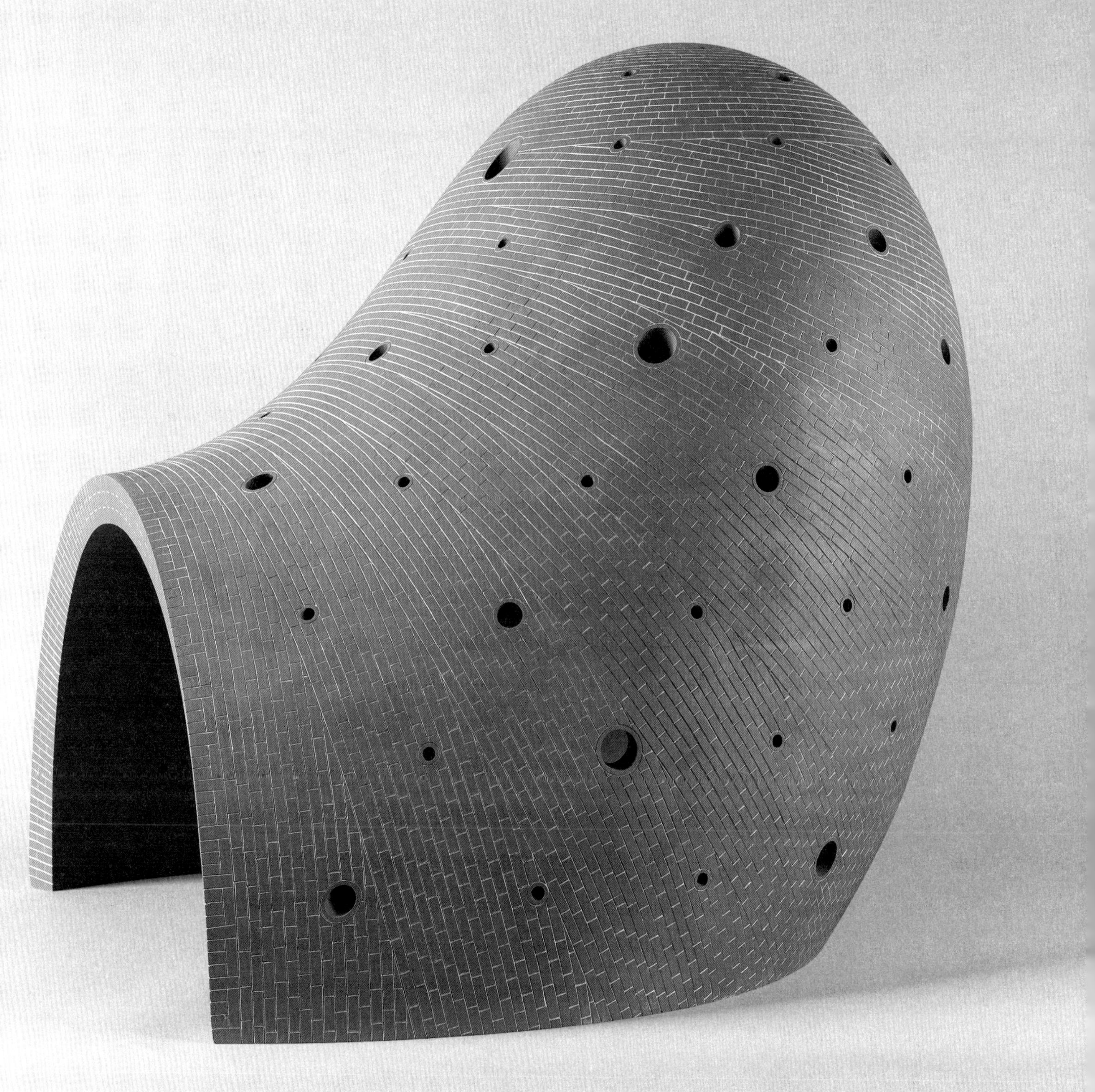

CITATIONS FOR MARTIN PURYEAR QUOTES IN "PROCESS AND SCALE"

Unless otherwise noted, all Martin Puryear quotes are from a conversation with the artist, Nora Lawrence, Amy S. Weisser, Adela Goldsmith, John P. Stern, Eric Booker, Jeanne Englert, and Rob Horton at the artist's studio, February 8, 2023.

p. 76: Martin Puryear, in conversation with Lawrence, Weisser, Goldsmith, Englert, and David R. Collens, January 20, 2022

p. 80: Martin Puryear, conversation with Lawrence, Weisser, Goldsmith, Englert, and Collens, January 13, 2022

p. 82: Martin Puryear, *Pavilion in the Trees*, video produced by the Association for Public Art (formerly Fairmount Park Art Association), 1995

p. 86: Hugh M. Davies and Helaine Posner, *Martin Puryear* (Amherst: University Gallery, University of Massachusetts at Amherst, 1984), 35

p. 94: Martin Puryear, "Notes for a proposal for the exterior plaza of the U.S. Holocaust Memorial Museum," November 11, 1991

p. 102: Jan Garden Castro, "Martin Puryear: The Call of History," in *Sculpture: The Publication of the International Sculpture Center*, December 1, 1998

p. 136: "Artist Statement," *Martin Puryear: Big Bling,* Madison Square Park Conservancy, 2016, 11

p. 140: Martin Puryear, text accompanying *Slavery Memorial, Brown University*, 2014

p. 150: Martin Puryear, in conversation with Lawrence and Goldsmith, September 22, 2023

p. 154: Martin Puryear, in conversation with Lawrence, Weisser, Goldsmith, Englert, and Collens, January 20, 2022

Checklist of the Exhibition

All works by Martin Puryear (American, b. 1941)
© Martin Puryear, courtesy Matthew Marks Gallery

PLATE 1
Box and Pole, 1977
Graphite on paper
29 × 21 in. (73.7 × 53.3 cm)
Drawing for temporary installation at Artpark, Lewiston, New York
Page 77

PLATE 2
Box and Pole, 1977
Graphite on paper
29 × 21 in. (73.7 × 53.3 cm)
Drawing for temporary installation at Artpark, Lewiston, New York
Page 78

PLATE 5
Maquette for "Stone Bow" (unrealized), 1980s
Painted wood
9 × 36 × 18 in.
(22.9 × 91.4 × 45.7 cm)
Page 81

PLATE 7
Maquette for "Pavilion in the Trees," 1981
Wood
16 × 38¾ × 10⅞ in.
(40.6 × 98.4 × 27.6 cm)
Commissioned by the Fairmount Park Art Association; installed at Cliveden Park, Philadelphia
Page 83

PLATE 9
Maquette for "Sentinel," c. 1981
Painted wood
10¾ × 8¼ × 3½ in.
(27.3 × 21 × 8.9 cm)
Commissioned by Gettysburg College, Pennsylvania
Page 87

PLATE 12
Bodark Arc, 1982
Graphite on ivory wove paper
6 × 9 in. (15.2 × 22.9 cm)
Commissioned by Governors State University
Installed at Nathan Manilow Sculpture Park, University Park, Illinois
Page 91

PLATE 13
Gog & Magog (Ampersand), 1987–88
Granite
East column: 13 ft. 7 in. × 36 in. × 36 in. (414 × 91.4 × 91.4 cm); west column: 13 ft. 11 in. × 36 in. × 36 in. (424.2 × 91.4 × 91.4 cm)
Walker Art Center, Minneapolis
Page 93

PLATE 14
Proposal for the Holocaust Memorial Museum (unrealized), 1991, refabricated 2023
Charred wood (to have been cast in bronze and patinated black)
7 × 7 × 7 in. (17.8 × 17.8 × 17.8 cm)
Page 95

PLATE 15
Proposal for the Holocaust Memorial Museum (unrealized), 1991
Graphite on ivory wove paper
23 × 29 in. (58.4 × 73.7 cm)
Page 97

PLATE 16
Maquettes for "North Cove Pylons," 1992
Wood, wire, and paint
North pylon: 25½ × 2 × 2 in. (64.8 × 5 × 5 cm); south pylon: 19½ × 2⅝ × 2⅝ in. (49.5 × 6.7 × 6.7 cm)
Commissioned by Battery Park City Authority, New York
Page 99

PLATE 19
Maquette for "Everything That Rises," 1993
Wood
20⅛ × 21½ × 9⅜ in.
(51.1 × 54.6 × 23.8 cm)
Commissioned by the University of Washington, Seattle
Page 103

PLATE 21
Untitled, Oliver Ranch, c. 1993
Black conté crayon on Strathmore white wove paper
23 × 29 in. (58.4 × 73.7 cm)
Commissioned by Oliver Ranch Foundation, Geyserville, California
Page 107

PLATE 22
Untitled, Oliver Ranch,
c. 1993
Graphite and pen on paper
12 × 23 in. (30.5 × 58.4 cm)
Commissioned by Oliver Ranch Foundation, Geyserville, California
Pages 108–09

PLATE 25
Maquette for "Bearing Witness," 1994
Pine
59¾ × 15 × 19½ in.
(151.8 × 38.1 × 49.5 cm)
Commissioned by the General Services Administration; installed at the Ronald Reagan Building, Federal Triangle Plaza, Washington, DC
Page 113

PLATE 27
Tokyo International Forum Proposal, 1995
Graphite on tracing paper
15⅛ in. × 7 ft. 9½ in.
(38.4 × 237.5 cm)
Pages 116–17

PLATE 29
Maquette for "Meditation in a Beech Wood," c. 1995
Wood
8 × 12 × 9 in. (20.3 × 30.5 × 22.9 cm)
Commissioned by Wanås Foundation, Knislinge, Sweden
Page 120

PLATE 30
Maquette for "Meditation in a Beech Wood," c. 1995
Wood
9⅛ × 10⅝ × 6¾ in.
(23.2 × 27 × 17.1 cm)
Commissioned by Wanås Foundation, Knislinge, Sweden
Page 121

PLATE 31
Drawing for "That Profile," c. 1997
Graphite on vellum
29 × 23 in. (73.7 × 58.4 cm)
Page 123

PLATE 32
Maquette for "That Profile," 1997
Steel wire and wood
23 × 48 × 38 in.
(58.4 × 121.9 × 96.5 cm)
Commissioned by The J. Paul Getty Trust
Page 124

PLATE 34
This Mortal Coil, 1998
Graphite on thin paper
14 × 11 in. (35.6 × 27.9 cm)
Commissioned for the Festival d'Automne à Paris; temporary installation at the Chapelle Saint-Louis de la Salpêtrière, Paris
Page 127

PLATE 37
Maquette for "Guardian Stone," 2002
Painted wood
22 × 17½ × 14 in.
(55.9 × 44.5 × 35.6 cm)
Commissioned by TV Asahi, Tokyo
Page 131

PLATE 39
Shackled, 2013
Iron
27½ × 30⅝ × 8⅜ in.
(69.8 × 77.8 × 21.3 cm)
Page 135

PLATE 40
Big Bling, 2014
Graphite on paper
50 × 42 in. (127 × 106.7 cm)
Commissioned by Madison Square Park Conservancy
Page 137

PLATE 42
Maquette for "Big Bling," 2014
Birch plywood, maple, and 22kt gold leaf
40½ × 9⅛ × 40 in.
(102.9 × 23.2 × 101.6 cm)
Commissioned by Madison Square Park Conservancy
Page 139

PLATE 43
Maquette for "Slavery Memorial," Brown University, 2014
Ductile cast iron and stainless steel
9 × 15½ × 16½ in.
(22.9 × 39.4 × 41.9 cm)
Page 141

PLATES 45, 46
Maquette for "Connecting," 2016
Stainless steel and painted wood
50 × 68¼ × 68¼ in.
(127 × 173.4 × 173.4 cm)
Commissioned by FAPE; installed at the U.S. Embassy, Beijing
Pages 144, 145

PLATE 49
Paving Pattern for "Connecting," c. 2016
Graphite on paper
23 × 23 in. (58.4 × 58.4 cm)
Page 147

PLATE 50
Proposal for Site in San Francisco (unrealized), 2017
Wood
27½ × 30⅝ × 8⅜ in.
(69.8 × 77.8 × 21.3 cm)
Page 149

PLATE 51
Maquette for "Swallowed Sun (Monstrance and Volute)," 2018
Oriented strand board, pine, maple, paint, and laser-cut acrylic
17½ × 33¾ × 16¼ in.
(44.5 × 85.7 × 41.3 cm)
Temporary installation at the U.S. Pavilion, 2019 Venice Biennale
Page 151

PLATE 54
Creature from Iddefjord, c. 2014
Graphite on paper
12½ × 19 in. (31.8 × 48.3 cm)
Page 155

PLATES 55, 56
Maquette for "Creature from Iddefjord," 2020
Poplar and paint
29½ × 18 × 31½ in.
(74.9 × 45.7 × 80 cm)
Commissioned by Sparebankstiftelsen
Installed at Deichman Library, Oslo
Pages 156, 157

PLATE 59
First Wooden Model for Storm King Commission, 2016
Wood
9¾ × 9¾ × 9¾ in.
(24.8 × 24.8 × 24.8 cm)
Page 161

PLATE 60
Brick Sculpture for Storm King Art Center (Thirteen Segments), 2018
Graphite on paper
23 × 29 in. (58.4 × 73.7 cm)
Page 162

PLATE 61
Maquette for "Lookout," 2018
Painted high-density urethane foam and painted wood
19½ × 32 × 34 in.
(49.5 × 81.3 × 86.4 cm)
Page 163

PLATE 62
Brick Sculpture for Storm King Art Center (Nine Segments), 2021
Graphite on vellum
23 × 29 in. (58.4 × 73.7 cm)
Page 164

PLATE 63
Final Nine-Segment Masonry Maquette for "Lookout," 2023
Painted high-density urethane foam and painted wood
40 in. (101.6 cm) high
Page 165

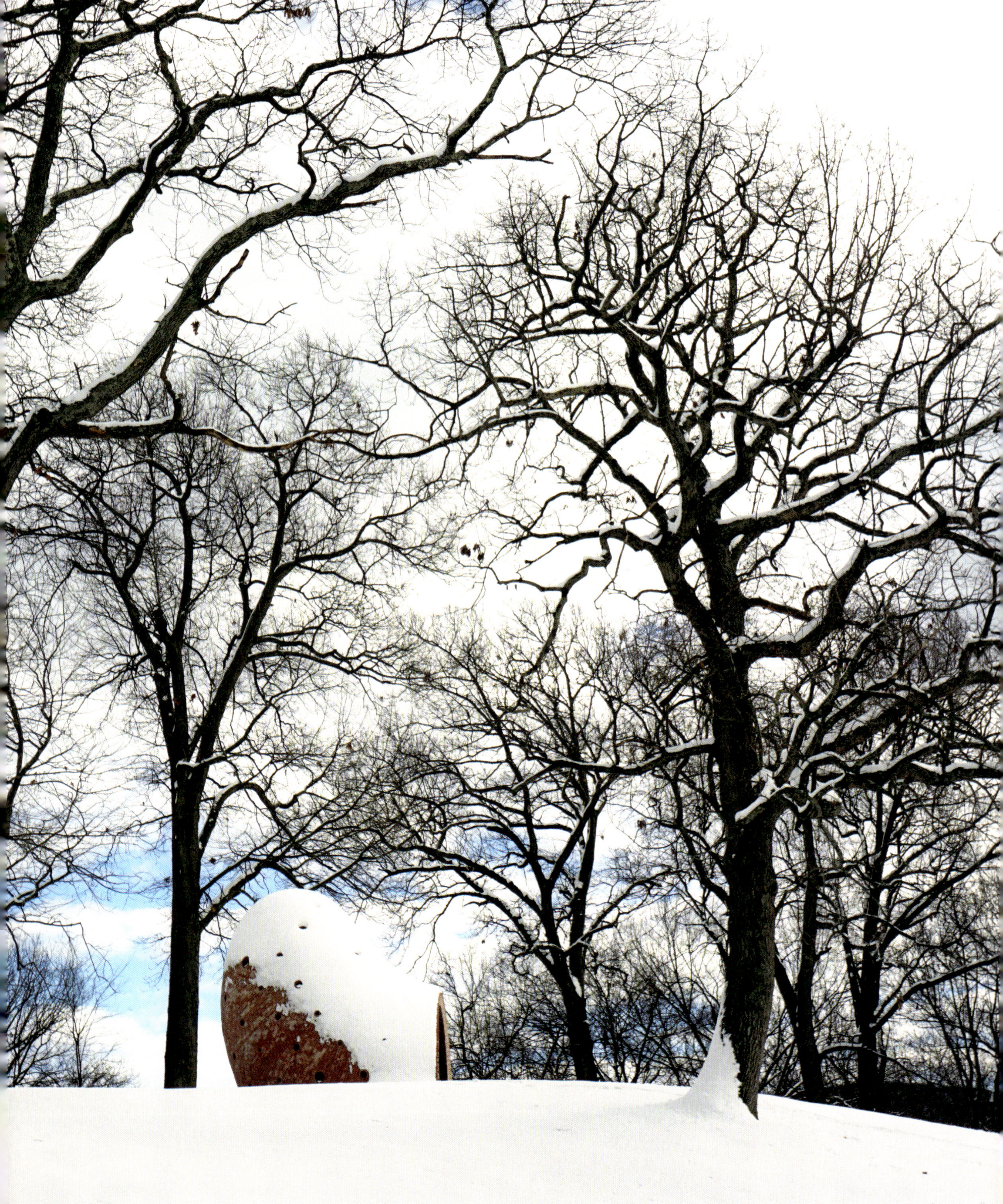

Biography

MARTIN PURYEAR (b. 1941) has created a body of work over five decades that defies categorization, creating sculpture that examines identity, culture, and history. Departing from the impersonal and machined aesthetic of Minimalism—the dominant sculptural movement of the artist's formative years—Puryear's work combines modernist abstraction with methods of making inspired by traditional trades and crafts. With shapes informed by the natural world and by ordinary objects, and made by direct engagement with materials such as wood, wire, tar, granite, bronze, cast iron, steel, and granite, his work is quiet but deliberately associative, inspired by his extensive travels and his endless curiosity about the world, and drawing on a huge and varied reserve of images and ideas.

Puryear was born in Washington, DC. His first one-person exhibition was in 1968, and since then he has exhibited throughout the world, including public commissions in Europe, Asia, and the United States. His work was featured in Documenta 9 (1992), and in 1989 he represented the United States at the São Paulo Bienal, where he was awarded the festival's Grand Prize. In 2007 the Museum of Modern Art in New York organized a survey of his work, which traveled to the National Gallery of Art in Washington, the San Francisco Museum of Modern Art, and the Modern Art Museum of Fort Worth. In 2015 the Art Institute of Chicago organized an exhibition of fifty years of his works on paper, which traveled to the Morgan Library and Museum in New York and the Smithsonian American Art Museum in Washington. Puryear received a MacArthur Foundation award in 1989 and a National Medal of Arts from President Obama in 2011. In 2019 he represented the United States at the 58th Venice Biennale.

Contributors

NORA LAWRENCE is the Artistic Director and Chief Curator of Storm King Art Center, leading its curatorial program and providing vision and guidance for the artistic functions of the institution.

AMY S. WEISSER is Deputy Director, Strategic Planning and Projects at Storm King Art Center, where she incubates projects focused on the institution's strategic growth. Weisser holds a PhD in art history from Yale University.

GLENN ADAMSON is a curator, writer, and historian based in New York and London. He has previously been Director of the Museum of Arts and Design and Head of Research at the Victoria and Albert Museum. Dr. Adamson is Artistic Director for Design Doha, a new biennial festival for Qatar, and editor of *Material Intelligence*, a quarterly online journal published by the Chipstone Foundation. He will serve as Curatorial Director for Design Miami in December 2024.

ADELA GOLDSMITH is the Curatorial Assistant at Storm King Art Center. Their work explores art and nature through a queer ecological lens.

Storm King Art Center

Storm King's commission and exhibition by Martin Puryear are made possible by generous major support from Janet Benton and David Schunter, Bloomberg Philanthropies, Roberta and Steven Denning, Bridgitt and Bruce Evans, Glenstone Foundation, Ellsworth Kelly Foundation, Ohnell Family Foundation, the Hazen Polsky Foundation, Thomas A. and Georgina T. Russo, and Margaret VB Wurtele.

Lead support is provided by Agnes Gund, Barbara Bluhm-Kaul and Don Kaul, The Ronald and Jo Carole Lauder Foundation, and Matthew Marks Gallery.

Support is also provided by Robert Lehman Foundation and Sidney E. Frank Foundation and supported in part by Allison Berg, Jennifer Brorsen and Richard DeMartini, Andrew L. and Gayle Shaw Camden, Tommy and Dathel Coleman, Martha Gabbert, Debby and Rocco Landesman, and the Ralph E. Ogden Foundation.

This project is supported in part by an award from the National Endowment for the Arts.

Bloomberg Philanthropies

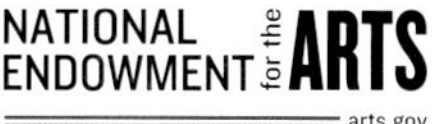

Artist's Acknowledgments

I am thrilled to have my brick sculpture, *Lookout*, join the sculpture collection at Storm King Art Center, and my thanks go to David R. Collens, Director Emeritus, for the initial invitation.

For their sustained support from start to finish of this challenging project I'm especially grateful to the following members of the Storm King community:

John P. Stern, President
Amy S. Weisser, Deputy Director, Strategic Planning and Projects
Nora Lawrence, Artistic Director and Chief Curator
Mike Seaman, Director of Facilities and Conservation
Adela Goldsmith, Curatorial Assistant

My assistant, Jeanne Englert, was an essential link between Storm King and my studio from the earliest planning discussions over a dozen years ago until *Lookout*'s completion in September 2023.

This project could not have been realized without the skilled team who collaborated on its execution.

Lara Davis of Limaçon Design and my studio assistant Rob Horton organized and led the brickwork on-site, together with Scott Cafarella and Mario Magana of Hudson Valley Mason Works, supported by Aaron Getman-Pickering and Donovan Palmquist.

John Ochsendorf provided crucial structural engineering support, together with Rebecca Buntrock from Silman.

Kurt Wulfmeyer and Chris Powers of KC Fabrications designed and constructed the stainless steel reinforcement that supported the construction.

Architectural concrete specialist David Kucera developed and produced composite concrete tubes for the ninety circular openings through the work.

The sculpture was integrated into its natural setting thanks to the site planning of landscape architects Reed Hilderbrand.

I owe a very special debt to Charles Taylor and Steve Blankenbeker of Taylor Clay Products, Salisbury, North Carolina, for formulating the custom bricks for the project.

Finally, I join Storm King in collective gratitude to the many donors and benefactors who made *Lookout* possible.

Martin Puryear

Published on the occasion of *Martin Puryear: Lookout* and the accompanying exhibition, *Martin Puryear: Process and Scale*, September 23–December 17, 2023, at Storm King Art Center, New Windsor, New York.

Design and production by Miko McGinty and Rita Jules, Miko McGinty Inc.
Copyediting by Libby Hruska
Proofreading by Marian Appellof
Publication production support by Adela Goldsmith and the Martin Puryear Studio
Prepress, printing, and binding by Trifolio, Verona, Italy

A version of "A Conversation with Martin Puryear," by Glenn Adamson with photographs by Carlton Davis, was first published in *Upstate Diary*, no. 17, October 2023.

STORM KING ART CENTER

Storm King Art Center
1 Museum Rd.
New Windsor, NY 12553
stormking.org

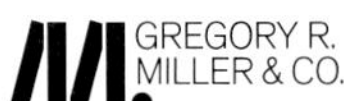

Gregory R. Miller & Co.
62 Cooper Square
New York, NY 10003
grmandco.com

Distributed worldwide by
ARTBOOK | D.A.P.
artbook.com

ISBN 978-1-941366-64-6

Library of Congress Control Number 2024932364

Photo Credits

pp. 2, 8, 20, 22, 23, 24 (left and right), 29 (top), 30 (left and right), 36, 41, 55, 56–57, 58–59, 60–61, 62–63, 65, 66–67, 68–69, 70–71, 72–73, 74, 81 (top and bottom), 83, 87, 91, 95, 97, 99, 103, 107, 108–09, 116–17, 120, 121, 123, 124, 127, 128, 131, 135, 141, 147, 155, 156, 157, 162, 163, 164, 165: Jeffrey Jenkins
p. 10: Nicholas Knight
p. 11 (top): © Haverstraw Brick Museum
p. 11 (bottom): The Century House Historical Society
pp. 12, 170: Adela Goldsmith
pp. 13 (top), 82, 84–85: Wayne Cozzolino, courtesy the Association for Public Art
p. 13 (bottom): Nick Micros
p. 14: Corcoran Gallery of Art
pp. 16, 110, 111: Oliver Ranch
p. 17: Paulson Fontaine Press
p. 25: Amy S. Weisser
pp. 26, 27 (left), 31, 149: Martin Puryear
p: 27 (right): a-plus image bank/Alamy Stock Photo
p. 28: Jerry L. Thompson
pp. 29 (bottom), 151, 161: Jeanne Englert, Martin Puryear Studio
p. 32 (left): courtesy the Modern Art Museum of Fort Worth
pp. 32 (right), 144, 145: Ronald Amstutz
p. 33: Andrew Shurtleff
p. 34: incamerastock/Alamy Stock Photo
pp. 43, 44, 45, 46, 47, 48, 49, 50, 51, 53: © Carlton Davis/Trunk Archive
pp. 77, 78: Buffalo AKG Art Museum
p. 79: Artpark
p. 89: Sarah Wells
p. 90: Nathan Manilow Sculpture Park
pp. 93, 105: Donald Young Gallery
pp. 100, 101: Jeff Goldberg
pp. 113, 139: Jamie Stukenberg
p. 115: Robert Lautman
p. 119: Anders Norrsell
p. 125: Lynn Davis
p. 129: Pascal Victor
p. 133: Shigeo Anzai
p. 137: Madison Square Park Conservancy
p. 138: Yasunori Matsui
pp. 142–43: Warren Jagger
p. 146 (top and bottom): Stefen Chow
pp. 152, 153: Joshua White
pp. 158, 159: Carsten Aniksdal

Cover and back cover: Jeffrey Jenkins